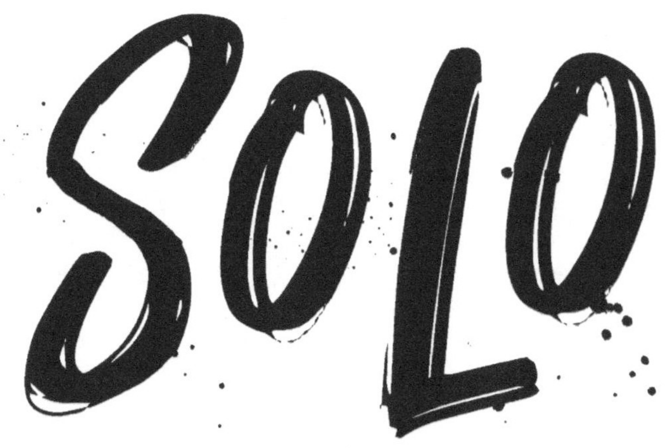

Survival Guide
for Creative Freelancers

SOLO

Survival Guide
for Creative Freelancers

By Palle Schmidt

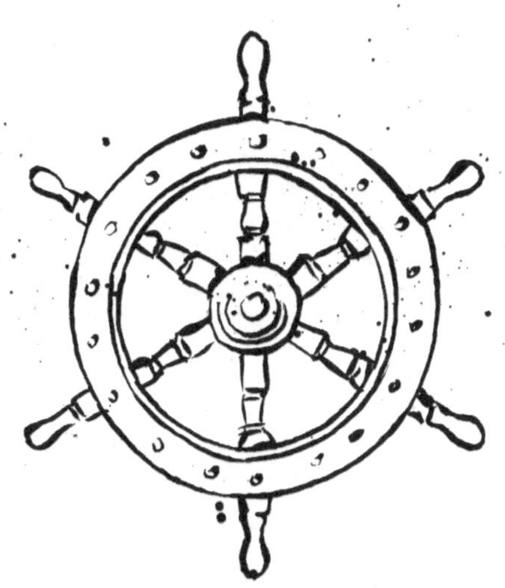

SOLO - Survival Guide for Creative Freelancers

Edited by Greg Tumbarello
All illustrations by Palle Schmidt
Graphic design supervision and ebook conversion: Slaven Kovacevic

ISBN: 978-87-93737-19-8

Thanks to:
Chris Miskiewicz, Dean Haspiel, Peter Snejbjerg, Kim Fupz Aakeson, Ole Comoll, Greg Tumbarello, Anders Matthesen, Jon Skraentskov, Anders Bronserud, Jakob Melander, Jim Dane, Sohail A. Hassan, and Line Leonhardt

Test readers:
Kevin Deitz, Juhana Lumme, Ian Su, Johnie Rohwedder, Irena Majcen, Ron Johnson, John Edingfield II, Adrian Patangui, Enrico Vattani, Liam Harper, John Poehler and Robbie Vermillion

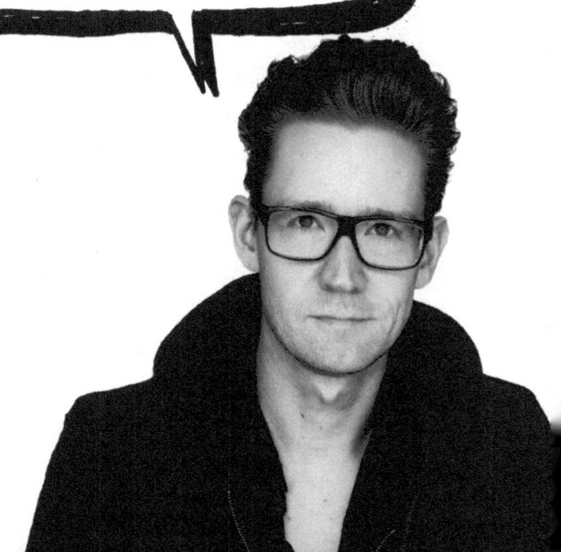

Ahoy!

Thanks for picking up this book!

I'm Palle Schmidt, artist, writer and comics creator (and teacher, and podcaster, and father, and a lot of other things). I'm based in Copenhagen, Denmark where this book was first published in 2017. This English language version is rewritten for artists and solopreneurs everywhere considering I often get asked for advice from non-Danish people as well (and let's face it; Denmark is a small market — the entire population are fewer than people living on the island of Manhattan!).

Even though I've been making a living from my creativity for twenty years, I still found myself looking for the perfect book on the subject, inspiration on how to make the most of my skills, and advice on how to ultimately do something I care about while still putting food on the table. I never found that book, so I attempted to write it myself. And while it's by no means a recipe for success, I hope you're able to find inspiration for your own creative career in some of the tools, tactics and techniques that I use.

Approach it like a smorgasbord (Swedish word, not Danish) of ideas to pick and choose from.

Let's dive in!

Table of Contents

Foreword

In the summer of 2014 I spent three weeks at Periscope Studio in Portland, Oregon. My family and I had rented a small apartment for the duration, and every day I took the bus downtown to work on *Thomas Alsop*, the monthly comic that I was doing with writer Chris Miskiewicz. I'd met Chris at the MoCCA Festival in New York in 2011. We eventually pitched *Thomas Alsop* to an editor at BOOM! Studios and, a year later, the book was available in stores all over the US.

Over lunch one day at Periscope, cartoonist Lucy Bellwood and I were talking about our careers. With her mouth full of bean salad from one of the food trucks across the street, Lucy said something that really stuck with me:

"I've started to say 'no' to things that don't fit into my overall goal."

It wasn't just that her decision made total sense. It was the fact that I'd never heard another freelancer talk about an overall goal. In Denmark this type of unapologetic ambition is somewhat frowned upon, certainly not mentioned in passing over lunch with someone you barely know.

I myself was starting to be more mindful about the direction my career was going and had started prioritizing my own projects rather than incoming illustration work, something that had paid my rent the past fifteen years or so. I was writing more, I'd taken a master class in screenwriting at the Danish Film School and published several YA novels.

I had changed paths in many respects, looking for inspiration in new places. This had led me to Portland, where I knew I would gain experience and insights by embedding myself with other creative pros. I knew, because I had done the same before, spending a couple of weeks at Dean Haspiel's Hang Dai Studios in Brooklyn, New York.

While there are obviously different challenges to freelancers and creators living in the US—the lack of a unified public healthcare system like we have here in Denmark springs to mind—Americans tend to have a more entrepreneurial mindset. An idea for a project is not immediately met with the concern and skepticism that Danes tend to have. Maybe I've just been lucky with the Americans I met, but it seems they are more likely to cheer you on than to dissuade you. Other than sheer praise and encouragement from peers, I've had people give constructive feedback and ideas, and share tips and even contacts. Me, a foreigner, basically there to steal American jobs… and the locals help introduce me to a publisher. I find this network economy fascinating. Rather than a scarcity mindset where "if YOU get success, there is less for ME," the people I've met in the US comics scene have an abundance mindset of, "we help each other out." That's the kind of mindset I'm hoping to pass along with this book.

There is no contradiction in being a professional and a creative. While there's inspiration to be found in books on entrepreneurship and start-ups, the growth aspect is something that few artists can identify with. Most of us are simply looking to build a sustainable career for one person, not attempting to build an empire. We are not only focused on getting as many sales, customers or clients as possible, but also on our personal expression.

SOLO is written for people who believe in creative living on their own terms. It will focus on people who want a sustainable career, mixing freelance work with creating and selling their own art. My promise is that diving into the tactics and strategies of this book will help you set realistic, actionable goals and give you the tools to carve out your own creative career path.

Navigation

First, a few disclaimers. I'm not a lawyer, an accountant or a business expert. I've failed several attempts to get a degree and numerous other things, but I have managed to pay the bills from my craft since 1998. While I'm not a guru on creativity, I've blogged and created podcasts on the topic, as well as held numerous workshops, panels and lectures. In fact, I often give free lectures over lunch at my studio, at the request of no one.

This is a wildly personal book and I strive to be painfully honest. After all, I'm trying to let you learn from my mistakes as well as my findings. I'm sure you'll find some of it useful, and some of it irrelevant. Some of it will be gold, some of it you'll downright disagree with.

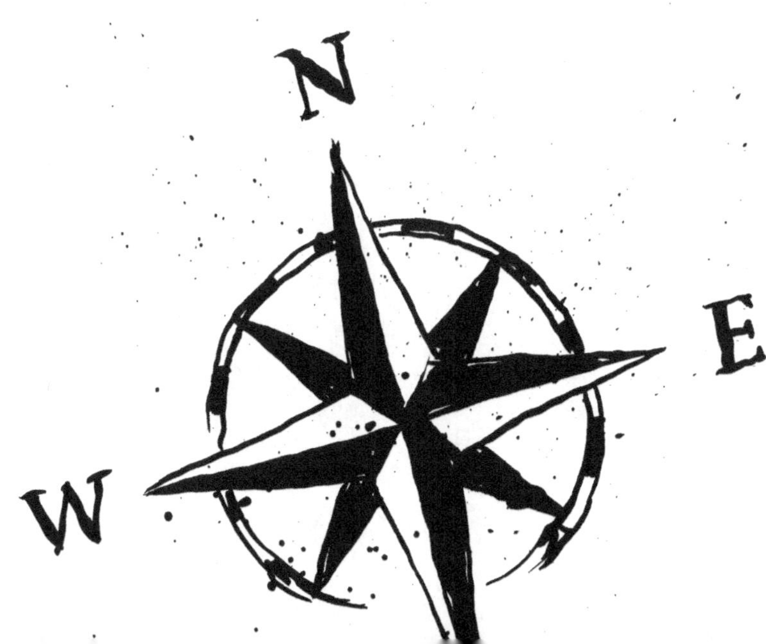

SOLO is divided into three major parts:

Part I: Before you go SOLO

What are you getting into? What does a creative career entail? What is your talent and what should you focus on? What should you be prepared for before you jump in?

Part 2: The first year of SOLO

Tried and tested strategies for kickstarting your career, all the practical stuff—getting clients, marketing, mentors, invoicing—and examples of things you don't need to spend time and money on.

Part 3: SOLO forever

Long-term strategies to keep afloat through the ups and downs of your creative career. Suggestions for income streams, dealing with bad clients, managing your time and growing as an artist, and taking your prowess to the next level.

In the back of the book you'll find a resource section with useful links and other tools.

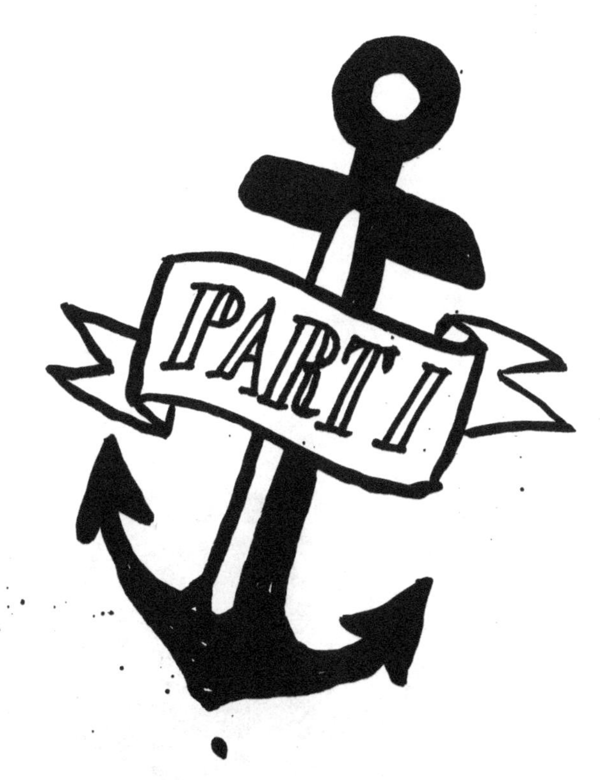

Before You Go SOLO

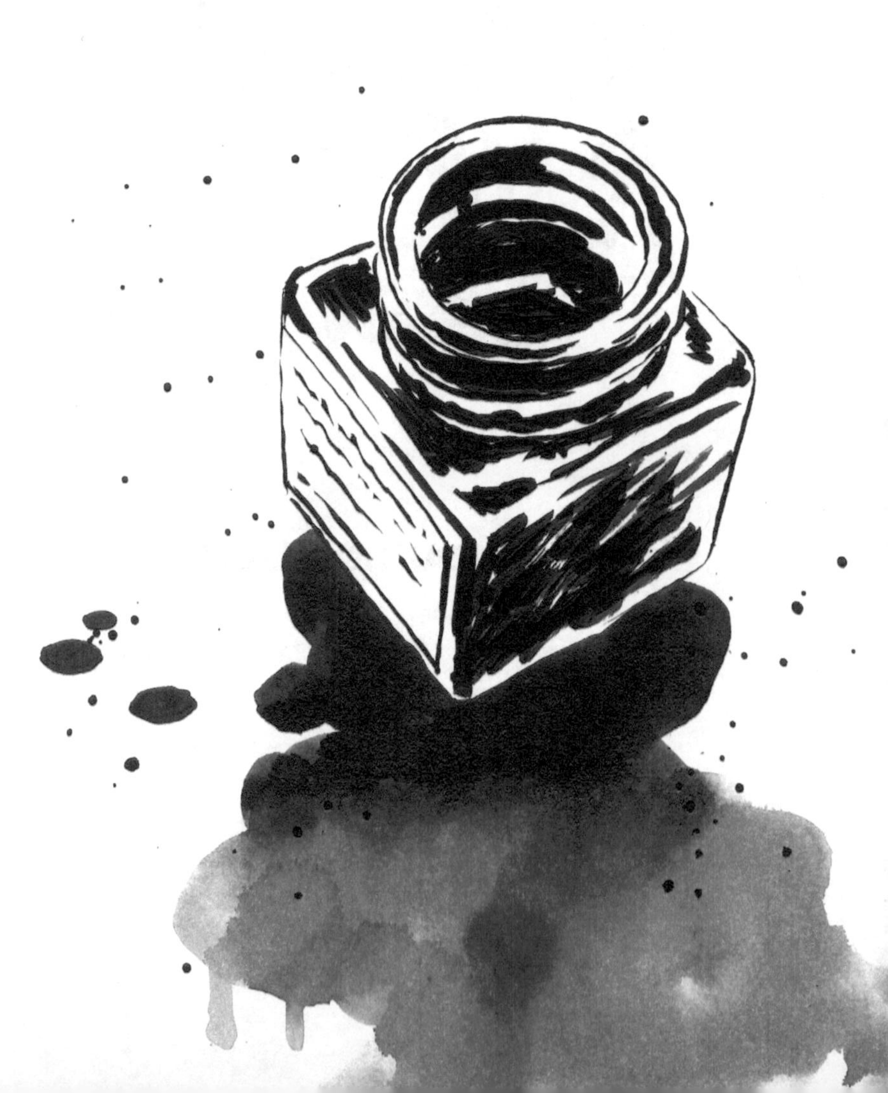

CHAPTER 1

Why Go SOLO?

The Best Part of My Job...

...is that I don't have one!

I've been making my living as freelancer since 1998. That's over 20 years of being "unemployed," something I am immensely proud of. I started out in illustration and comics but in later years have turned my focus more towards writing and I also do some teaching (mostly online at *ComicsForBeginners.com*), and public speaking. I go back and forth between commercial (storyboard work, corporate workshops etc.) and the hopelessly uncommercial (comics that sell 4-500 copies or podcasts I create for free). And it may sound like I'm living the life all over the globe as an international man-of-mystery! In fact, I'm writing this very paragraph in an apartment in Paris (I don't own the place, but still). But only in recent years has it dawned on me that being freelance can mean a great deal of *physical* freedom as well as mental. The technologies we have at our fingertips today has made it a lot easier to be location independent.

My favorite time of the week is Monday morning, when the kids are in school and I'm at my office with a cup of coffee and a day's work ahead of me. And however boring or frustrating that day's work may be, it is always something that I myself put on the calendar. Because I said "yes." Most of the time, I decide when and how to work. I don't have to deal with a psycho boss or crappy work environment. Until I have to pick up the kids from school, I am the boss.

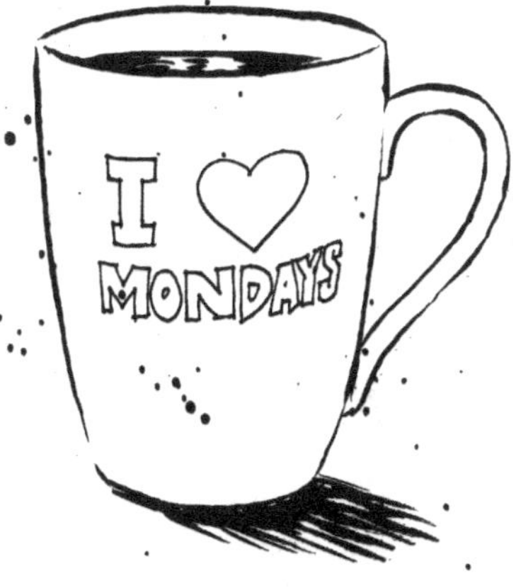

I don't have *a* job, I have *many* jobs. If one of my clients goes out of business or decides never to work with me again, I have other sources of income. When my industry changes course, I can change with it, speeding along in my little motorboat, where a big corporation would have a hard time turning the ship around. In periods where there's no incoming work-for-hire, I relish the opportunity to focus on my own projects. That attitude has saved me from many sleepless nights, by the way. I know fellow freelancers who freak out when the order book is empty—I only freak out when my bank account is empty.

Another reason I don't envy the guy with a traditional 9-to-5 job, is that I see how quickly their expenses match up to their income. Having more money means *spending* more money. I'm pretty frugal with my money 'cause I don't know when there's more coming in. I sometimes ask people in so-called real jobs how much money they put aside every month and a staggering amount of them say "none." I work very hard to have a buffer so I'm not reliant on incoming work from month to month.

We tend to judge our success (and the success of others) by the amount of money we have. But another very underrated currency is *freedom*. The freedom to choose how to work and what to work on. Where to work, when to work—and when *not* to work! The fact that I don't have to ask anybody's permission makes me a very, very rich man.

I'm incredibly grateful for my freelance life and can't imagine not being self-employed. But it wasn't always that way. When I was starting my creative path, I had no role models and little encouragement. It took years before I had the guts to jump in.

"We Can't All Play the Bongos"

This headline is stolen from a friend's dad who was trying (probably in the best of intentions) to stop his daughter from a career in the arts. This is pretty much the reaction from all parents everywhere.

An education, a steady job and a mortgage is what most of us are told to pursue. A freelance career is usually seen as insecure (which can often be the case) but the beaten paths have their downsides too.

A long education is no guarantee to get a well-paying job. Just ask your friends who spent years in academia only to get rejected for a job waiting tables because they don't want a professor hanging around making everyone else in the workplace feel stupid.

A steady job? Well, those used to exist. Remember the auto industry? In 1950's Detroit, a job at Ford or General Motors was pretty much a guarantee for lifetime employment and a gold watch at the end of it. Not so anymore. Job security is a thing for the history books and you risk having the rug pulled out from under you faster than you can say "outsourced."

A mortgage? Owning your own home may very well be a great investment, what do I know. But it may also end up being a noose around your neck if your industry moves and you can't sell at the price you paid for it. And that is completely beyond your control. You're stuck. Renting at least leaves you with the opportunity to up and leave whenever you want.

The world economy and job market is not the same today as it was in our parent's youth so it's hard to take any of their advice to heart. Likewise, the bank is much more likely to lend you money if you can show a steady income, rather than a fluctuating one that may even be bigger. I find this particularly weird since if you want to invest, diversification is the norm. But diversification of income? Oh no, that's way to risky!

These days we hear a lot about entrepreneurship and you can find tons of advice for self-employment online. But most people still ask me how I sleep at night, not knowing where the next check is going to come from. I don't know how *they* sleep at night, having put all their eggs in one basket!

The Smell of Fear

When I told my mom I planned on launching a freelance career, her reaction came pretty close to a full-on panic attack. I'd been a really bad student for 5-6 years at that point (studying English at university and later architecture, graduating from neither). But I had worked as an illustrator for magazines and personal projects on the side, so I'd technically been a freelancer for years already. I just needed to learn how to make money on it.

Who knows, maybe your family will have a greater understanding of your artistic ambitions than mine. But I'm willing to put money on them not getting it and trying to talk you out of it. Your friends and colleagues will likely have the same reaction. They probably have a real job and when you turn your back on that, you make them question their own existence. You're rocking the boat.

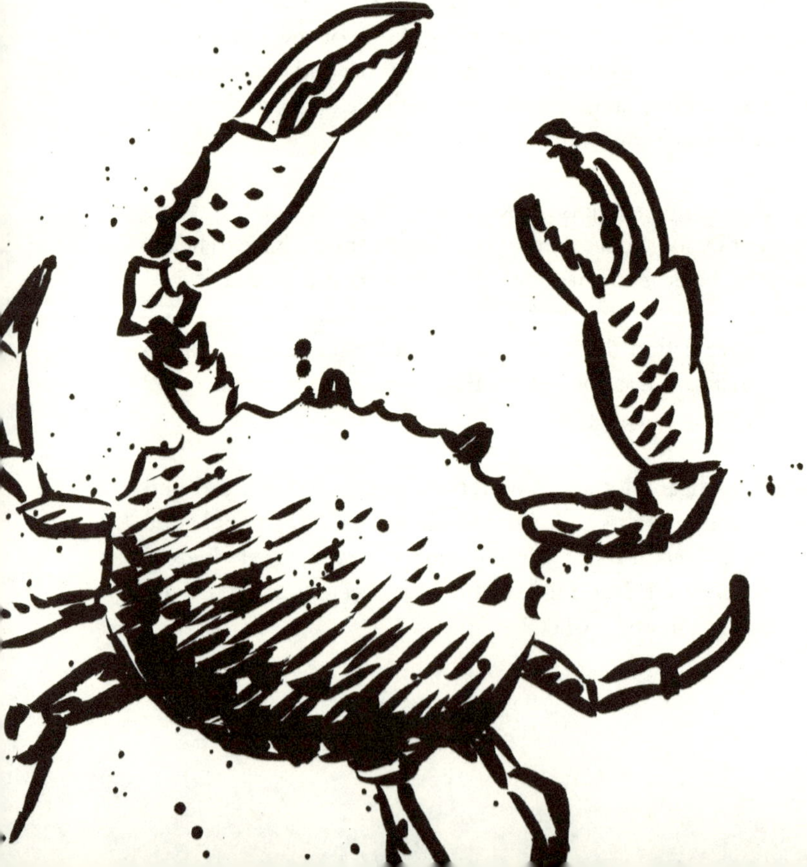

Let's stay with the maritime for a second and let me tell you a story about crabs:

Allegedly if you catch a bunch of crabs and put them in a bucket, you don't need to put a lid on it. The moment a crab tries to claw its way out of the bucket, the other crabs will pull it back in.

That's pretty much how humans work too. Where I come from it's certainly frowned upon if you're too ambitious, too artistic and too out of the ordinary. Stay in the bucket with the rest of us, come on!

"Can I make a living doing it?" is a relevant question you'll ask yourself, sure. But it's very hard to answer if you've never tried. Art is not an exact science.

I know plenty of people making a living doing art as I have been for twenty years now. I may not exactly be raking it in but I'm doing something I like and am relatively good at, while making clients and readers happy along the way—that's more than a lot of people can say about their jobs! And I certainly wouldn't have been able to say it if I'd finished my education and become a mediocre (or rather, unemployed) architect shamefully creating comics on the side.

This book is my response to the "can you make a living" question. There's lots of ways, lots of opportunities and potential for creating your own job and peddling your artistic skills in a delicate balance. Never exactly Zen, but always interesting.

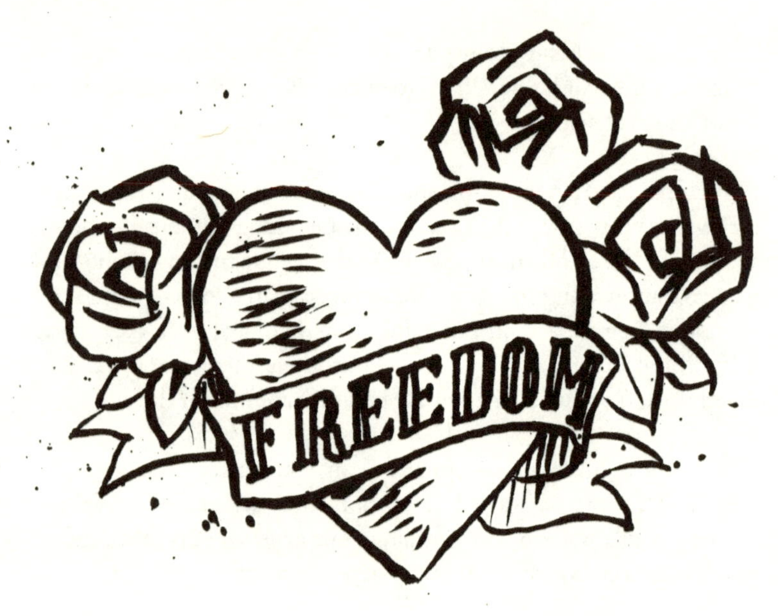
FREEDOM

CHAPTER 2

How to Go SOLO

In the previous chapter I kind of unfairly blamed societies norms (and my mom, sorry) for not going solo a lot sooner. But in hindsight, it was more likely my own insecurities and the lack of role models that kept me back. I didn't know a single self-employed person let alone an artist. This was before the internet, mind you!

As a youth I had the very simple ambition of completing some kind of education leading to some kind of employment, allowing me to write and draw whatever I wanted in my spare time. And while that may have worked had I not been such a hopeless student and completely unemployable, I'm sure I wouldn't have been very happy.

Without ever asking anyone's opinion, I rejected the thought of ever earning a living from my art. I simply couldn't imagine it being possible. I managed to convince myself that art was my hobby, my safe space and that it would be a corrupted and joyless activity the minute I started monetizing it. I honestly can't say where that delusion came from. Maybe it was the mentor I briefly had back in 8th or 9th grade who had a big house by the ocean. He'd made his fortune painting hyper-realistic romance novel illustrations for magazines, featuring beautiful women crying big, fat tears of heartbreak. I was by no means envious of his fortune. I couldn't imagine a fate worse than painting big, fat tears of heartbreak. Yeah, I sure lacked imagination back in those days.

Beyond the fear of becoming a romance novel artist, I also feared ridicule. Putting yourself out there is not an easy thing, especially for artistic souls with low self-esteem. Making money from art seemed a distant dream. Until I met people who were living that dream.

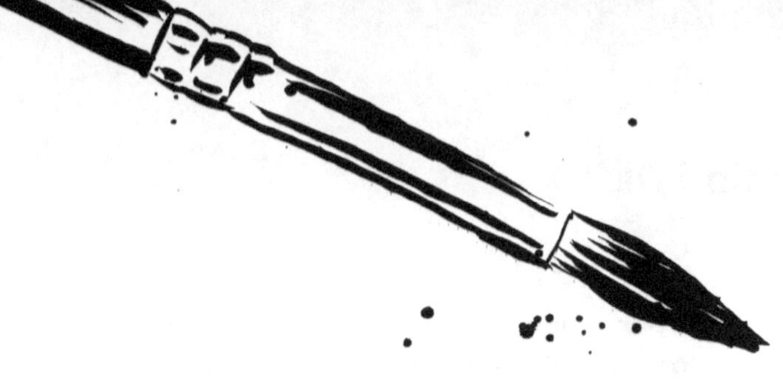

I treated the lessons my first mentor gave me like I treated any other homework—avoid at all cost and/or delay till last minute. The romance novel artist only really managed to deter me from pursuing a career in the arts.

It wasn't until I met Peter Snejbjerg (artist on *Books of Magic*, *Starman*, *A God Somewhere* and a bunch of other US comic books) that I realized there was a career to be had without selling out. Through Peter I started hanging around Gimle Studios in Copenhagen, where a dozen or so freelancers sat bent over their desks, creating comics for a living. While this may seem less than glamorous to you, for me it came close to a revelation. I had found my tribe!

I joined Gimle in 1998 and worked out of there for the next twelve years as a freelance illustrator and comics artist. I basically paid for a studio space and it wasn't like we worked together, but the people there were crucial for getting my career off the ground. And I still get advice or referrals from my old studio mates from time to time, just as I refer clients to them whenever I can. Even if you can't join a relevant studio or office space in your area, I recommend you seek out peers and mentors in your field (see page 37 for more). They've been where you are and understand your struggles and ambitions. They are more than likely to be supportive, if you are committed to the craft and respectfully ask for their advice.

FAQ

If you are considering a freelance career but haven't yet made the jump, you probably have a ton of questions. In this section I'm taking a wild guess on some of them. And don't worry, we'll go into more depth later on, I just want to begin by setting your mind at ease.

What do I go freelance with?

I can't tell you where your passion or talent lies, but you're probably already doing something on the side. If it doesn't matter to you what you sell, you're not the kind of entrepreneur that this book is meant for. But even the most artsy of artists has to think a bit like an entrepreneur to make it. You have to think in terms of clients and market, whether you want to or not. Here's a very biz type of illustration known as the Venn diagram:

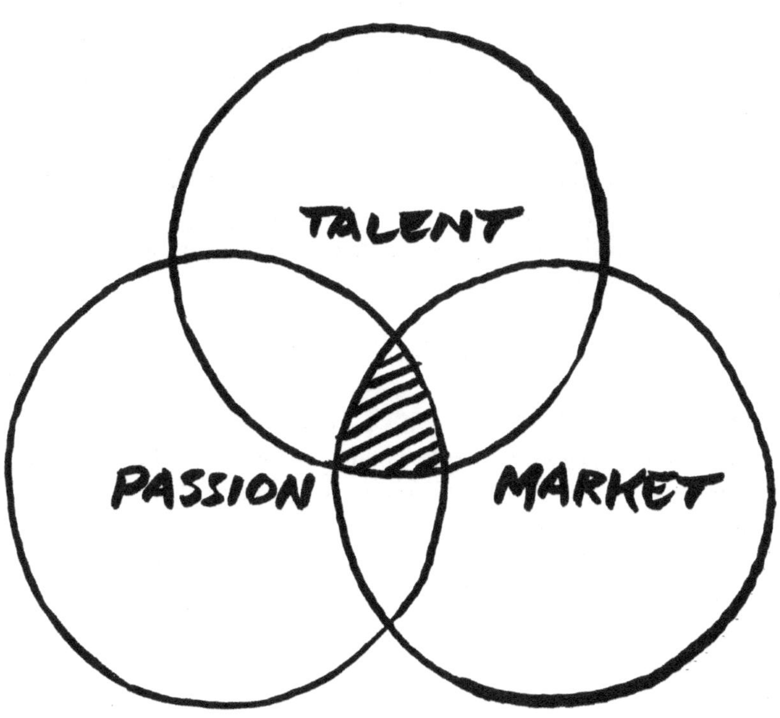

Wherever your passion and artistic merits overlap with what some people are willing to pay for, you have a career. This book is intended to help identify and expand this overlap.

Am I good enough?

No one can tell you for certain if you have what it takes. Asking your Mom is not an option! You could ask a pro in your field but they probably can't tell you either. A portfolio review only tells you if you have the basic talent for drawing, not if you have what it takes to make it as a freelance artist. Talent is one thing but there are dozens of other factors—mindset, discipline, stamina, luck and intuition, to name a few.

How do I get started?

If you're reading this book, chances are you already have something going on, even though you may not be making money on it. Whether it's painting, writing, playing guitar or making things out of clay, the common denominator is you can basically just sit down and effing do it. What's stopping you? Other than your own fears and doubts, that is. Let's see if we can't shut those up by the end of this book.

No one is born with a clear voice and a completely unique style. We find our voice through practice, lots and lots of practice. By stealing from other artists and combining in new and surprising ways. You just have to *start*.

You don't learn to swim by standing at the edge of the pool.

What if I fail?

We all hit bumps in the road or periods of despair. The trick is to learn from it. You know the Edison quote, right? "I have not failed. I've just found 10,000 ways that won't work." Failure is your best teacher. If you go freelance and you find it too stressful or just not as fulfilling as you thought, there's no shame in getting a job. At least you'll know and you'll have gained valuable insights from trying it out. More about failure and setbacks on page 188.

But I'll need an education, right?

I have no doubt that going to an arts college or whatever will immensely help build your skills and your confidence and grow your network. And in some fields more than others, certain educations are considered a stamp of approval. Having a degree from Julliard will likely help you get a Broadway audition. But then again, I see many examples (myself included) of successful creative people with no formal education or highly educated people who don't use their degree for anything.

Before you apply to an arts college you need to ask yourself what the purpose is. Is it to build skills and network? Or is it just to put off the scary decision of going full freelance? An education can be used as procrastination too, you know!

The culture in arts education varies of course but I've learned from experience, and from talking to others, that a lot of times these institutions live in their own bubble. You'll spend an enormous amount of time just getting to know the rules of the place, on socializing and understanding the idiosyncrasies of the staff.

I went to the Danish School of Architecture in Copenhagen and I'd say it took me the first three years just figuring out what was expected of me and how how the school worked. I learned the hard way to set my own agenda for what I wanted to learn from each project rather than try to second-guess the teachers or live up to some unspoken expectation. I also found that most of what they had us do was very theoretic and far removed from what the real world would have us do once we got out of school. The real world does not care about your school projects, believe me!

> You don't learn to swim by standing at the edge of the pool.

An unpaid internship or struggling along with freelance work may end up getting you further than your friend who got in to that prestigious school. She's starting from scratch while you know everybody in the business. You'll also begin your career with a lot less debt that way.

Being your own boss requires a great deal of confidence. I didn't build mine from being a "D" student at the School of Architecture. I consistently failed courses and felt like a loser out there. When I took a master class in screenwriting at the Danish Film School (after more than a decade of making a living as a freelance writer and artist) it did wonders for my skill set and confidence as a storyteller. But at that time I was much older and more grounded and I knew what I wanted to gain from the course.

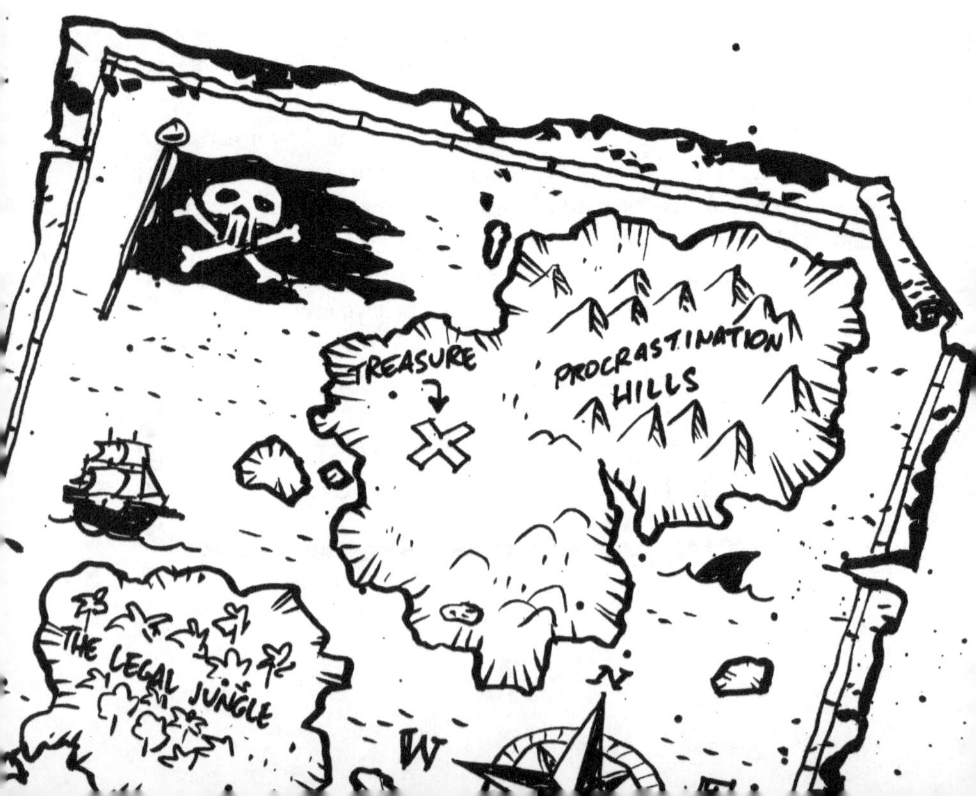

My point is this: Don't let it discourage you if you don't get accepted to the school you'd hoped. There are many ways to make it without a "proper" education and I have yet to meet a client who asked to see my exam credentials. The *work* I put out there is what matters, not if I have a degree in anything.

What about taxes and finances?

If you're the kind of person who is incapable of putting money aside, self-employment is going to be a challenge for you. Freelancers don't have a steady paycheck coming in the first of every month. We have money going *out*, because we have to pay rent and other expenses. So we need to be mindful of how much we spend. The tax system in my part of the world is probably different from yours, but basically you have to set aside money to pay later or pay up front based on an educated guess of what you might earn. I cover more on page 58 but for now let's just say it's not as complicated as you're likely to think.

What if I can't earn enough money?

The myth of the starving artist didn't come from nothing. It can be friggin' hard to get the cash flowing. But if you're talented, persistent and able to keep cool under fire, it is by no means impossible. I want this book to be your guide in finding and sustaining freelance work, as well as an idea catalogue for generating income streams from your own art (see page 177).

First you have to find your own definition of what "enough" is. How much do you need to bring home to stay afloat? Without a clear goal in mind it can be really hard to know when you've reached it. Try to make it realistic and concrete, put a number on it. With some kind of budget and a plan, you'll be all right.

How do I put a price on my work?

It's always a good idea to ask other professionals in your field. If the average hourly rate for sound technicians is $100, you should feel alright about charging $70. Check the market, or set your price high and then dial it back down if no one is buying.

Remember that you're not just selling your time but your expertise, built up through years of focused practice. Drawing a logo in Adobe Illustrator or creating a jingle may seem easy to you—but to your clients, it's damn near impossible. You are a trained specialist, just like a surgeon or a plumber. Charge accordingly. How can you expect anyone else to take you seriously if you don't?

Know Your Niche

Getting to know the language of your field is a good investment of your time. I'm sure there are courses for start-ups or entrepreneurs in your area, online or off. Whether it's governmental or arranged by trade organizations, you should be able to find something for free. Just be aware that most of these courses are designed for a different breed of entrepreneur than freelance artists, which is part of the reason I wrote this book! But I can't know the major players or unspoken rules in your particular area or niche market. So you have to do your own research.

Some of this research can be done from your couch by surfing the web, signing up for newsletters or joining Facebook pages or the like. I myself am a member of a few online forums for cartoonists and several guilds like the Danish Writer's Guild and Danish Comics Creators. I'm also signed up to newsletters like the Danish Arts Council, letting me know what's trending and what new opportunities for work and travel grants are available.

In addition to lurking on these platforms I use a service called Talkwalker. (talkwalker.com/en/alerts). It works like a Google alert but way more stabile and easy to handle. You can set up an alert for your name, the name of your new book or any series of words—a great way of getting a feel for a particular niche market. If you teach Spanish guitar you can set it up to get an alert every time somebody blogs about "how to play Spanish guitar." You'll get an idea of supply and demand as well as how others approach that market.

Know Yourself

Self-knowledge is probably even more important than knowing your market. What is the thing that only *you* can do? When do you create your best work? What needs to be in place in order for you to be most creative and prolific? Do you thrive juggling multiple projects or do you feel better digging in and focusing on just one thing? Do you like networking at social events or does it drain you and take you days to get back in the groove? Do you need a clean working environment or is a messy desk part of your creative process? What are your bad habits and blind angles?

I know some of this soul-searching can be hard and you don't have to answer the above questions right now. But if you want a creative career that is sustainable over the long run, you need to be mindful of what it is you do, what brings out the best in you. Knowing your own process means you can repeat it. Knowing how long each task usually takes makes pricing and keeping deadlines possible. Knowing the pit falls means you can avoid them.

As a creative freelancer, you'll be creating your own work life. Might as well make it fit who you *are* instead of what others think you should be.

Register Your Company

As I've mentioned earlier, I live and work in Denmark. Chances are your system for creating a company and paying taxes is different than ours. But I'll go out on a limb and say you probably have some way of writing off business expenses, and you probably need to be registered as a business to do so.

My math skills are below average. In fact, they are almost laughable poor. Yet I manage to do my own finances. Do I like doing it? No. Can I live with spending an afternoon twice a year balancing my takes and reporting it? Yes.

I understand perfectly if the whole tax thing and balancing books make you cringe. If it lets you sleep better at night, by all means get an accountant or a bookkeeper. Just note that those kinds of people tend to want expenses and invoices presented in an orderly fashion and they don't know your business as well as you do. I'll go deeper into the whole financing thing on page 58.

Jump In!

Preparation is good but there are a lot of things you can't think your way out of. You have to get your boat in the water and kind of have to build it along the way. I've tried drawing up a map of where the reefs are and what things to pack for your voyage, but the weather can be unpredictable and so can the captain (that's you, by the way). Nobody knows how you'll handle the changing tides but you'll only learn by giving it your best shot.

In the next chapter, we'll take a closer look to your first year as a solopreneur. Even if you're already years into your career I recommend you read along. Maybe you've skipped important steps or maybe there's something that needs to be refreshed in your mind. A creative career is not a linear journey and one size does not fit all.

Your First Year of SOLO

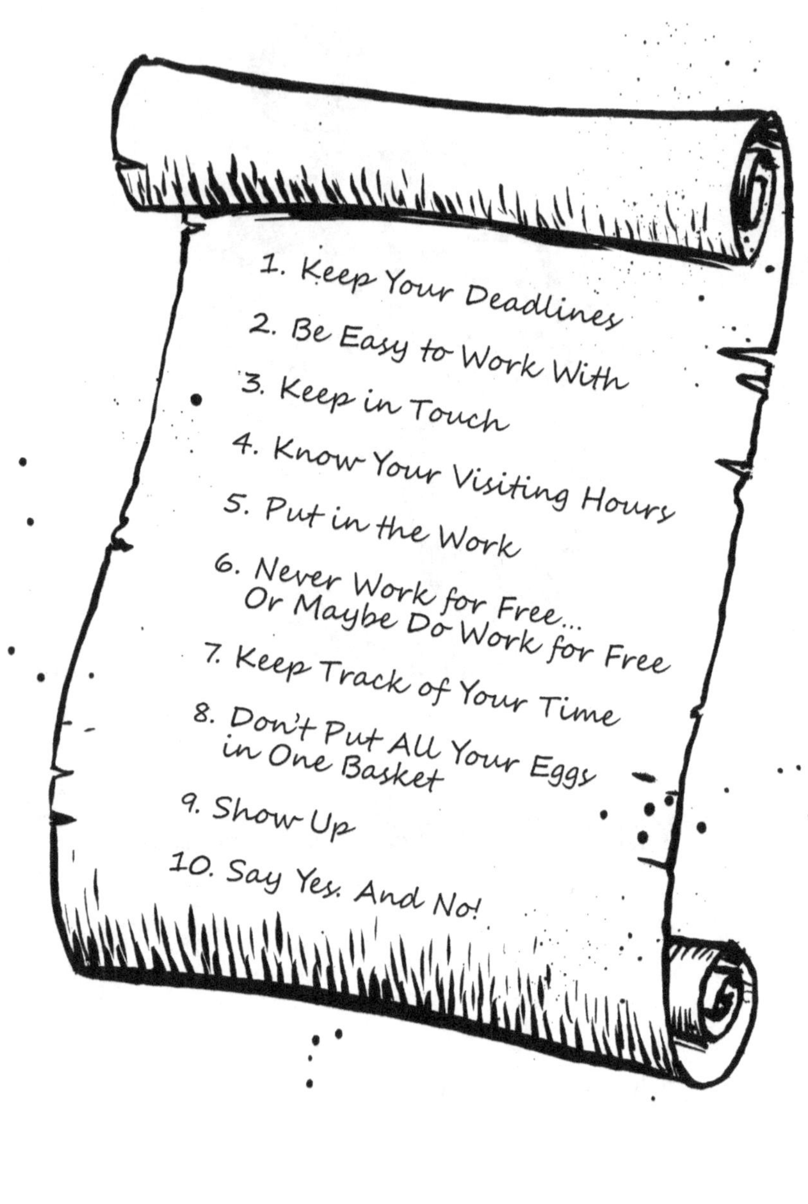

1. Keep Your Deadlines
2. Be Easy to Work With
3. Keep in Touch
4. Know Your Visiting Hours
5. Put in the Work
6. Never Work for Free... Or Maybe Do Work for Free
7. Keep Track of Your Time
8. Don't Put All Your Eggs in One Basket
9. Show Up
10. Say Yes. And No!

CHAPTER 3

The Good Freelancer

The Ten Commandments

This book is an attempt to gather all the experience I've gained in the past twenty years as a freelancer. But if I had to distill it down, this section is the most essential advice I have to give—my ten commandments for anyone attempting to make a living as a creative freelancer.

Let's go through them one by one:

1. Keep Your Deadlines

Accountability is the no. 1 thing clients are after. Talent is on the list, sure, but waaay down. If what you hand in isn't your best work, chances are they won't notice. But if you don't deliver on the agreed time – you bet they will notice! Reliability is crucial for a freelancer.

If for some reason you can't keep your deadlines – call! Most editors and clients are reasonable people who understand if your kid is sick or something made it impossible to make your deadline. Give a heads up if things look tight, ask if your deadline can be postponed. It usually can. Do *not* stick your head in the sand by dodging phone calls or ignoring emails.

If you get overwhelmed or strained on a project, bringing in another freelancer to help out is often a good solution. You could have someone in your network help out or take over the job completely, if the client agrees. Usually what they're after is getting the job done and if you can't deliver, bringing in someone who you vouch for is the next best thing, hopefully ensuring that the client will still call you another time.

2. Be Easy to Work With

Nobody likes a prima donna who rolls his eyes every time there are a few changes to a project. Clients can be a pain, not knowing what they want and not understanding how you work. You have to be lenient, flexible and forthcoming. If they keep moving the goal posts or change things on a whim, you are perfectly entitled to bill for the extra workload. But if you agreed to the terms and messed something up, you have to own it.

I once had to redraw almost all illustrations I did for a book because I had consistently drawn people with shoes on. Problem was that everyone needed to be depicted barefoot. Nothing in the brief from the editor about that. I charged for the extra changes and the publisher was forthcoming. In another case I'd drawn the wrong people in several illustrations and this was totally my own fault. I had read through the brief too quickly and messed up the names of John and Jack. So I had to redraw on my own time, owning up to the responsibility.

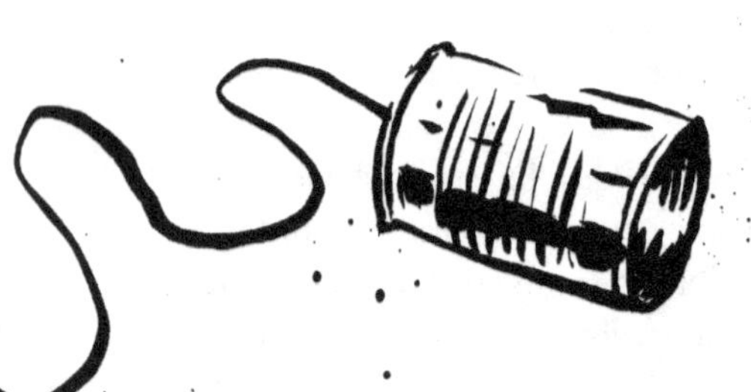

3. Keep in Touch

Out of sight, out of mind. This is especially true for us freelancers who don't bump into our clients at the water cooler. Keeping in touch with your network is a long-term sales tactic.

Nowadays it's easy to stay in touch via social media. When I've met someone through some professional capacity I usually add them on Facebook, thereby increasing the chances they'll remember me in the future. They might see something I post, and vice versa. It can be a great source of research or a way to break the ice when you meet somebody in person. And I still believe that face time (the activity, not the app) is the best way to connect with other people.

Something as old school as sending a physical Christmas card has proven a great way to let clients know I appreciated working with them. A lot of people like the extra effort of a postcard, believe it or not!

4. Know Your Visiting Hours

Some editors like that you pop by for a cup of coffee. But you don't want to outstay your welcome. I myself can be a chatterbox, so even though I recommend face time or even calling people on the phone once in awhile, I try to remind myself to have an agenda. Jot down a few notes before getting on the phone and wrap it up when the issue you called about is resolved. You need to find your own balance between personal and business.

5. Put in the Work

In the words of artist Molly Crabapple: "Remember that most people who try to be artists are kind of lazy. Just by busting your ass, you're probably good enough to put yourself forward, so why not try?"

You will undoubtedly experience periods of time when no clients are calling and you worry about where next month's rent is going to come from. Don't sit around waiting for clients to call, biting your nails and worrying. Why not use the opportunity to make some headway in your own projects? It will sharpen your skill set and help keep anxiety at bay.

6. Never Work for Free . Or Maybe Do Work for Free

Especially early in your career you will meet truly charming people who want you on board for their exciting projects—unpaid projects, that is. They will tell you of the great opportunities for long-term jobs and the amazing exposure you will get. Er, no. Ninety percent of these offers are bullshit that won't pay the bills now or ever. As it turns out, it's almost impossible to convert a low-paying client into a high-paying one. Getting your foot in the door will only result in achy toes.

I'm sure there are some circumstances where working for free can have long-term benefits but I'd be very skeptical of these charlatans. Asking someone to work for free is just not professional and you want to work with professionals, if you want to be one yourself. If, on the other hand, you get a chance to work with someone you admire or can see it as a learning experience, go right ahead. Especially in the early years you need to keep an open mind and give clients the benefit of the doubt. Just be aware of the ones who want to sucker you into working for free. More about spotting bad clients on page 97.

7. Keep Track of Your Time

As a freelance artist you can easily end up spending all your waking hours huddled over your work. And you can just as easily end up goofing off all day not getting anything done, beating yourself up all the while. You need some kind of structure, especially if you want to keep the aforementioned deadlines. Decide when and how you're going to work on any given project, set up some boundaries and keep the appointments you make with yourself.

Being your own boss requires a great deal of discipline and the calendar and the to-do list are among your most important tools. More on productivity and planning on page 129.

8. Don't Put All Your Eggs in One Basket

If you only have one major client, your small business is very vulnerable to the changes of your industry. Keep several sources of income, so if a client decides to try something new, you still have ways of getting food on the table.

This goes for your personal projects as well. If you bet everything you have on that one novel, that one exhibition or album, you could end up taking a devastating blow to your confidence if it fails to deliver the success you'd hoped for. Once you send in that novel to the publisher, start writing the next one! That way, when the rejection letter comes (and it will, trust me) you're already so far into your next project that it doesn't crush your soul. Keeping that flame of confidence alive is crucial in order to thrive as an artist. Keeping multiple projects going is the best defense against rejection and failure.

9. Show Up

Woody Allen is quoted of saying: "Eighty percent of success is showing up." He's not all wrong!

It's easy to fiddle away at our art in the comfort of our own studio. That modesty you pride yourself in having can just as soon make you invisible. If you want to make a living from your craft, you have to flaunt it. You have to look up and say hello to strangers, let the world know what you're up to. Yes, you can do that on Instagram but if you really want to pivot, you have to put on pants and go meet people in person.

If you don't show up to the party, no one's going to invite you to dance.

10. Say Yes. And No!

Early in your career you can't afford to say no a lot. You need the experience and you need something to put on your resume. Just be aware that whatever you do most of, you will get more of. In time you need to choose more wisely between offers–at least if you have a goal in mind of what you want to be doing long term.

Once you've got the basic needs taken care of, it's perfectly fine to turn down work you really don't want to be doing. Especially if you can pass it off to someone in your network who would appreciate the work. Pay it forward. More about saying no on page 206.

Checklist for Pros

Other than the Ten Commandments above there's a list of things I feel are needed in order to be perceived as a professional. You may have a different opinion, but here goes:

An Elevator Pitch

As you probably know, the elevator pitch is a short description of what you do or what you're trying to sell. It should only be two to three sentences, clear and concise enough that you would be able to communicate it in the time of an average elevator ride (hence the name). If it's a story you're selling a publisher or reader, it can be as simple as, "It's *Paddington* meets *The Matrix*!" Or if you're describing yourself, "I'm a graphic designer by trade and I mostly do intros for independent movies."

I realize this may seem douchey and annoying and I agree completely! But it is just as annoying (for you and whoever you're talking to) if you haven't given a moment's thought to how you'd describe who you are and what you do. You'll find yourself hemming and hawing while the person in front of you is looking for the exits. Do a little bit of thinking ahead of time, please. And while you're at it, write down a short and a longer bio as well. You may need it for press or grant applications later on.

A Registered Company

Again, I don't know exactly how this works in your part of the world. But if someone is going to hire you it helps if you know how to get paid. If a plumber can figure out how to send an invoice, you can too.

A Plan

Not a detailed plan! You'll be changing it along the way anyway. Constructing a long-winded business plan is either going to be a roadblock or a means for procrastination. Don't go there. What you need is a list of maybe five things you can do to get clients right now. Obviously you then have to actually do those five things.

A Homepage

Having a central hub you can direct people to is today's equivalent of being listed in the phonebook. It's non-negotiable. Doesn't have to be anything fancy.

There are lots of free blog templates or basic webpage setups. See if you can get your own name through whatever domain seller you prefer. To begin with you don't need more than an "about" page and a way for people to get in touch with you. If you have a way to add a portfolio and a list of your services, even better.

Creating a webpage is the number one thing I see people get stuck on, trying to make it perfect. Don't! Just get something up and running, pay someone to do it if you have to. You can always add to it or change it later. But if a client tries to find you on Google and all they find is a Facebook page, odds are they'll consider you a wannabe.

If you need inspiration for what your webpage should look like, go check out someone else in your niche and see what theirs look like. Use a free template from Wordpress or Squarespace and don't spend weeks fiddling with learning html or whatever.

If you're trying to run a webshop or sell yourself as a visual artist you may need more than a glorified business card as a web page. But if it's not your core competence, I'd recommend hiring someone to do it.

The Right Equipment

It's really important to keep your expenses low when you don't have a steady income. But you have to have some kind of equipment in order to run your business. If you're planning any big purchases, like a computer, a camera or a mixing board, again it's a good idea to have set up your company so you can write it off as a business expense.

Think twice before you shop yourself silly though. Overspending on stuff you don't really need is a stupid way to run your business into the ground before you even get started. I myself have made plenty of irrational purchases over the years. Here are a few of them:

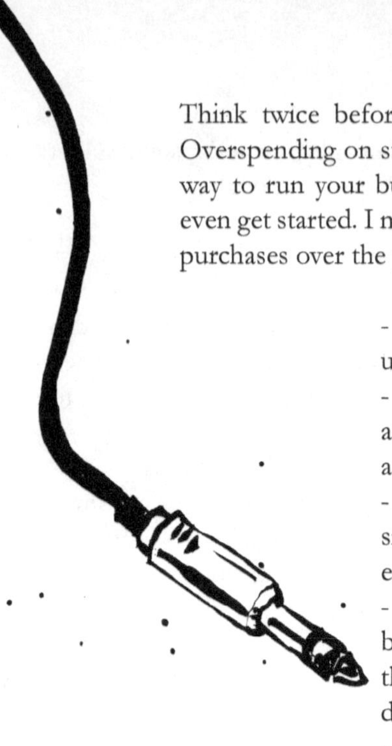

- Multiple domain names I don't use.
- Tons of watercolor pads, folders and notebooks neatly tucked away in a drawer.
- A video camera I only used for 7 small videos and then decided it was easier to use my phone.
- A digital recorder I stopped using because I bought two (no wait, three) other microphones that plug directly into my iPhone.
- A new iPhone I honestly didn't need.
- Several shoulder bags and travel bags to replace the last one that wasn't *exactly* what I was looking for.

From where I'm sitting right now, I can also see at least twenty books on writing, reference books and other craft handbooks that I barely opened since Amazon delivered them. Not counting all the novels and comics I bought for "inspiration" and that are now threatening to crash my bookshelves. File that under "it seemed like a good idea at the time."

So before you make the same mistakes I did, take a long, hard look at your shopping list and decide whether things are need-to-have or nice-to-have. The clients don't care what kind of equipment you have, as long as you get the job done.

A Social Media Presence

The obvious way to start branding yourself and your services is online. It's free and somewhat expected that you have a social media presence. By no means does it have to be a designated Facebook page or anything fancy. You just want people to be able to find you.

I can't tell you what platform will create the best—if any—results for your business. It depends entirely on what it is you sell and to whom, how much time and effort you put in and how enjoyable you find it.

As with anything, social media is a learned skill. I won't say I'm an expert, I'm not very active on Facebook, rarely check my Twitter and haven't logged into LinkedIn for years. I try to use as little time as possible on social media but if people want to find me, they can.

Some artists and writers value secrecy and exclusivity, it's part of their brand that they're hard to find and they don't have a website or a Facebook profile. While that strategy may work for Banksy or Alan Moore, I'm willing to bet good money it won't work for you. I'll go into more detail on the use of social media as a freelancer on page 84 but for now let's just say that in this day and age it's kind of a must.

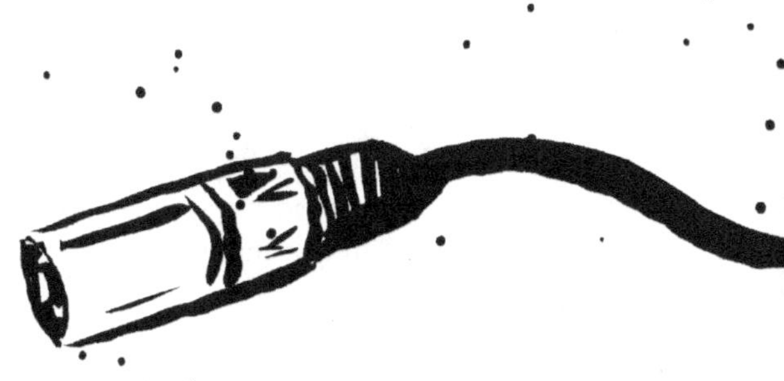

A Decent Profile Pic

No, a selfie doesn't cut it. Get a pro to take a good headshot, that's money well spent (and tax deductible). Have them take a few shots of you engaged in your work while they're at it. It's nice to have if you ever get a chance for some media exposure. Make sure you get the digital files in high resolution.

By the way I'd recommend you use the same profile pic for all your social media platforms. It gives a nice feeling of interconnection and makes one less decision for you to worry about.

A Business Card

How can a piece of cardboard with your info make any difference for your business? Well, *not* having it makes you seem less pro, that's for sure. You don't want to be running around looking for a pen and a napkin to share your info if you run into some high profile person. It's more important that you get *their* info, but having a card is just a great way of signaling you're serious about whatever it is you do.

Backup

As a solopreneur there's no IT department standing by to save your ass. If your computer crashes and you lose an entire weeks work that's all on you. Your client might be sympathetic that you can't deliver on the promised date but they might also not use you again. Better safe than sorry.

Dropbox has become one of my favorite tools and I save almost every ongoing project there, as it is accessible everywhere I log in, on every device. It has saved me a ton of trouble over the years. Like the time I was at my home in Copenhagen, when I saw an email from the publisher in L.A. saying they hadn't received the latest issue. I found the finished pages in a Dropbox folder on my phone and was able to move them to the shared folder. Problem solved in less than two minutes.

When I meet an agent at a convention and they ask for a PDF of my book, I can share a link directly from my phone and in ten seconds time they have access to the file from their email.

When the memory on my phone is almost full and I'm nowhere near my computer. I've set it to automatically upload pictures when I'm on a Wi-Fi connection so after a quick pit stop at the hotel I can safely erase old pics and clear space on the phone.

Or when I was working out of a New York apartment coloring comic pages in Photoshop and wanted to be sure they synchronized.

At this time you can get 2GB storage on Dropbox for free or get 1TB at a very reasonable price. Again; tax deductible. If you want extra security you might want to get an external hard drive or two, maybe even keep them in different locations in case there's flood or fire. But also keep in mind that every hard drive you ever own will eventually fail because it's their nature to wear down with use over time. Being prepared with multiple backups in different formats will save you from unwanted stress and potential disaster in the future.

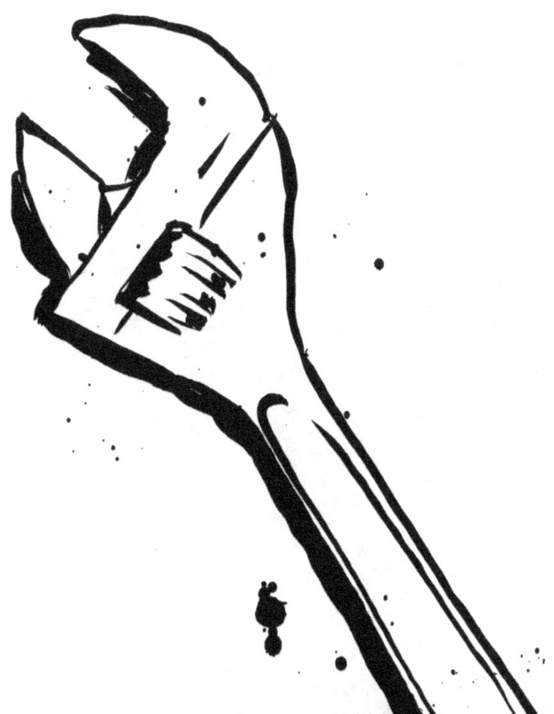

Create Your Own Workspace

As I mentioned earlier, I wouldn't have had the career I have today, if it wasn't for my time at Gimle Studios. This is where I learned from the best, grew my network and got the jobs that laid the foundation for my business. Most importantly, being surrounded by other hard working professionals was how I built my work ethic and self-confidence as an artist.

Later on I got a spot at the larger co-op Republikken, which was as far from what Gimle was as I could get. I needed to shake things up a bit and sitting with designers, photographers and other types of creatives as well as entrepreneurs certainly helped me get a new perspective. This is where I came up with ComicsForBeginners. com and where I started to really focus on my own projects.

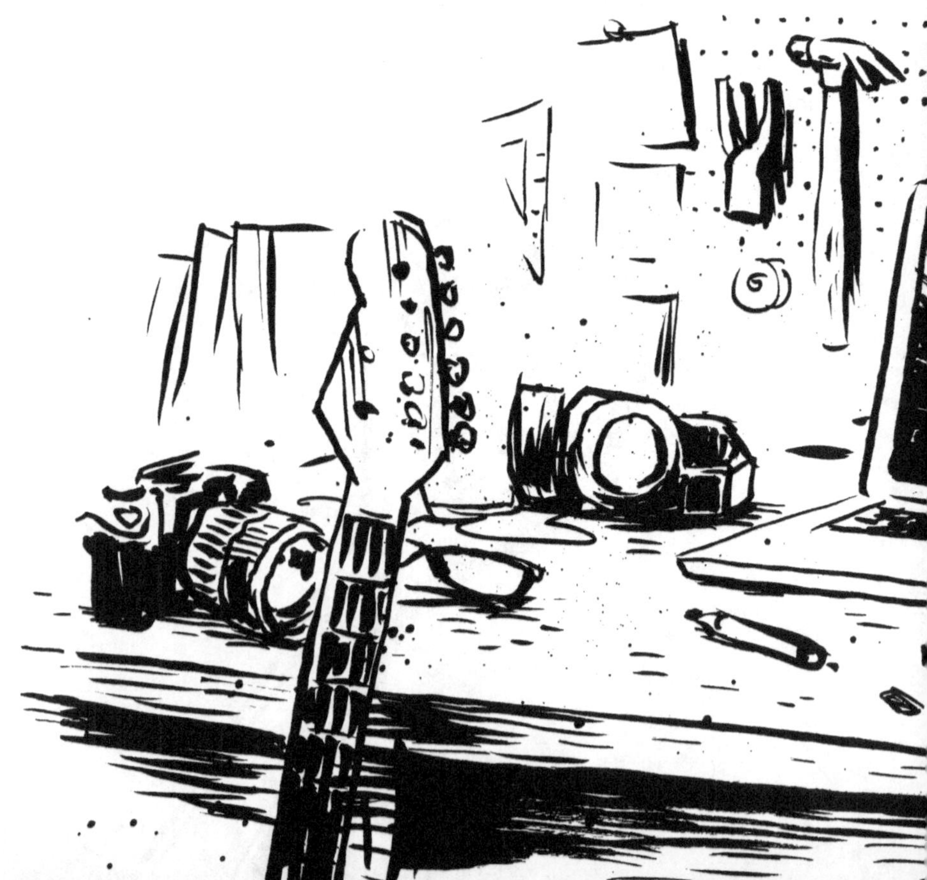

After working out of my house for a year while I studied at Film School (yet another way I started to think outside the box) I'm now back at a studio space with a handful of other creatives—illustrators, designers, photographers and another writer. I have a whole room for myself which is perfect for when I'm writing and need to concentrate, when I have people over for podcast interviews or when I'm filming videos. In hindsight, I would probably have benefitted from isolating like this sooner, as I tend to get involved in conversations if I'm in an open office environment. I love having an office in town as it helps my focus to have a dedicated workspace and it's good for me to get out of the house every morning.

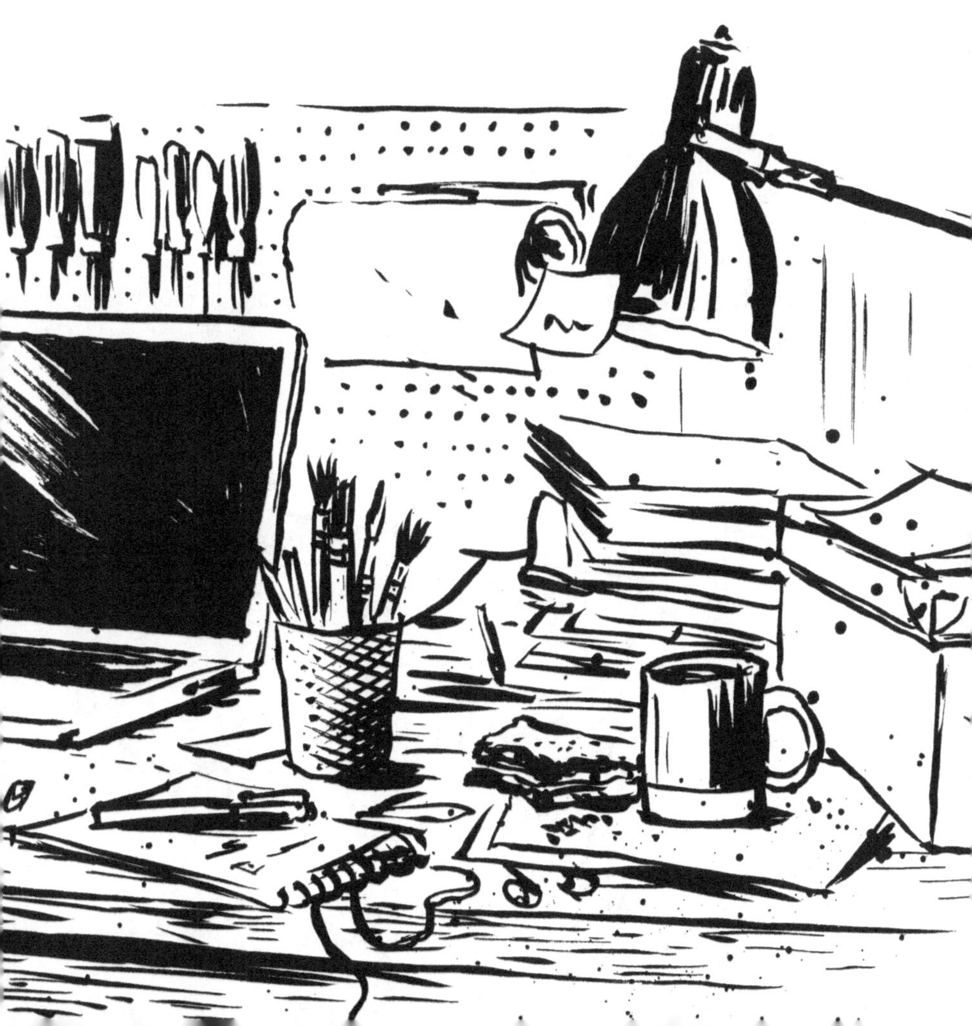

Whether you want to work from your house, an office space or the local coffee shop is up to you. Of course it depends on what you do, what area you live in, what your economic options are, and what kind of set-up your work requires. I'm sure an opera singer will have a harder time working from a café than a blogger.

Pros and Cons

To help you decide where to work from, here's a list of some of the advantages and disadvantages.

Home office pros:
- A pretty quiet work environment, no office chatter or ringing phones besides your own.
- No extra rent (and maybe even a tax deduction—check with your relevant authorities).
- You always have all your tools and files at hand and can work anytime—even after the kids are put to bed.
- Speaking of kids, you may find it convenient to be able to take care of your young ones at home, while you're running your business.

Home office cons:
- Lonely lunch hours and probably nothing interesting in the fridge.
- Work habits can be hard to maintain and things can start to slide.
- Working alone, no one will notice your procrastination.

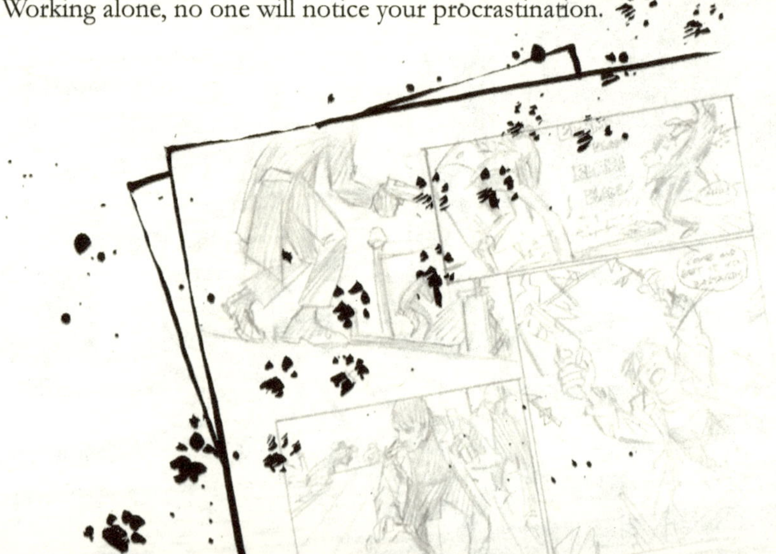

Office space pros:
- Getting away from your house chores can do wonders for your productivity.
- You can take longer days and not be interrupted when the kids come home.
- Your friends tend to leave you alone and not lure you out for drinks if you're in an office.
- No obligation to do dishes or laundry, you can focus on the work.
- Procrastination is harder to fall into when everyone around you is working.
- You have a support group of peers handy if you get stuck creatively or run out of work.
- You have the opportunity to collaborate and bring in skilled help on projects.

Office space cons:
- Commute.
- Rent.
- Other freelancers can be noisy and/or lazy too.
- Water cooler chatter can eat up your days.

Alternative Working Spaces

More and more business hotels and co-ops are popping up, where you don't have to have a desk but rather just plop down wherever is available. A lot of freelancers take their laptops to the local library or set up office at Starbucks. Some people find it hard to work with a noisy espresso machine going on in the background, others find the buzz of people inspiring and appreciate the constant supply of coffee available. The coffee isn't free though. You could end up spending more money on lattes than you would on an office space—and gain twenty pounds!

If getting a spot at a studio or a co-op is out of reach, try finding a peer group online that you can check in with on a regular basis. Committing to a weekly hangout or uploading new art every Wednesday can help you stay on track and keep you motivated.

Accountability and moral support is solid gold for a struggling, self-doubting creative.

An online support group could be as simple as a Facebook group, a mailing list or a weekly Skype call with a handful of likeminded people in the same type of situation. More about this kind of network in the chapter on master minds (page 147).

Get the Family on Board

Working out of the house requires some sort of framework, especially if you have a spouse or other family members who need your attention. Routines and a dedicated workspace can help create boundaries and a better understanding from the rest of the family. It's great that you're at home and can keep an eye on the kids or take care of a few house chores during the day. But it can be a source of constant interruption and lower productivity, gnawing away at your relationships, both professional and personal.

You need to set expectations and explain your side of the story to family members, and stick to the agreements you make. It's a give-and-take. If they promise to leave you alone during work hours, it's not fair that you sneak off after dinner or your attention drifts too much during family time. If a closed door means you're working, you better be working and not playing World of Warcraft!

I'm lucky that I met my wife when I was already working freelance, so she knew what she was getting in to. Being a writer herself (and now also working freelance) she understands the irrational need to go off and create something. It can still create some tension when I work late nights or leave her with the kids while I go off to Comic Con (although it's likely that she's just envious). We give each other space and respect each others needs. When my wife goes off to a writing refuge for a week, you'll hear no complaint from me either.

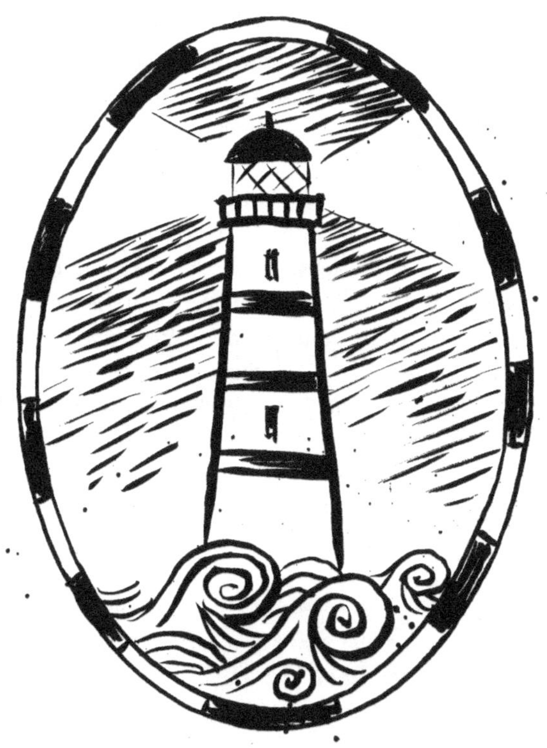

CHAPTER 4

Mentors

I can't stress the importance of mentors and peers enough, especially when you're starting out. Being able to follow in someone's footsteps, realizing it can be done, is huge. That's the main reason I wrote this book, to show a path for others who might not have the amazing network I did.

While I did my best to include all the best advice I could think of, you may still need guidance and expert opinion on your exact situation. This works best in a one-on-one situation with people you respect and admire. And luckily it's easier than ever to reach out to someone like that.

Of course your biggest idol is super busy. But most people like to help others. They like feeling needed, feeling wise and important. And odds are they've been exactly where you are at some point and been fortunate enough to have the help of a more experienced peer or mentor.

When reaching out to someone you respect, admire (or envy), be mindful of the JFK doctrine; ask not what they can do for *you*, but what *you* can do for them. And at the very least, be serious about it. If you've never played the guitar, it makes no sense for you to want career advice from a rock star. You have to show up with dedication to the craft, some talent, and some work to show for it.

Here's a template for an unsolicited email you could send (edit as needed):

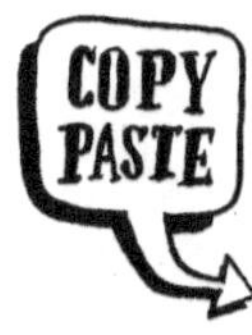

Hi (name),

I've been following your career as a (cartoonist/writer/musician/whatever) for quite some time now and I must say I'm floored by your (results/skills/work ethic/ability to keep upping your game). I'm heading towards becoming a (cartoonist/writer/musician/whatever) myself and would be eternally grateful if I could (buy you a coffee/buy you lunch/get you on a quick call) some time. I have a handful of short, concrete questions I want to ask you.

Let me know if it's at all possible to (meet up/sit down/hop on Skype) some time in the coming weeks. Whatever is convenient for you!

I know you have a busy schedule but a few pointers from you would mean the world to me.

Best,
(Your name)

As the above email template shows, I want to remain humble yet confident. I want to keep it short, making sure not to include any questions yet, but letting them know that I have concrete questions I want to ask and not just "pick their brain." You want to make it convenient and non-committal for them. If/when they ever get back to you, you might want to include a link to your website and/or some suggestions for times and places to meet up. Again, to make it easier for them to just say yes and show up instead of unloading the responsibility of arranging the meet on them. You need to be flexible and forthcoming, obviously.

If you don't hear back immediately, don't discourage. Try them again a couple weeks later and if you still get no reply, let it go. And don't take it personally. They're busy people.

Meeting with a potential mentor is sort of like a blind date. You might want to keep food intake to a minimum, so you can focus on the conversation instead of wrestling with a gigantic club sandwich. A coffee is less of a commitment and can be kept short and sweet if there's no chemistry or conversation starts to lull.

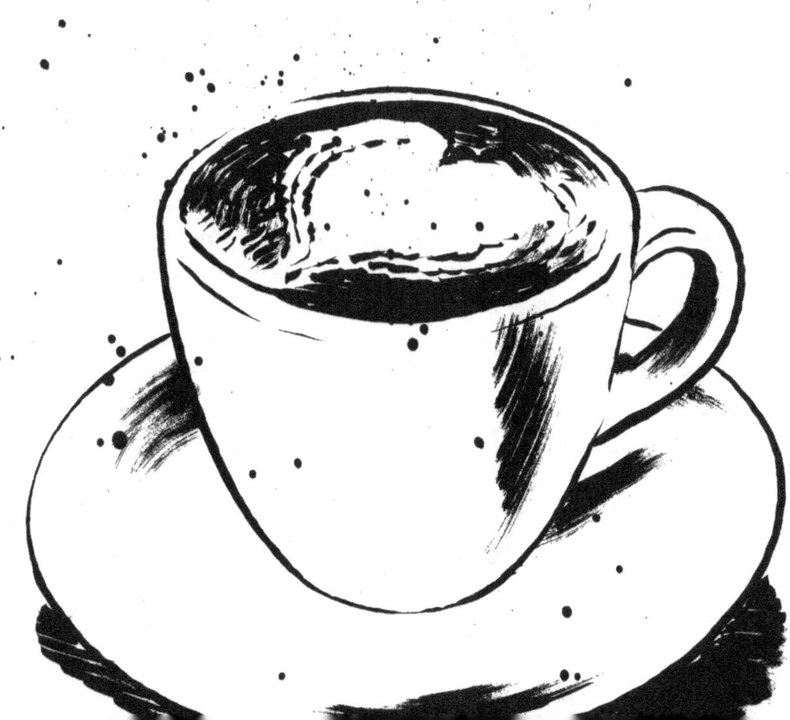

I purposefully didn't mention the word "mentor" in the above message, because I don't believe any one who hasn't met me would commit to such a thing. You don't want to scare anyone off. And you don't want to commit to anything long term with someone you haven't met either. See what comes of it and let the relationship build slowly.

If/when you manage to get a sit-down, here are some pointers:
- Show up on time!
- Have specific questions ready. At least one, no more than ten. Not having an agenda is a waste of time, yours and theirs.
- Do your research so you know who you're talking to and can ask better questions.
- Praise wins the day. You don't have to suck up or anything but I'm sure there's a reason why you picked that person specifically. Maybe it's not that you admire their art, but a phrase like "you do the thing that I'm aiming at" can suffice. I don't want you to be dishonest but appreciation and enthusiasm is better than playing it cool.
- Don't spend the whole time talking. You're there to listen and learn, not to tell them your life story. They don't care and it won't help you get any wiser.
- Take notes. On numerous occasions I've had people ask me for advice and it always blows my mind that they just sit there nodding, not writing anything down. What a wasted opportunity! I doubt they'll remember any of our conversation. I need to remind myself of the same thing as I've often also been so consumed with listening that I forgot to take notes.
- Get in, get out. Not letting the meeting drag on for hours is your responsibility. You need to respect their time and let them know that you do so. You can always follow up by email if there's anything you forgot to ask.
- Pay for the coffee/lunch/whatever. This may seem silly as they're likely more well-off than you, but you're the one who asked for the sit-down. Picking up the tab is the least you can do. And you can probably write it off as a business expense.

Questions for Your Mentor

I'm sure you have a bunch of questions already, but here's some general examples for your inspiration:

- How did you get to the level you're at in your career?
- What do you think would be a logical next step for someone in my situation?
- Where do you see my art needing improvement?
- Is there anything I'm missing in how I perceive this business?
- How can I improve my online presence?
- Any resources or people you can recommend I reach out to?
- What's the one piece of advice you give most to people who want to achieve what you have?

Again, remember to say "thank you." And maybe follow up a few weeks or months later, letting them know that you followed up on the advice they gave, maybe with examples of how it affected your work or helped in some way. *That's* the main thing you can do for them—letting them know that their guid-ance matters, that you took it to heart and it made a difference.

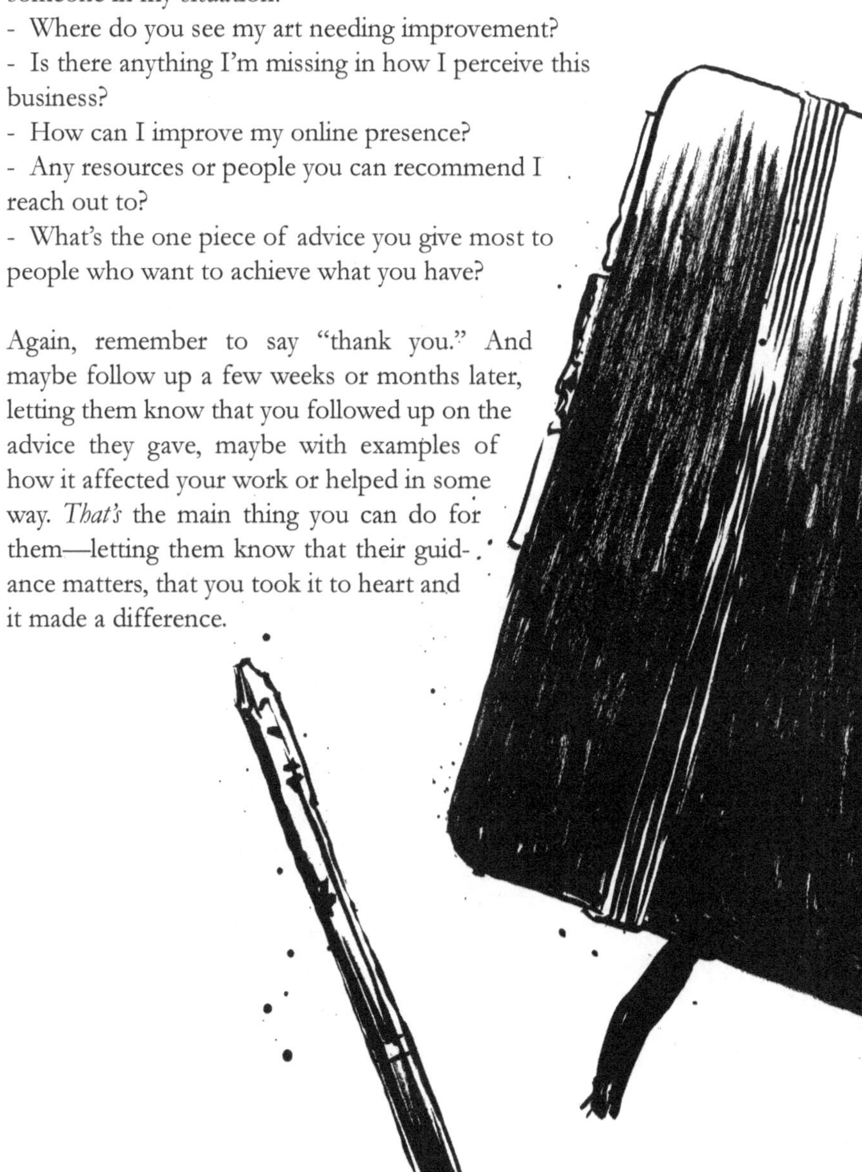

CASE STUDY: THE DEVIL'S CONCUBINE

This book was over ten years in the making, a perhaps overly ambitious project designed to kick down the door to the US market.

I wanted the book to look like a music video and be as stock full of gratuitous violence as an early John Woo action movie. I wanted to create a book that my 13-year-old self would find impossible not to pick up. I had a dogma that no matter where you opened the book, there should be someone getting shot, something blowing up or someone taking their clothes off. I struggled to find the right drawing style, often asking my studio mates and specifically my mentor and long-time idol Peter Snejbjerg for feedback and advice. Looking back it's obvious that although I carried myself with a cocky arrogance and razor-sharp sarcasm, I was super-insecure, always looking for validation and praise from my peers.

For years I tried the traditional route of mailing sample pages (this was almost before the internet!) to US publishers, getting rejection slips or no reply at all. I tried publishers in France and the UK as well, getting close to a deal a couple of times but never anything set in stone. And no, dropping Snejbjerg's name in the cover letter didn't make any difference. The industry seemed far away and didn't seem very interested in what I had to offer.

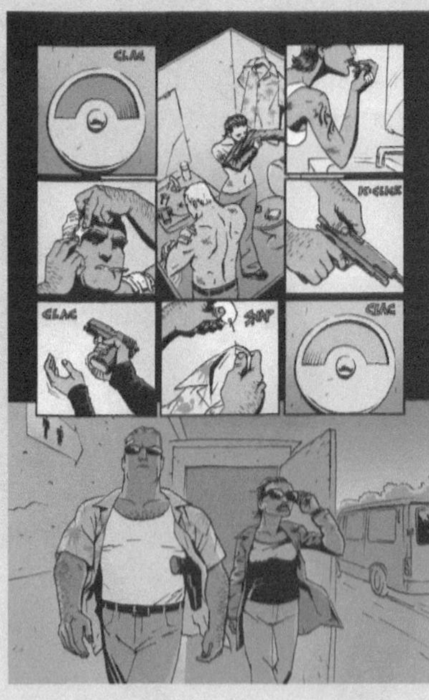

I knew it would take years (with no incoming salary) to finish *The Devil's Concubine* and was almost ready to give up. It just seemed like it would never happen. Then one night out drinking with a bunch of comics guys in Copenhagen, I got to chatting with small press editor Paw Mathiassen of Fahrenheit. He asked what I was working on and I told him the woeful story of *The Devil's Concubine*. I'm sure this dead-end project of mine was a running joke amongst my peers at this point but apparently Paw hadn't heard it. "Send it to me," he said and as it turned out that slight interest from an editor was enough to kick me back into work mode.

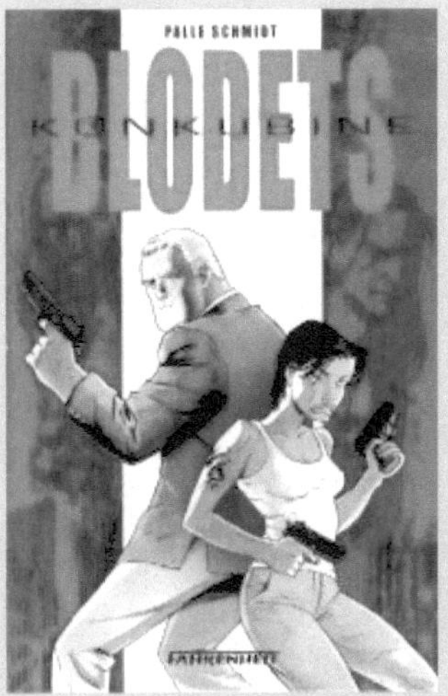
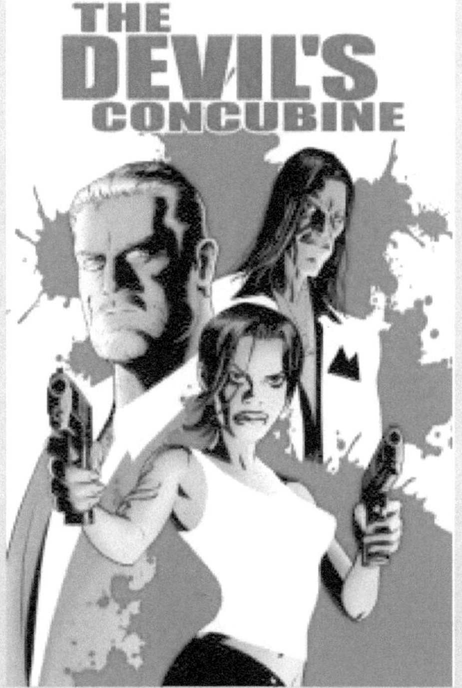

I translated the script to Danish (it was originally written in English) and rough sketched the entire book in a few months, so I at least would have something readable to present. Paw agreed to publish the book and although it was a back-end deal that never made me any money as far as I recall, I could now see the finish line and was able to drag myself out of the ditch and finish the race. I worked on the book any chance I got for the next year or so and *The Devil's Concubine* was finally published in Denmark in 2009, more than a decade after I came up with the initial premise and main characters.

With the book finished, I was now able to present to US publishers with a little more confidence. Time and technology had worked in my favor because now most publishers could be reached via email and I was able to send a full PDF with links to a cool trailer a friend of mine had made in After Effects and both a Danish and English version of a website (created by another friend, still available at devilsconcubine.com). IDW showed interest and we reached an agreement after about a year of going back and forth. The book finally came out in the US in 2011. Peter Snejbjerg did the cover art for the US edition.

Lessons Learned:
Ambition is great, finishing something is better. It's also a whole lot easier to sell a finished project than an idea. If you want to create something, do it for your own sake in your style rather than trying to cater to any market.

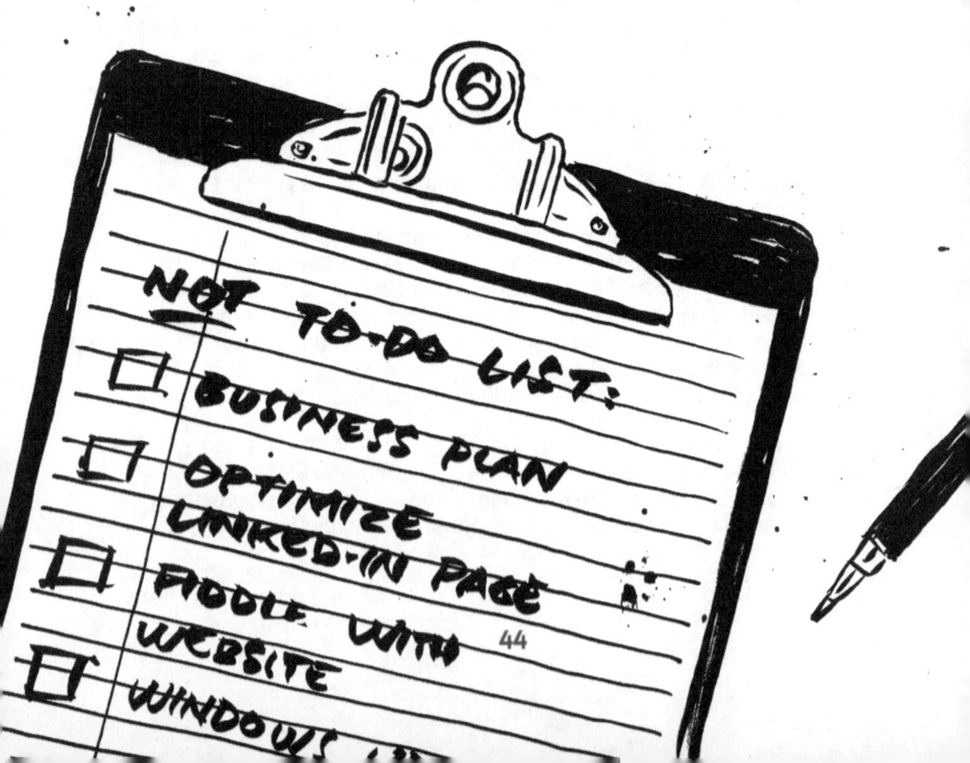

NOT TO-DO LIST:
BUSINESS PLAN
OPTIMIZE LINKED-IN PAGE
FIDDLE WITH WEBSITE
WINDOWS
44

CHAPTER 5

The Not-To-Do List

Maybe you're already reeling from all the advice and things you feel like you should be doing. But a lot of these things you don't need to worry about for the first years of your career. So let's strike some of those tasks from the list, leaving you with more time and energy to focus on what's important right now.

Logo Design, Webpage Graphics, etc.

It's tempting to hire someone to make a company profile for your business or to spend months fiddling with it yourself. Don't get derailed by letterheads and business card design at this point. Better to spend your time reaching out to peers and potential clients or creating something you can sell. Nobody cares if you have a cool logo or not, believe me.

If you're a designer yourself, perhaps your webpage or business card shouldn't be butt-ugly but you should think it through: Is it necessary or just a source of procrastination rather than doing the scary, real work? Once you grow your business a little and have some money to burn, maybe it's a good investment. But for now, use whatever free resources like Canva.com for graphics.

Having the best looking webpage will not help you land the best jobs. Fiddling with it will more likely drain your creative energy and bog down your whole business.

SEO

You've probably heard that Search Engine Optimization can help brand your business and boost sales. What if you could get to the first page of Google and quadruple the number of visitors to your site? Sounds great, right? Sure. It would also be great if you could build you own moon rocket. It's not gonna happen, let it go. I know SEO experts will fight me on this (as they should), but I don't believe it makes a huge difference what your ranking is, if you're not selling the cheapest version of a product that people are searching for on Google. I could be number 1 for "cartoonist" or "crime writer," but guess what, nobody's searching for that term. They might search for my name though, and my website comes up first. Never spent a dime on SEO for that.

Unless you have a webstore, whatever traffic you attract is pretty much worthless. And unless you have an interest and/or talents in SEO, forget it. Even if you pay some expert to do it for you, it's very hard to discern what they actually did for what you paid them and the results will be just as vague.

Crowdfunding

I know a lot of people who've had great success with running a Kickstarter or an IndieGoGo campaign. But it is A LOT of work. Unless you already have a huge following or your funding goal is a very small amount, I'd recommend making your money elsewhere and channeling them towards whatever project you want to create rather than focusing on running a crowdfunding campaign that will be very challenging at the early stage of your career. This is not to discourage you from crowdfunding in the future, but unless you have a co-collaborator on the project who can give your project the signal boost it needs to reach your target audience—or you have a unique and easily identifiable hook that will get people on board with your goal right away—it's going to be a lot of time and effort that might be better used in another way. More on crowdfunding on page 181.

Blogging

Had you asked me a few years ago, I'd have put my money on blogging. And while it may drive some traffic to your website and help you build an audience and status as an expert in your field, it could just as easily backfire. Unless you consistently update it, your blog could end up signaling that you either died or gave up on your business.

I'm no great example, I keep three or four blogs going (or rather, limping). Being a blogger and making my living from that is not my dream. If it's yours, great, knock yourself out. For me it's just another chore with diminishing returns.

Facebook Pages

Besides having a private Facebook profile, a lot of professionals have a dedicated writer page or business page. The idea is you can keep things separate, get more likes and reach a wider audience. I have an artist page as well and I'm guessing eighty percent of the people who've liked it are my other Facebook friends. It doesn't make a whole lot of sense to have two places to update other than the fact that I can plan posts ahead of time on my artist page. Which I rarely do.

If you like fiddling with this kind of stuff and you can see it works, great. If you're like me, you'll get tired of posting stuff in both places and your followers will end up seeing the same post twice—if at all. Facebook keeps changing their algorithm and the tendency right now is pay-for-play. The business pages don't show up in the feed unless the company decides to boost the post.

How about you strike the idea of building a Facebook following for now and just live with the fact that people will see both the personal side and the business side of you. If you do have a more personal post, you can always change the setting from "public" to "close friends."

Job Banks and Other Forums

Yes, networking is important. Yes, learning the ins and outs of your particular field is helpful. No, you don't have to be active in every Facebook group or sign up for every online community. Unless you have the money to burn and the free time to invest in getting to learn the lingo and the people involved.

Any forum who offers freelance jobs attract a lot of douchebags hoping to hire cheap labor and a lot of desperate creatives willing to fight for scraps. It's a race to the bottom. Unless you have no other ways (and I mean NO other ways) to get work, I'd steer clear of places like that.

Media Coverage

If you can get your story on the morning shows, by all means do it. And of course it is possible, people do it all the time. But that usually only occurs for people who spend a lot of time and energy on chasing the media and have a uniquely personal story or groundbreaking product. Or people with a clear press strategy and other people working for them. I've sent my share of press releases and media kits out, none of it has had much of an effect.

The few times I've had media appearances like TV or radio it has either been through a publisher or through personal contacts. And while I've enjoyed talking about my comics on live TV (and I would do it again if I ever get the chance. Call me!) I doubt that it's moved many books. Media coverage certainly doesn't hurt and can help build your platform, but you just can't bank on it ever happening. Don't spend your time chasing the big networks. Focus on creating your art and if the media ever calls *you*, great.

Articles, Links, Books, Newsletters, Trade magazines

Of course it's important to stay updated on what's going on in your business. Right? Or maybe it isn't. You don't *have* to click on every article people post on Facebook, even if it's relevant to your niche. You'll end up spending days consuming knowledge rather than creating content. And will you retain any of that knowledge, really?

There's this term called "just-in-time learning," can't remember where I picked it up. The idea is to research when you *need it* and not on the fly. Why spend three days looking at YouTube for tutorials on Wordpress, if you're not currently building a Wordpress site? If the actual work on a project is six months from now, all that research is time wasted. You won't remember any of it and it could have been made redundant by software or business changes anyway and you have to read up on it again. Huge potential for time suck here, folks.

Business Plans

You'll likely hear this term thrown around in entrepreneurial circles. If you're selling physical products and need to raise capital or get investors on board, you *do* need something like that. For the rest of us, it really doesn't make any sense and it's something you could get stuck on for months. Maybe the daunting task of creating a business plan will make you abandon your ideas all together. Even if you're able to pull it off, it will likely consist of pure guesswork, useless in any practical sense.

I've never created a business plan and nobody has ever asked to see one. What I'd recommend you do is think about what you're offering and to who. Make a list of three things you could do to generate some income. Get started and course correct later.

Before you throw time and money into a task, consider this small diagram:

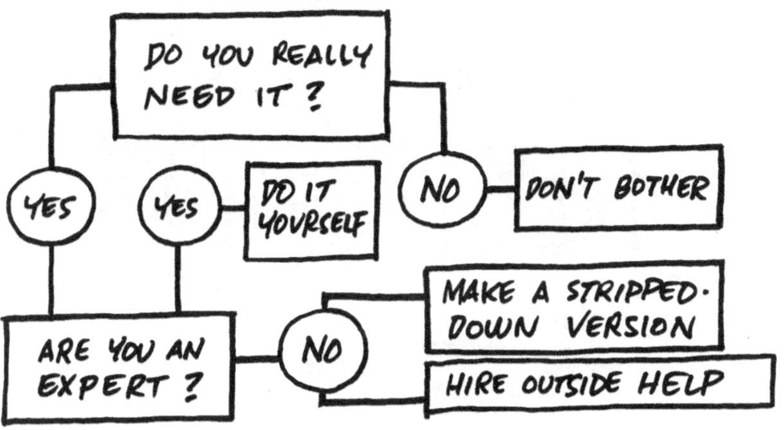

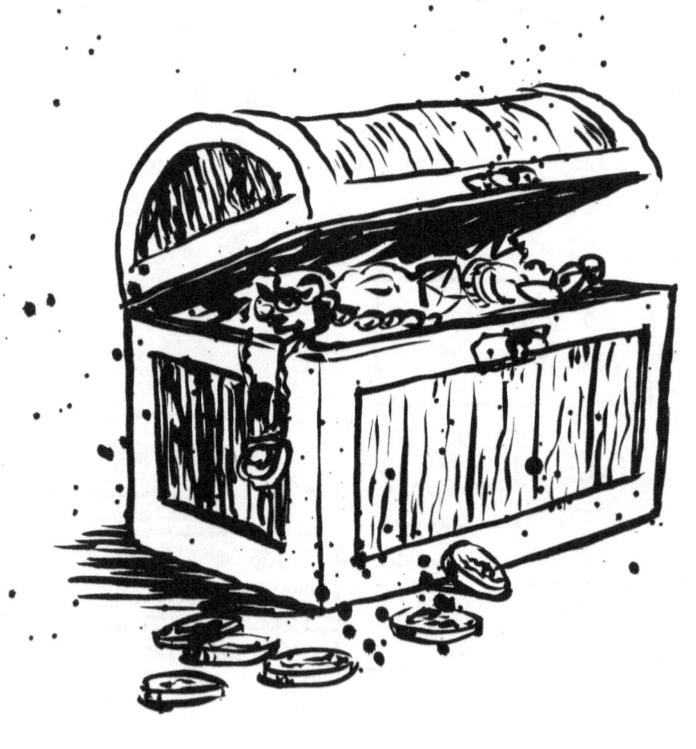

CHAPTER 6

All About the Money

In the beginning of your career, gaining work experience and bringing in some cash should be your main focus. But the most important thing is to be able to keep cool, calm and collected.

Swimming alone in open waters, you need to just take one stroke at a time. If you start worrying about how far it is to shore and how deep the water is, you'll likely panic and drown. So strike a course and stick to it. Maybe decide on a specific time when you're allowed to reevaluate your plan and your tactics. Like if three months go by and nothing shows up on the horizon, maybe you need to change direction a little bit.

Having been a full-time freelancer for twenty years I can tell you that there *will* be periods of little to no income. There *will* be periods of severe self-doubts. I've kept swimming and made it so far. You can too.

Have a Buffer

For you to keep calm and focus on creating your art it's important that your expenses are somewhat covered. If you don't know where the rent is coming from, it's very hard to just sit down and write poetry or play amazing music. That's why a lot of people start their career in arts as a side hustle, making their money at a regular job—preferably one that helps develop their artistic skills, allows them build a network, or at the very least doesn't drain them completely of creative energy.

I've had a few soul-sucking jobs in my early twenties, where I was too tired and depressed to get any work done after I clocked out. If you have to work that kind of job, try batching it together so you have a few full days off every week to focus on your own creative endeavors. Figure out what works best for you and try to scrape by. Apparently screenwriter Kay Cannon wrote the script for *Pitch Perfect* on her commute by train over several years.

If you can create a runway or save up enough for three months with little to no income, you'll be able to focus more and do better work thereby increasing your chances of success.

Keep a Lid on Your Expenses

You don't have to be completely frugal to be a freelancer and you don't have to be an accounting genius either. You just have to be wary of regular expenses like rent and not buy new shoes every three weeks. Unless you can somehow write it off as a business expense.

My spending has never really been tied to my income. To be perfectly honest I don't keep track of my expenses, I just have an inner brake that tends to work. If it's absolutely necessary for me in order to do my work or it's not too expensive, I just spend the money. My rent is pretty cheap and I don't go out a whole lot. Partly because I don't have a shitty job that I need to treat myself for living through another week of.

Plans and Back-up Plans

Like I mentioned earlier, I'd consider a business plan a giant waste of time. But in terms of money, it might be a good idea to whip out the old calculator and think ahead just a bit. How much do you need to pull in to cover your basic expenses? What is the low number that will keep you "ramen profitable," and keep yourself fed?

Just as there are ways to clear time in your schedule, there are probably expenses you could cut and live fine without, like that Netflix subscription or the membership to that gym you never go to. You could also think of alternative methods of income, like renting out a room.

Back in the early Nineties, some friends and I made a role-playing game magazine. We sold subscriptions, had advertisers and everything, even though we were just kids at the time. But we hadn't done the math.

None of us were paid a salary and we didn't have offices or any other major expenses—but we had printing costs. After the first issue, we were in the hole by about $1,500 and after the second issue, our debt had risen to $3,000. $4,500 by issue 3. Ouch. Needless to say, the magazine soon folded.

I also self-published a few books back in the day and while I covered printing costs from what retailers paid, I hadn't thought of shipping costs. So I ended up spending about $3 on every book I sold.

Some obstacles are to be overcome. Others are a hint from the universe that you need to change your strategy.

While I never had a business plan, these days I spend a lot of time thinking through the next couple of steps in whatever I'm doing. And what steps to take if things don't go according to plan. What's my next project going to be, what will be my focus in the coming weeks or months, what do I need to learn, what would the best and worst case scenarios be, what opportunities or people could be leveraged if my current strategy doesn't give the results I was hoping for.

Invest in Yourself

I'm sure you know the term "bootstrapping," getting by with what you already have, rather than bringing in a bunch of investors. You can most certainly bootstrap your creative career; you don't need venture capital to become an artist or a musician. And you don't need the most expensive guitar in the store in order to learn to play.

If an investment in a course or a piece of equipment will help you get to the next level, by all means go for it. It took me years if not decades to understand the value of going to conventions and other network events or paying extra for a tool that would improve my work. Today I'm more prone to think of these things as a long-term investment and an opportunity rather than an expense and I'm more likely to throw money at a problem rather than trying to do everything myself.

With and Without Money

Every freelancer I know has their own story on how they got started. There isn't one clear path to follow and what works for me won't necessarily work for you. It all depends on your field, your life situation, your attitude and your priorities. Someone with kids and a mortgage will be in a different spot than a young, single person with a trust fund.

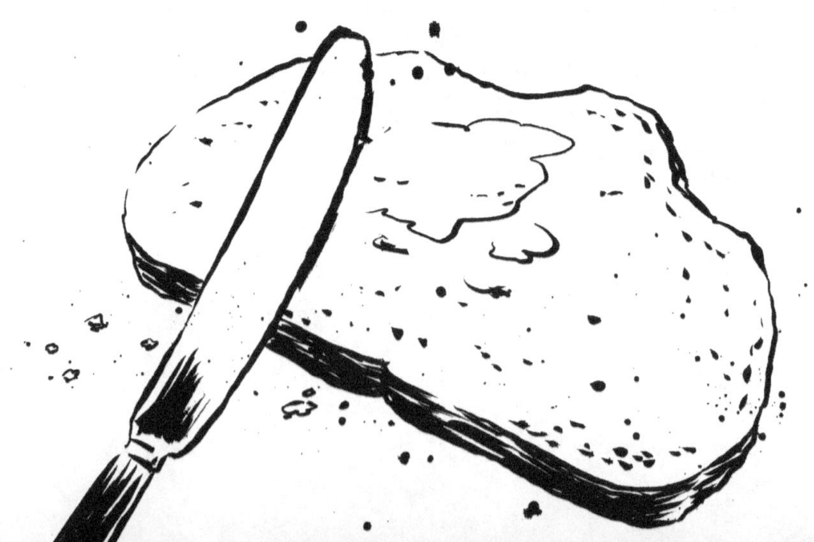

There are a few ways you can build a runway to get your creative career off to a good start:

With a Relevant Creative Job

Being in a job or long-term contract could be a great way to learn the craft, build a network and gain valuable business insights. You can find your footing while building a portfolio and long-term relationships to peers and clients, while saving up to go out on your own. This way of starting out is full of advantages but also has a few pitfalls. The biggest one being: you get used to having a steady income. But you also get used to office banter, the free lunch or the benefits. Like the health insurance that many countries rely on employers to help provide.

Unless you're extremely disciplined and have a clear goal in mind, you could end up getting stuck in that job for years as your values and friendships become more closely attached to the company. You need an exit strategy if you plan on jumping ship eventually.

Working Part-Time

A lot of artists have regular day jobs while building their own thing on the side. This might help you sleep better at night but it can also be extremely draining, leaving little energy to become prolific at your craft. If you can find a job where you can sort of phone it in or work a few hours a week to cover your expenses, great!

Here's a list of low-stress jobs:

- Transcribing (No-brainer work that isn't physically demanding)
- Teaching night school (Better pay than regular teaching and you have the day to work on your art)
- Phone interviewer (Not salesperson! That's way too draining)
- Babysitter or house-sitter (You can work on your art when the kids are asleep)
- Hotel desk clerk (Nights pay better and there's less to do—just be aware that night work is draining and you need a day to recuperate)

- Parking lot attendant or other attendant (Especially not too busy places)
- Personal care aide (Especially night watches—see above)
- Virtual assistance or anything you can do from home

For different ideas for craft related income go to page 177.

With Money Saved Up

If you feel like you need to give it your full attention, there's no other way than to build some runway before you strike out on your own. Perhaps you could get a grant or someone in your family is willing to fund you for a while. I would be wary of taking out a loan. Interest rates are high and chances of getting a loan are slim. Banks still consider people with one job way more safe to lend money to than someone with many jobs. Go figure. Perhaps you can get a credit agreement so you at least don't get charged an arm and a leg if cash flow is low for a few weeks.

It takes time to build a client portfolio and when you do start sending out invoices, it takes a while for the clients to pay too. With about six months worth of income tucked away you should be able to manage even the rockiest of starts.

If you're the kind of person who gets sweaty palms and an irregular heartbeat every time you think of finances, either stop thinking about it (my personal go-to strategy) or reconsider your ambition to become a freelancer.

Jump in With No Life Vest

Some people are highly motivated by necessity. If that's how your mind works, be my guest. Burn the boats and take the island, with no back up plan or money in the bank. Then you HAVE to make it work, right?

I wouldn't personally recommend this approach but I do know a few people who've managed to pull through with fear of starvation as their primary drive.

Insurance and Risk Mitigation

Yeah, I know it's boring, but we have to eat our veggies too! Please note that I am not a lawyer, an accountant or insurance expert. You need to talk to other people in your area to find out what they do but rest assured that you are probably *not* covered if there's a fire in your studio. Seriously. Business insurance and private insurance are two different things. And if you do get business insurance, it will cost you more than you think. I've sometimes gotten special travel insurance as my personal insurance will not cover any damages if they find out the trip was business related.

We all know we should protect our passwords too, change them every few months. But do you? Getting your Instagram or Facebook hacked is a hassle but getting your email hacked can be disastrous. If they can get into that, you could lose years of correspondence and contacts. And through your email they could get access to basically all other services you use by requesting a new password.

I'm not trying to make you paranoid, just a friendly reminder that having the same password for your PayPal as you use ordering take-out is probably not a good idea. And I'd think twice about handing in your phone for screen repair without making sure there's no easy access to email and the like.

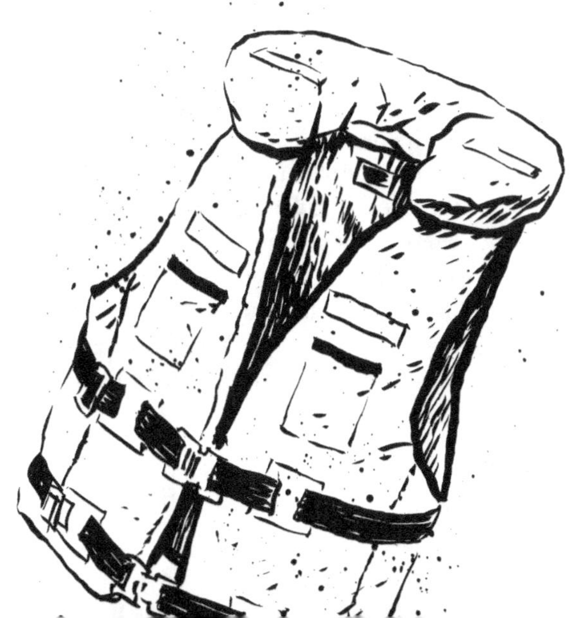

Unemployment Security, Health Insurance, Maternity Leave

However important these things are, the rules vary from country to country (or even state to state, if you're in the US), it's not for me to give advice on any of it. There are likely measures you can take to mitigate risks or prepare for emergency situations (public or private insurance, taking advantage of a spouse's insurance, etc.). Ask around and see how other freelancers in your area handle these things. You'll likely encounter a good number of people who haven't thought about it for a second—ignore them and find the sensible freelancer who doesn't just stick his head in the sand.

Accounting for Dummies

As a business, you're likely obligated to hand in yearly or bi-yearly accounts. It varies what the demands are. I'm so low on the income scale that my tax authorities just want to know the end result, I don't even use Excel or anything fancy like that. I do my accounts by hand using a plastic calculator from the dollar store.

To make it super simple, your accounts consist of two things:

A: Income
B: Expenses

Basically you just subtract B from A and you have the gross income from which to pay your taxes.

Having expenses in your company means less tax to pay, so make sure you file that receipt for printer toner for later. I can't tell you what the specific rules are in your country but my guess is you can write off more things than you probably think. And should you write off something that later turns out you can't, I doubt they'll fine you for it. You just need to take it out of your business accounts and pay the extra taxes, no biggie. At least in my country! Your tax authorities can be a different bunch of bastards, but you'll know this better than me.

When I do my accounts, I put expenses in different categories:

- Office supplies (stock paper, watercolor, pencils, note pads, etc.)
- PR (print costs on business cards, flyers, Facebook boosts, etc.)
- Computer (if I bought one that year)
- Inventory (such as a lamp for my office)
- Rent (my office space)
- Transportation (bus and train tickets, cab fare)
- Travel (plane tickets, hotels, car rentals)
- Postage (packages, etc.)
- Day-to-day operations (web hosting, everything else)

These categories don't really matter but they make the piles of receipts less overwhelming. And some categories have VAT included and others don't so I need to sort it through anyway. I'm required by law to save my accounts going back five years, but I don't have a fancy filing system, I just put them in a folder labeled that year, so I can find it if anybody ever asks to see it. As of yet, nobody has asked.

Before all my invoices and receipts go into that folder, my "filing system" consists of two drawers. One I put my crumpled up receipts in, all of them. The other contains print-outs of my invoices, so every time I send out one of these (usually by email these days) I make a hard copy for the drawer. It just helps me to have it all in one place when I sit down with the calculator twice a year (which is when I have to report my VAT).

Other than those two times a year, I spend my days *not* thinking about my finances. I try very, very hard not to. It just doesn't seem productive for me to worry about these things when I'm nose-to--the-grindstone working on something that requires focus and skill.

If you're the type of person who needs financial clarity and you like budgeting and juggling numbers, knock yourself out. I'd recommend setting aside maybe once a week or once a month so it doesn't eat away at the time you need to actually do the work you're supposed to. I know a lot of creatives who batch together admin work for a specific day every week. Friday seems like a good idea for that so you can take the weekend off feeling good about having updated whatever needs updating and know where you are in terms of invoices sent and bills paid.

Some people have a separate business account (some places require it by law) and pay themselves a monthly wage through that. I don't, but I don't have a budget either. So far it's worked out. But whatever your system, please, *please* remember to put money aside for taxes. It's no fun to get an unpredicted tax bill if you already spent all the money you earned. I pay a percentage up front based on my self-assessment but this too can vary from country to country.

By the way, bookkeeping for self-employed and small businesses has gotten a lot easier with online accounting programs and services such as Freshbooks or QuickBooks but I don't have any experience with it. You can also find apps that enable you to quickly scan a receipt and send it directly to your accounts, like Forreceipt (links up to Google Drive) and Verify (links up with QuickBooks).

Budgeting

Unstructured artists with their head in the clouds can greatly benefit from having a budget so they know what their expenses are and expected income is. It's a good idea to know how much you have to bring home. I personally just try to bring home as much as I can every given month and put most of it away like a squirrel stockpiling nuts for the winter. Sometimes (a lot of times, actually) there are no nuts coming in, so I just take from my stash. As long as there are some nuts left in there, I try not to worry too much.

Some things are beyond your control, like if the phone will ring or not. You can (and you should!) try to put jobs and projects in the pipeline but you'll often find diminishing returns in chasing work. In my experience, you need to make yourself known and available and then be ready to say yes or no to incoming projects.

In the beginning of my career I basically said yes to everything, nowadays I almost always say no. I find that creating my own projects is both more fulfilling and more predictable than hoping and praying for work to come in. It's like waiting for rain. I wait for nothing, I get to work. Sometimes it rains and I go fill my bucket with water but the rest of the time I just try to not drink all of it.

A recent example: I was writing this book when upon checking my bank account I realized I had about $230 left before I would have to take out a loan or sell a kidney. I just nodded and said to myself: "Interesting." And then I went back to work. It wouldn't make me richer or poorer to go into panic mode, but the book would likely be delayed. A few weeks later I got a grant and a major job fell into place, securing my income for the rest of the year.

I know this sounds like dumb luck but sometimes you have to trust in the universe and things will work out. Of course these opportunities didn't just fall into my lap, I had planted the seeds by researching and applying for the grant in the first place and now those efforts paid off. I'm always placing little bets but not banking on them. The real reason I sleep soundly at night is because I own a home in the city and could probably take out a second mortgage or a loan to keep me afloat for another six months. And my wife (who is also a freelance writer by the way) brings home some of the bacon. We each contribute what we can and try not to worry about finances too much.

Even people in "real" jobs can get hit by disaster. It just seems like those people are able to rest safely as long as they have a steady income—the minute they get fired is when they start to panic. And they have no skills for dealing with it, where we freelancers live with that insecurity every day.

It's like they've been comfortably floating on an air mattress giggling at the idiots in the water next to them. The minute that air mattress sinks, they're screwed. How is that better than having learnt to swim?

Tax Deductible Expenses

Another thing regular working people don't get to do is write off business expenses. While it obviously has to be relevant to your type of business (and again this varies from country to country), you can probably write off a lot more than you think.

Here are some examples:

Musicians:
Instruments, CD's or other music purchases such as streaming services, note paper, studio rental, transportation to and from gigs, rented equipment.

Illustrators and fine artists:
Drawing paper, canvas, studio space rental, art books, paint, computer, software like Photoshop or Clip Studio Paint, museum visits.

Writers:
Computer, writing software, books on writing or other fiction, theater tickets for screenwriters, research trips or writing refuges.

Designers and Photographers:
Cameras, lights, software like Photoshop or InDesign, printing costs for art prints or posters, studio rental, location travel expenses.

If it's business related, you can also probably write off:

- Computer purchases
- Web page hosting
- Guild memberships
- Courses and coaching
- Office/studio rent
- Accountant assistance
- Transportation costs
- Print and copy costs
- Apps and software
- Business related books (like this one!)
- Freight and postage

If you're facing a major purchase or investment, perhaps now is the time to set up that business, allowing you to write it off. Please note that this does not mean your new computer, synthesizer or ceramics oven suddenly comes at no cost—it just means less of your income you have to pay taxes on. In my part of the world, we have a very high tax percentage so that means I save almost half on business purchases. That's worth a lot.

Whether or not you can write something off will always be a judgment call, depending on your type of business and tax system. Before you put something in your business account, you first need to make that call yourself—will it hold up to scrutiny or are you straining your business credibility? If you have an accountant, ask them. If not, then ask your tax authorities (if you can get through the phone carousel).

Accountant or Bookkeeper

If your business has weird expenses like real estate, foreign markets, drop-shipping services or employees of any kind (other than invoice-based work for hire) you may need to get someone else involved who knows the ins and outs of your tax code. It comes at a cost of course, but that's a write off too, I would think. If it helps you sleep better at night, it's a good investment. Just be aware that you need more structured bookkeeping in order for a stranger to understand what's what. Accountants and bookkeepers are from a different tribe than most artists I know, so try to find someone who at least understands what being creatively self-employed entails.

Having to do your accounts is one of the major hurdles self-employed people face... at least psychologically. Like I mentioned earlier, math is by no means my core competence yet I manage to do my own accounts. So it's probably not as tricky as you think.

You don't have to know every rule and while you may get audited, I doubt that you'll get in trouble if you're not juggling millions or are deliberately trying to cheat. Plead stupidity! But I still implore you to do your due diligence in the first place so you don't get caught up in that.

In some cases, like if you're several people involved in the company or you sell physical products, it's a good idea to separate your personal from your business finances. Talk to your tax authorities to find out how you need to set it up.

Invoicing

You need to be able to bill a client in order for them to pay you. And the sooner you bill them after a job ends, the sooner the money will likely show up in your bank account. I find that sending an invoice when the project and client are fresh in mind is not just easier but also more professional. If several weeks pass after you hand something in, the client is likely to forget what the deal was and be annoyed at this blast-from-the-past expense. I know I would.

I send my invoices by email. Some prefer a PDF, others need a specific client number or job title on the invoice in order for them to process it correctly. You just have to put whatever they say on it. You might like the invoice paid within eight days or whatever, but again that varies a lot from company to company. I tend to let thirty days go by before I bug the client on an unpaid invoice. I should keep better track of when something gets paid but again I put my trust in the universe. Usually people pay eventually—and if they don't there's a template on page 66, I can use as a friendly reminder.

This may differ between countries but for me an invoice contains:

- An invoice number
- The date
- The company name (meaning mine) and address
- My VAT number (my value-added tax ID number that is unique for the company)
- The client's name and address
- Possibly a person reference

- Job description (what I'm invoicing for)
- Billing (hourly or flat rate, specified if needed)
- Added VAT if applicable
- Total invoiced fee
- My bank account number, possibly EAN or PayPal
- Last day of payment (because why not try)

That's pretty much it. Like I said earlier, I print a copy of every invoice I send for my accounts, just to be sure I have it all in one place. I also save all my earlier invoices in a Dropbox folder, not on my computer.

INVOICE TEMPLATE

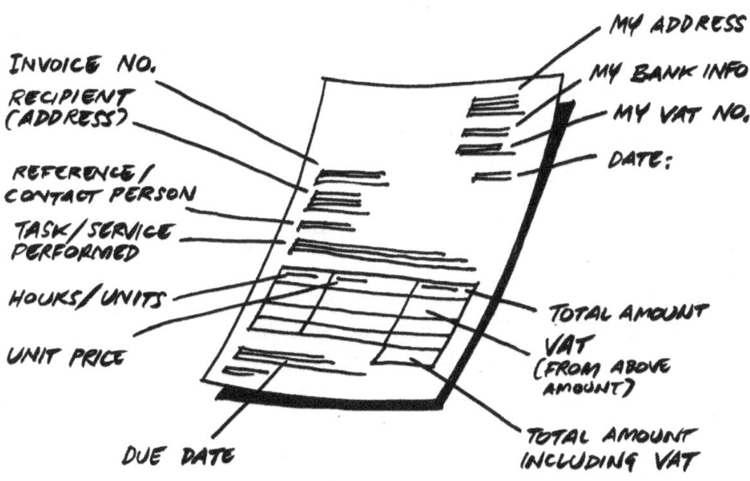

Payment

Clients often have their own internal payment system. Rather than demanding or expecting a certain payment date, I usually just suck it up if the client has some weird 45-day payment rule. Some freelancers add a late fee to their invoices. And while that may be fair, to me that seems a bit aggressive not to mention cumbersome, to have to send a $5 late fee invoice—and then have to keep track of whether they pay *that*. If it makes your clients cough up the money on time, go right ahead. And if you're a better man than me, you mark your calendar when you send off an invoice and keep track of payments on a regular basis.

If for some reason a client "forgot" to pay your invoice, here's a template you can steal:

Hi (name),

I was just going through my accounts and as far as I could see I haven't received the payment on the attached invoice. Would you check to see if something went wrong on your end?

Thanks!

Best,
(Your name)

I used to worry a lot about wording these kinds of messages, now I use my own template. Smart, huh? And while the above is pretty respectful and leaves a back door open for "glitches," I include something I'm usually very careful not to put in emails: a question mark. The reason I include it here is I expect and demand a reply and will keep following up if I don't get it.

Only a few times in my career has a client refused to pay. In one instance I kept calling them on the phone and getting the run around and ended up sending a discounted invoice of half of the original amount just to get it out of the way. In at least two other instances I realized the client was a scammy bastard and/or insolvent and I decided to let it go. I didn't want to spend another minute of my time with these people and just wrote it off as a painful learning experience.

A last example from a few years ago frustrated me to no end, because the client implied I hadn't delivered as promised. Mind you, this was after months of them ignoring my invoice and all my emails. I found it damn insulting and unfair, an excuse they pulled out of a hat after not having expressed any dissatisfaction earlier. I ended up sending an email higher up the chain and cc'ing a lawyer friend of mine—whom I never paid and didn't need to. My invoice was cleared after that.

If I have to give one piece of advice on these things, it's to consider the cost before you pull out the big guns (metaphorically). And don't pull out a gun (still metaphorically) unless you're willing to use it. You may also want to try to vet the client before you work with them.

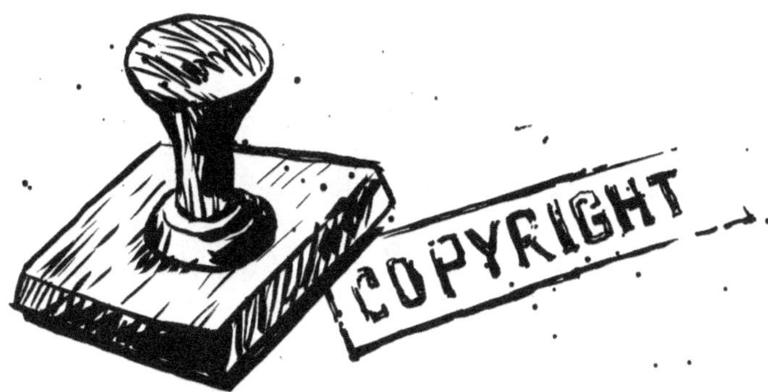

Copyright and IP

In most cases, an artist hired to do a specific job retains the IP (Intellectual Property) of their work. Creating a jingle, a op-ed illustration or a short story for a magazine doesn't mean signing off ownership. It means you lease the work you did to a client for a specific purpose and/or time period. If there's a contract involved this should specify exactly who owns what right but as a rule of thumb, it's you as the creator.

In comics, there is work-for-hire (in which case the publishing company owns all the rights) and creator-owned (in which case, you bring the project to the publisher and sign off the publishing rights but retain the intellectual property). If you've been on retainer or creating something while working for Disney or Microsoft, you bet they will keep the IP—and trying to fight them on it will cause you a lot of time and headaches… and likely bankruptcy.

If on the other hand, you were hired to design a poster and the company decides they want to use it for a banner ad or a free giveaway sticker, you'll likely be able to get more money or get them to cease and desist, since you still own the IP. Theoretically you could sell the same piece of work twice but you risk pissing off both clients, were they ever to find out. Comics artists do this all the time, selling original artwork that was printed in a book and I'm sure it's similar in other industries.

If a client should present you with a waiver or contract leaving them with all the rights to your work for all use in all eternity and known universes, I'd be very wary of signing it. And if I did, I'd expect to be well compensated. Some clients will try to get all the rights but it's usually negotiable if you push back. If you do sign off on say publishing rights, make sure the rights revert back to you after a period of time—the standard is two to three years.

Some of my earlier clients have thought they just owned whatever they bought from me, to use for whatever. I've sometimes introduced the idea of rights and been able to charge a higher price for my work, by offering broad usage with no time limit—mostly in cases where I cared less about the artwork, and had no use for it myself. The client might find it more convenient to buy you out from the beginning instead of having to negotiate a new rate every time they find a new use for your jingle, illustration or whatever. And that's totally fair, as long as they pay a premium.

Copyright is another can of worms but basically no one is allowed to steal your work and present as their own or use it for commercial purposes without your explicit permission. There's something called "fair use" which means if a blogger reviews my comic I can't very well sue them for using an image from the book.

If you're a semi-pro artist I'm sure you use stuff like Instagram to promote your art. Some artists are wary of putting their content on these platforms as it might get stolen or copied. And while it certainly happens, I wouldn't worry about it too much. You can post work-in-progress or detail shots rather than finished artwork and your followers will be just as happy. Besides, the more loyal fans you have out there, the bigger the chance that they will let you know if your work shows up in weird places.

If you do find your work popping up somewhere online you can take two different approaches:

1. Let it go. Usually there's no ill intent behind it, people just don't realize that you can't copy/paste whatever you find online. Or maybe they're evil bastards (like the people who put my book *The Devil's Concubine* on a torrent somewhere in China), who knows? But the chances of you getting them to cease and desist are slim at best.

2. Send a nice email to the owner of the site, asking them either to take it down or at least credit you—or simply send them a bill! I wouldn't expect them to pay but it might help persuade them to remove your work from their page.

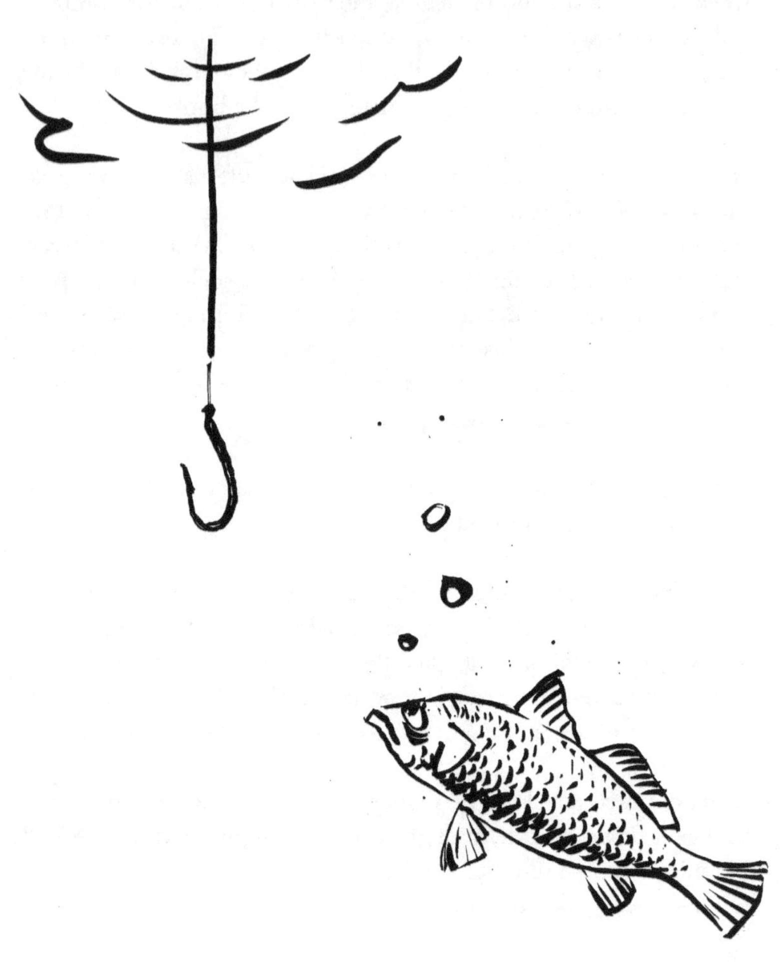

CHAPTER 7

Fishing for Fans and Clients

Visibility is extremely important, especially in the beginning of your career. It's tempting to think an online presence is all you need but in my experience it's meeting people face-to-face that creates the best opportunities. And it's not necessarily the big clients or decision makers you should go for.

Selling yourself is probably very low on the list of things you'd like to be doing, right above poking yourself in the eye with a pencil or getting a root canal. But you don't have to be salesy and douchey.

I once saw a guy at a dinner who nonchalantly spread his business cards across the table like a blackjack dealer. Needless to say, he didn't leave the best impression with the other dinner guests. All his business cards were still on the table after everyone had up and gone.

None of us want to be *that guy*. In fact, if you even have those reservations it means you're probably not that guy! Without knowing you, I'm willing to bet you can turn the knob ten percent more towards "car salesman" without becoming a total sleaze-bucket. If you're an artist, chances are you *hate* talking to strangers let alone promoting yourself. I get it! I hate it too. But you have to get out of your comfort zone if you want to earn a living as a freelancer.

Get used to the self-promotion aspect as part of your daily habits. While you may be drowning in work right now, six months from now could be a totally different situation. In fact it's when we're too busy working that we should be planting the seeds for upcoming work, counterintuitive as it may seem. When you *do* have the free time, chances are it's too late.

By "self-promotion" I don't mean "self-importance." You don't sell yourself by running around shouting: "Look at MEEEE!" You do it by being great at what you do and letting people know you exist. Keeping in touch with people, sharing resources, floating ideas for projects or grabbing the occasional coffee with an editor or a fellow freelancer. Like fishing, it requires a great deal of patience and persistence.

Connecting with Peers

The best spot for a freelancer to be in, is where the other freelancers are. By far, most of the jobs I ever got, I got through fellow artists and others in my field. Don't think of your peers as competition but as advisers and allies—your peeps. Buy them a drink, pick their brain and find out how you can help them out. It's a good long-term investment, believe me.

In the short term, how about shooting out a short email to friends and family, letting them know you started out on your own? Who knows, maybe Uncle Ernie or that friend from yoga class years ago could use someone like you some day. They certainly won't think of you if they don't know what you do. Letting them know is a service.

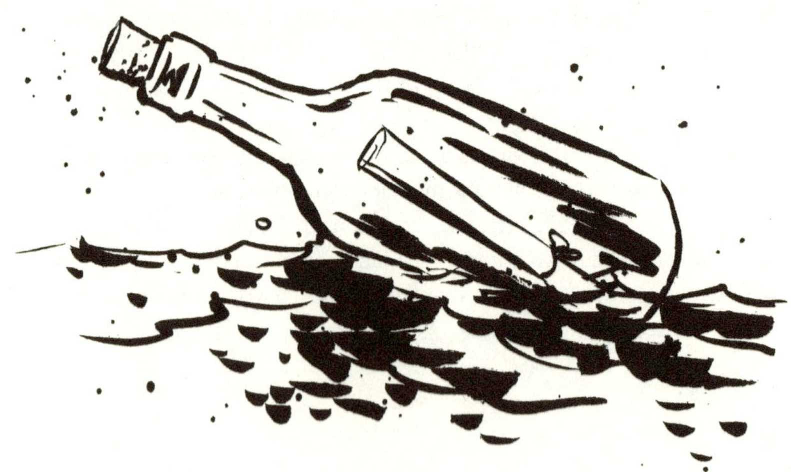

Here's how an email like that could look:

Hey (name),

I just wanted to let you know that I've taken a leap of faith and started out as a freelance (designer/artist/musician). Visit my website at (link) to find out more. You can still get in touch with me at (phone number/email).

Hope this finds you well and that you're enjoying (what's left of the summer/your work at whatever/life in general)!

Best,
(Your name)

And while you're at it, how about adding that new web page of yours to your email signature. Again, think of it as a service! You want to make it easy for people to find you.

Partnerships

Collaborating with someone on a project can be a great way to build a relationship and gain a foothold in your industry. It can also go south really quickly if you don't establish a good set of ground rules up front, like who is the main shareholder and who has ownership over the idea. Someone you meet and like may turn out to a flake or their initial enthusiasm fades once the rubber meets the road. Before you commit to a long-term working relationship with someone it might be a good idea to test the waters with a smaller project.

Be careful with making promises you can't keep and take mental notes along the way on how responsive and committed the other person is. I've worked with writers who gave me total freedom to do whatever I wanted and others who had corrections for almost every drawing I turned in. I've worked with collaborators who saw me as an equal partner and others who forced their will upon the project.

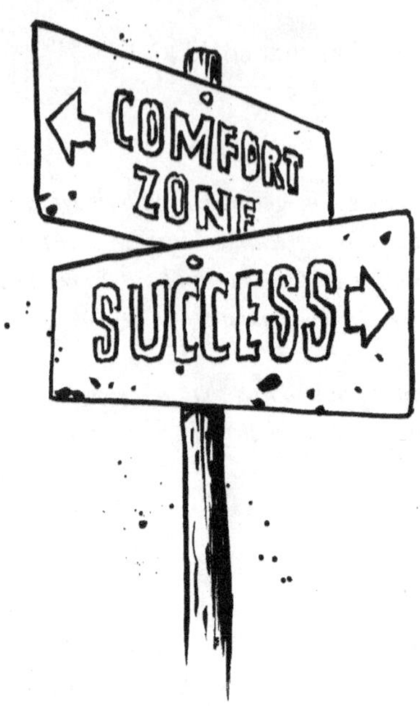

The best advice I can give is to make small commitments until you find someone who's great to work with—and then try your damnedest to try and work with them again.

I think a lot of people make the mistake of trying to cozy up to the top dogs, the gatekeepers or the rock stars in your industry. If you can get there, great, but don't underestimate the value of connecting with people at your own level, people who are trying to do the same thing you are. We have to help each other out! Just avoid the temptation to spend all night sitting in the corner with your friends—that won't help you get new ones.

I went to my first US con in New York in 2011, laying the foundation for an invaluable network. This is where I met Chris Miskiewicz who I did *Thomas Alsop* with—my first real paid work in the US comics industry. We were a bunch of Danes at the show but even though I would consider most of them friends, I pretty much dodged every chance to hang out with them. (I can do that any time in Copenhagen.) Instead I went where the locals went and found myself the odd man out in some bar.

Unlike Danes, Americans are much more open to conversation so I quickly found myself included in several group conversations. I just had to get over feeling like a complete loser and have the guts to say: "Hi, who are you?" to a complete stranger. It works!

At the show, I also spent most of my time away from the Danish booth, focusing instead on meeting new people. I'd done my homework and looked at the list of participants, even found pictures of some people on Google and brought a print out. This was the only reason I knew to say hello to Dean Haspiel and through him I met Chris. Chris has since become one of my best friends and that only goes to show this is not some cynical game of getting clients or winning the day. It's about *finding your peeps*, connecting about common interests, common goals or common personalities. I went in trying to learn as much as I could about how things worked—not with an agenda to get work. That came secondary and even somewhat reluctantly on my part.

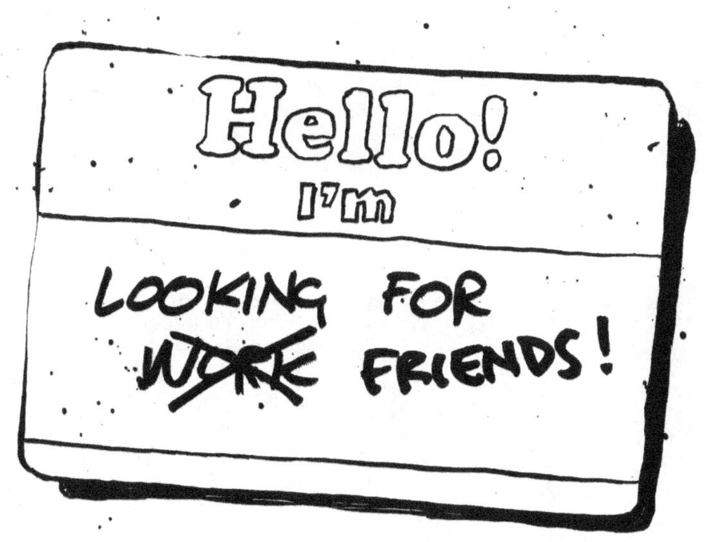

CASE STUDY: THOMAS ALSOP

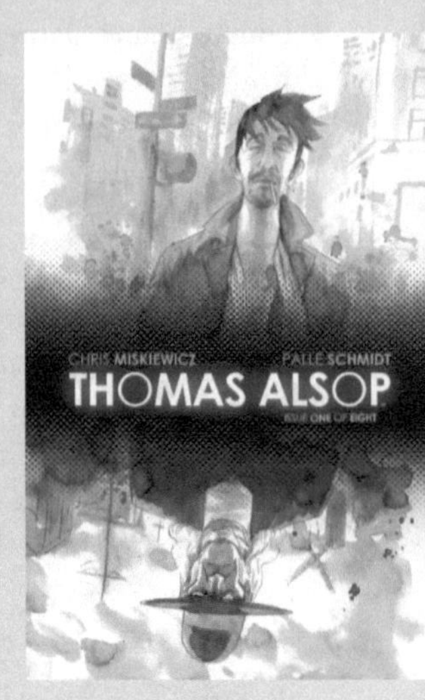

I met Chris Miskiewicz at the MoCCA Festival in New York in early 2011. *The Devil's Concubine* was set to be published in the US that year but wasn't out yet. I carried a print-out of the book with me, as well as a sample of my upcoming book STILETTO. I was blown away by the response. I wasn't used to that kind of praise, and for the first time, people seemed to really GET IT. It felt like I'd been in a box for ten years and now someone had finally taken the lid off. I didn't know what to expect from the show but I certainly wasn't looking for work.

I met Chris as he and Dean Haspiel were setting up a booth. Chris and I clicked immediately. He gave me a copy of his *Everywhere!* anthology

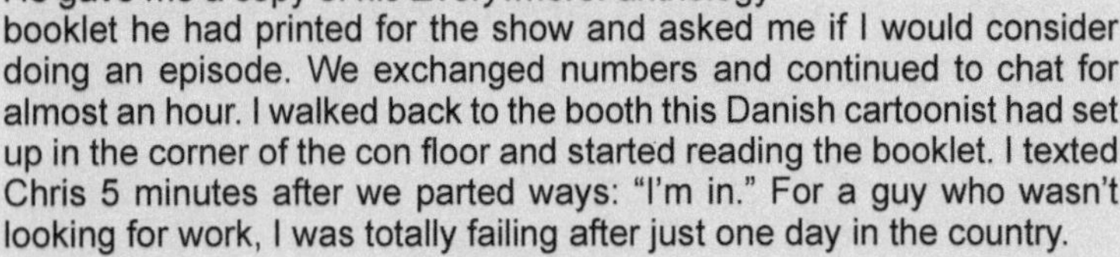

booklet he had printed for the show and asked me if I would consider doing an episode. We exchanged numbers and continued to chat for almost an hour. I walked back to the booth this Danish cartoonist had set up in the corner of the con floor and started reading the booklet. I texted Chris 5 minutes after we parted ways: "I'm in." For a guy who wasn't looking for work, I was totally failing after just one day in the country.

We stayed in touch over the next months via email and texts. Chris sent me a great script for an *Everywhere!* episode—a heist story that was more or less written with my taste in mind. It was a great experience and Chris continued to bring up *Thomas Alsop*, a concept he had pitched me on the con floor that first time I met him. I still figured it had nothing to do with me, not ready to commit to anything that major and not sure how to go about it.

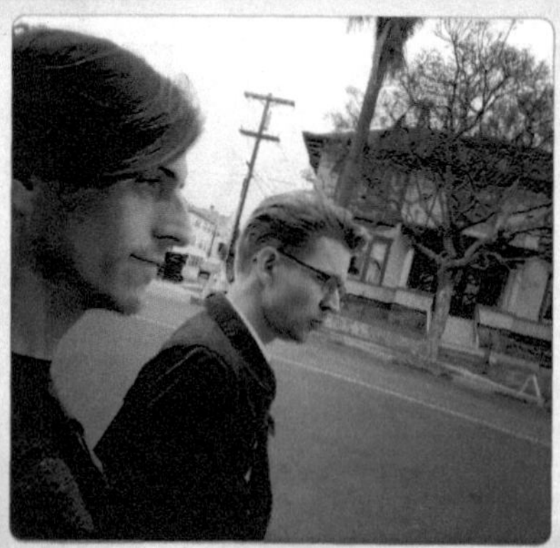

Later that year I heard of New York Comic Con for the first time and figured I would try to fly over for that. I'd already been to San Diego Comic Con and did a few signings on the West Coast. I reached out to Dean and asked if I could come sit at his studio for a few weeks before the con and he said sure. I went and got to know both Chris and Dean a whole lot better.

Scripts and photo references for *Thomas Alsop* started filling up our Dropbox and we did a little teaser episode for Trip City called *The Case of Dead Uncle.* Google it, I'm sure it's still out there. Again Chris was smart enough to lure me in with something short and doable rather than a full script for 8 issues.

Chris had already written the entire 8-issue arc before I even drew a single page. It was crucial to have the ending (and wow, what an ending!) in mind even as I was working on issue 1. Whether it would ever go anywhere was still in the wind, but when Chris spent his own money creating a live action trailer (viewable on the front page of thomasalsop. com) I was floored. It looked like a million bucks! This crazy New Yorker meant business and he clearly knew what he was doing.

In July of 2013 we pitched *Thomas Alsop* to BOOM! Studios at SDCC. We'd bumped into a friend of Chris' on the con floor who introduced us to Matt Gagnon and we chatted for like 20 minutes. Only after parting ways did we realize he was the company's Editor-in-Chief.

BOOM! eventually picked up the book and I started breaking down the script and drawing issue #2. We did hit a small snag when the publisher suddenly wanted to discuss a key point in the story revolving around 9/11. If it had been a minor element, we would have probably obliged to change it but since it was in line 2 of the pitch they bought and was a crucial focal point of the whole series, Chris and I stood our ground. We eventually agreed to add little essays as back matter, making it clear for the readers that Chris was not just some douche exploiting a national di-saster but was himself a New York-er, born and bred. The book went forward and the controversy never happened. On the contrary, the re-spectful handling of 9/11 in the sto-ry seemed to land us an even more committed fan base and the book was dubbed *Best Mini-Series of 2014* by *USA Today*.

Lessons Learned:
If I have any regrets in my career, it is not going to a US con sooner. Where the US has an actual com-ics industry, Denmark does not. I learned a lot from working with Chris, and found out I don't neces-sarily have to be the one behind the wheel to enjoy the ride.

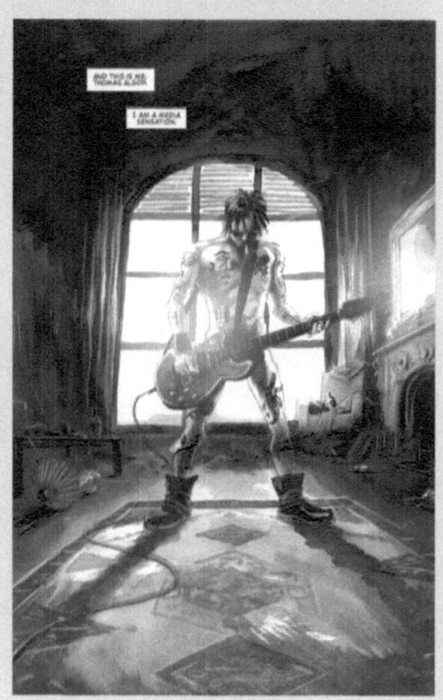

Meeting Clients

Having the right bait won't do you any good, if you're fishing in the wrong lake. You have to find out where there's a market for what you do, and then let that market know you exist. You can do that without a hard sales pitch (who likes those, right?). Letting a potential client know what you're up to should be considered a service. Should they ever need someone like you, they might like to have your info. That's helpful to them!

Instead of focusing on the sale, focus on getting to know the client and their daily life. Most people like to talk about themselves and their work. So ask them! About their company, about the business, about the challenges and opportunities they face. If you're honestly curious and open-minded, chances are they'll recall your conversation as pleasant. That's a good first step.

Messing about on Facebook or chatting with people on LinkedIn won't cut it, you need to show up in person. Conventions, book fairs or trade shows are a good way of meeting people. Or maybe you can just walk in off the street. For a clothes designer it might be a particular store you want to get into. If you're a musician, maybe there's a particular club in town. And if it's not the right spot for you, maybe they can help point you in the right direction. And they will, if they like you.

If you can get another freelancer or friend to introduce you, that's great. Having gone to a lot of comics conventions I think the first hurdle you have to get over as an artist, is convincing people you're not insane. There's plenty of insane comics artists out there, believe me! If someone the publisher trusts introduces you to them, they'll likely be more open to conversation than if you just pin them down at the booth showing your portfolio.

If you do have to pin someone down yourself, here's an example of an opening:

> *"Hi, I'm (name), I see you've got some (great books/cool products/interesting stuff going on) very much in line with what I do. Do you mind if I leave (a portfolio/some samples/a card)? Or maybe you can tell me who it would be a good idea to reach out to?"*

The above is an example of a classic cold call. Please note that it's way easier to approach someone you *know* so your main focus should be to get to know people.

When I go to a US comics convention or a Danish book reception I just try to have a good time and meet people, ask questions rather than pitch my own stuff. I also tend to spend less and less time at the show and more and more time at the bar.

I'm pretty good with faces and names but I meet so many people I can't possibly remember all of them. I've found one trick that helps and that is to take notes quickly after. I just take a moment and jot down the name, occupation and maybe a detail or two in the note app on my phone—a pretty discreet way of taking notes during a reception or a show. It helps me remember people and I can then find people on social and add them later. Maybe send them a quick message like: "Hey Josh, good to meet you yesterday! Hope you had a good show." I mainly use Facebook to keep in touch with what people are up to. Sometimes work relations or real friendships arise, other times not.

Stay Open

You never know where the next job, the next great insight or the next great friendship will come from. Instead of keeping all your focus on the cool kids, I'd recommend you look around you and see if there's another poor soul looking for a way in, someone you might be able to help out. Giving people the benefit of the doubt and treating people with respect—no matter where they are in the food chain—is a good long-term investment. The guy who's only looking out for himself and ignoring the people who are "below him" won't get as far as the guy whose success everybody is rooting for.

I'm not saying you shouldn't try to move up in the world or suck up to your idols, go right ahead! Holding back out of fear will get you nowhere. Especially in Scandinavia, we have a tendency to worry about what people might think, worry about making a fool of ourselves, so we don't talk to anybody—particularly people we admire. In my experience, even the most successful or cynical artist won't mind a respectful compliment. I'm certainly not against cheap flattery, especially if it's directed at me.

That Business Card

I know, old school. But having a business card just sends the signal that you're serious about what you do, it's a no brainer. You can get great, solid stock at places like Moo.com, where you can also upload a bunch of your own art. The price is the same whether you get fifty cards with five different motifs (ten of each) or the same on every card. The most important thing on the card is your website address, your email should probably also be on there, phone number is optional.

Tossing business cards around is not going to get you work (or friends for that matter) but it's nice to have if people ask for it. You should be the one asking for *their* card and own the responsibility of the follow-up.

Nine times out of ten, you don't hear back from people. That's just the way it is, people are busy. Hand a portfolio, sample or some other give-away to somebody, you can bet they'll lose it the moment you turn your back. Or they find it in their bag a week later and have no idea what that was about. *You* need to be the one to follow up, every time.

Get. Their. Info.

The Art of the Follow-Up

The real work starts when you get home from the trade show or whatever with your pocket full of cards and your phone full of notes. Whether you need to follow-up on every person you met is up to you. I'd say it certainly can't hurt to shoot people an email saying "hey, great to meet you." But instead of spending the coming days debating yourself or trying to figure out the wording, worrying what they might think if you say this or that, how about you just steal this:

> *Hey (name),*
>
> *Great to meet you at (the book reception/your store/the trade show) the other day! I think I gave you (my card/a sample of my work/a portfolio/my latest demo) but just in case you lost it, here's my info again.*
>
> *You can find more of my work at (link to homepage/link to You-Tube channel/Facebook page/LinkedIn profile).*
>
> *Thanks again for (your time/a great chat/an engaging conversation). Hope to see you again some time!*
>
> *Best,*
> *(Your name)*

The Interview Tactic

If you're feeling a little intimidated reaching out to a potential client, an important gatekeeper, I can't blame you. The last thing you want to be is that pathetic guy begging for work or attention from a high-profile busy person. But there's a way to do this that is really efficient and only requires a slight mindset shift.

Think of yourself as a *researcher*. Instead of trying to sell or pitch something, ask for advice and business insights. You'd be surprised how open most people are to someone who is genuinely interested in their work. It's a lot easier to say yes to an interview than someone trying to sell you something.

The more you know about the daily struggles and challenges of an editor, a producer or an agency, the better you can navigate. The more you understand the business you want to be in, the better your chances of achieving that goal. The more you approach networking with curiosity, the less nervous you'll be. Have the courage to ask the stupid questions and you'll end up smarter and leaving a better impression than someone trying to look cool.

How and when to reach out varies from industry to industry. If you're just starting out or graduating from school, you have a great excuse to set up an appointment, asking for fifteen minutes of their time. But you could also do it mid-career, with the opening line of:

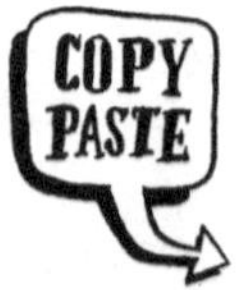

"I figured out I have some blind spots and would really love to get a deeper understanding of how the business works on your end of things."

Examples of questions you can ask are:

- Where do you see the big challenges for your company in the coming years?
- What tasks consume most of your time on a daily basis?
- Where do you see your industry heading?
- What core competences are you looking for in a freelancer?
- How do you prefer people contact you with business opportunities?
- What's the worst thing a freelancer could do in terms of retaining a work relation?

Make it about *them*, not about you. Save your pitch for later (way later in most cases) unless they specifically ask you what you've got going on. Instead get their info and use the template on page 81 for follow-up, thanking them for their time and the valuable insights you got from talking to them. What will likely happen is you'll leave a good impression and have possibly laid the groundwork for opportunities down the line. It's not about the quick sale, it's about the long game.

Bonus tip: If you followed my suggestion on page 40 and took notes during the meeting, you'll likely be in possesion of some gold you don't even realize: The lingo. If they use words like "stability" or "flexibility" to describe the perfect freelance contractor, you can totally steal those words for your "about" page—just be sure you actually are able to act it out as well.

Social Media

I'm kind of conflicted about this. On the one hand, Facebook, Twitter and Instagram are all great ways to reach a wider audience, keep in touch with friends and contacts and build your platform. On the other hand, it can be a huge time-suck and sometimes feels like another chore—and a way to compare your own crappy life to the success of others in an extremely unhealthy fashion.

You have to find your own way in the ever-changing online landscape but here's the best advice I have right now:

Be the Best Version of Yourself

This can of course be applied to offline life as well, but there is a difference: The internet doesn't forget. Craft an online persona but try to at least model that persona on who you actually *are*. Authenticity goes a long way.

Set a Time Limit

You need to find a balance between creating the actual work and promoting it. We can all fall in and watch days disappear sometimes, that shit is addictive! As a rule of thumb, I'd say you probably shouldn't spend more than ten percent of your time and efforts on social media—unless you have a clear strategy and a way to convert your likes into sales. And hey, if you do find out how to do that, let me know!

Think of the Added Value

Self-promotion is part of being a freelance artist and your friends can live with you posting a review or a piece of news once in a while. But if all you ever post is work-related you might stretch people's patience. I'm no great example to follow, but I do try to think of what people might find interesting, funny or insightful before I post something. If you can't think of anything clever to say, maybe there's no need to say anything. Or maybe just share a piece of content one of your friends put out. Your friend will appreciate it and maybe they'll return the favor one day, who knows?

Don't Brag or Whine

You don't have to pretend to be a huge success (although it seems that's what everybody else is doing) but be careful what you put out there. Vulnerability and authenticity are good but complaining of low self esteem or lack of jobs will likely make sure you stay unemployed. And posting twenty links to HuffPost articles or YouTube videos will send a clear signal that you have too much time on your hands. Yes, that's just like my opinion, man. I'm trying to be authentic here!

What's Private and What's Not

My notion of privacy is very different from older generations and probably different from a lot of you reading this. My kids are now the age that I find it most respectful to ask them before posting pictures of them. But I don't shy away from posting personal stuff, it's part of the whole picture. Just be mindful that future employers do sometimes check out people on social to find out what kind of weirdo they're dealing with. A little weird is fine, keeping it mostly professional is probably better. I tell people they shouldn't post about politics but I don't follow my own rules, go figure. Set your own boundaries. Or not, it's up to you.

Ignore the Trolls

Putting yourself out there is a surefire way to get hateful comments, as I'm sure any blogger or YouTuber can attest. Luckily most artists usually don't get the same heat a politician or a big brand can attract. Unless you decide to draw pictures of the prophet Muhammad or post a picture of yourself in blackface, you'll probably be fine. You just need to develop thick skin and selective hearing, whether it's "fan" comments or lousy reviews.

There will always be people who either try to get under your skin (out of envy, spite or boredom, who knows) or just don't like what you do. Ignore at will. Or if you can't help yourself, just reply: "I'm sorry you don't like this. Hope you find something you do like one day."

Create a Gang

Get a handful of friends or peers to commit to helping each other out in the online craziness. Share, retweet or at least just hit that "like" button, every little thing helps. If you can't start your own gang, sharing, liking and retweeting other people could be a way to join theirs. At the very least it will help you get on their radar. And one day they'll likely return the favor.

Use the Platform that Works

I keep mentioning Instagram and Facebook as it seems to be what I myself always go to, while my Twitter and LinkedIn lie dormant. Your experience and personal taste may differ. Go with what works for you, whatever gives you the most joy and whatever is the best way to connect with your audience.

For visual artists, Instagram seems to be the best place to be right now, as taking a pic of whatever you're working on is super-easy and everyone can follow along without you needing to confirm your friendship or whatever. You can even hook it up to your Twitter and Facebook, so in like two clicks you can be on three different platforms all at once. I'm sure you can add the feed to your blog as well.

Other than a convenient way for self-promotion, some artists, designers and even ceramists manage to leverage Instagram in selling physical products. You don't need an online store, just a PayPal account or other means of receiving payment. Obviously this is one instance where you *do* need to check the comments.

It seems that Twitter is the place to be if you're a writer (or a President). I don't use it at all these days but most of my US comics connections are addicted to it. The obvious benefit is that you can @ anyone from your mom to Tom Cruise and sometimes they even reply. And with a few retweets you could be reaching an audience of thousands. I have the distinct feeling that no one really reads Twitter but that's likely because I personally don't.

Musicians and other performers will likely find places like YouTube and Soundcloud is where they can gain the best traction. More about these platforms on page 167.

Thank You, Thank You, Thank You

While we're on the topic of how to behave in social situations online and off, I just want to remind you of the importance of saying thanks. If someone lends a hand, sends work your way or makes an introduction, don't forget to thank them. Do it by email or hand-written note, send a copy of your latest CD, a book, a bottle of wine or some flowers if you can afford it. Keep them in mind when you stumble upon a resource or an article they might like, shoot them a link and say thanks again. Don't be a stalker but let them know you appreciate the favor, always.

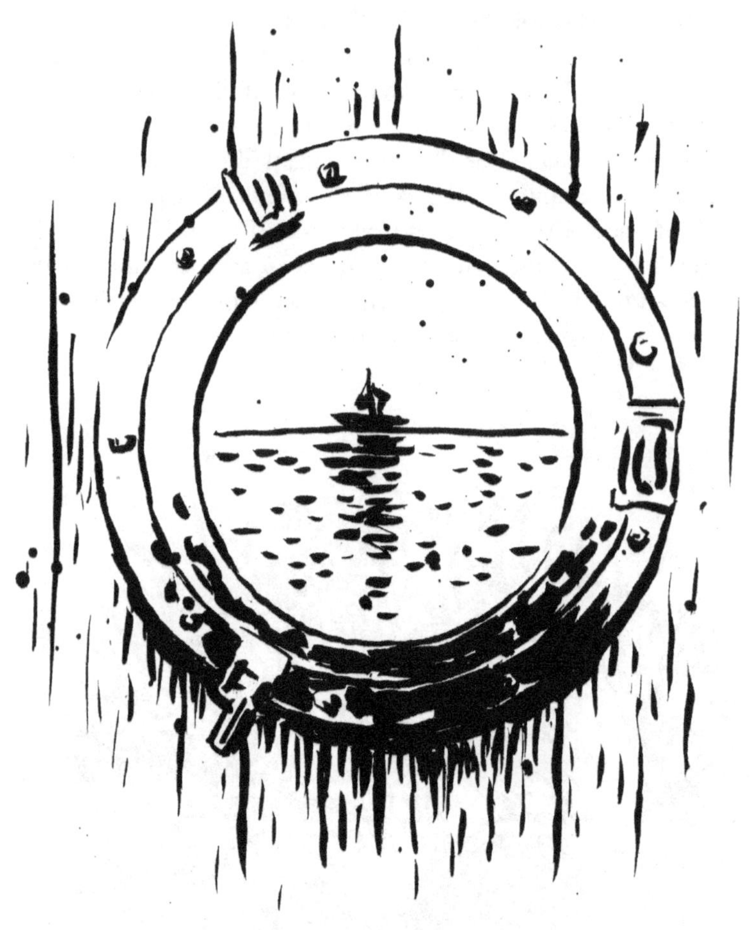

CHAPTER 8

Working with Clients

This chapter focuses on the professional relation between you as a freelancer and the client. You can't expect a client to immediately understand how you work, or what the ideal working conditions and delivery form is for you. Maybe they've never worked with a freelancer before or maybe they have a completely unrealistic set of expectations. Every new gig and every new client is a potential for getting paid, or getting screwed.

In the beginning of your career you can't afford to be too picky. You need the experience and the money. You have to put your best efforts into helping the client achieve whatever it is *they* need but also take care of your own needs. You have to evaluate the time and effort needed and be careful not to take on more than you can handle. As Seth Godin put it in an interview with Tim Ferris recently: "if you grab too many things, you drop the whole basket, and then you've got nothing."

If you bill by the hour, perhaps burning the midnight oil is an opportunity rather than a hassle but you still need to be able to vouch for the quality of the work and make sure you can sustainably perform. If things start to slide and the job is taking longer than they're paying you for, better to give the client a heads-up rather than run yourself into the ground.

When you're working on a deadline, this is usually not the best time to experiment too much in your art. Stick to the craft they hired you for and make sure you can deliver on time rather than reinventing yourself as an artist. More about how to organize your time and resources on page 129.

Pricing and Negotiation

The first few (or many) times you have to put a price on your work, you'll likely get it wrong. You'll likely also miscalculate the amount of time a given task will take. That's OK, don't beat yourself up over it. You can adjust along the way. You'll gain the experience and confidence needed over time.

While the hard part of acquiring a customer may be over, coming up with a price tag can be equally challenging.

In general, negotiating for pay always works best over the phone or in person, not via email. I'm sure you think email is way easier and communication will be much clearer, right? Wrong! Email and texts are a huge source of miscommunication. The friendly chitchat and tone of your voice is lost—and you may end up leaving money on the table. Get over your inhibitions and get on the phone!

When giving a price, make sure the client understands how many corrections are included or you can easily end up going back-and--forth for days and stretching yourself thin to accommodate their needs. And make sure you don't give them a discount without telling them about it!

There are basically two ways to come up with a price:

1: Let the client do it
The upside of this method is you dodge the difficult task of pricing altogether. The downside is the client won't necessarily get it right either and you end up not getting what you're worth.

It's great if you can find out what their budget is, before you give them a number. You need to know the scope of the task anyway so you might as well throw in the line: "I don't know if you have a fixed budget or not…" and leave it hanging. Maybe the client will jump in saying: "We've set aside $1,000 for the job." Which is good to know, if you were planning on asking for $500.

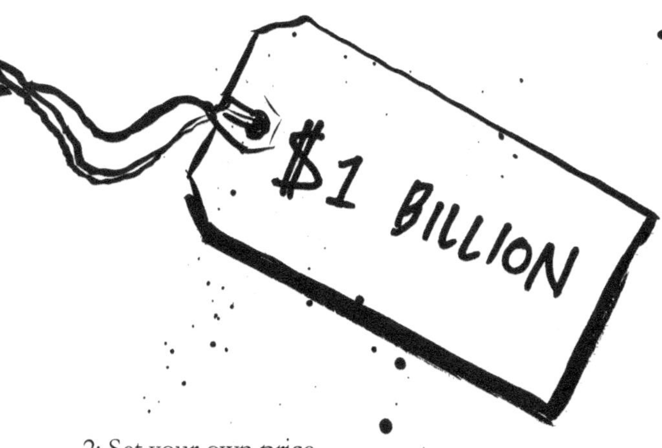

2: Set your own price

Some clients play their cards close to the vest or simply have no idea what things cost. In these cases you'll have to shoot for a number yourself. Some prefer a fixed price and others are fine with you billing by the hour or daily. Talk through the various options and be flexible. Remember that if it was *you* hiring someone to do a job, you'd be worried about going over budget and not getting what you paid for too.

Charging for your work is really hard, especially in the beginning. But you can prepare yourself by going through this checklist:

Hourly Rate

Ask other freelancers in your industry what they charge. And if you're just starting out, set your hourly rate slightly lower. Most people understand the concept of billing by the hour, so it can be a good place to start. To quell any worries of going over budget, offer up an estimate of hours or even a fixed number. You could also agree to give them a heads up when you hit a certain number of hours.

Daily Rate

Some times it makes more sense to bill for the entire day. If I'm live drawing at a corporate workshop or have a speaking engagement, I'll give my daily rate instead of hourly, because while the actual hours working may be few, it pretty much kills my entire day going back and forth. If I have to leave my office, they have to pay me more.

Working Hours

If you can't bill by the hour but have to give a fixed price on a specific task, it still helps to know how long it will take. In the beginning this will be an estimate and you'll likely miss the mark the first several times. But if you time yourself, you'll eventually have a better idea.

Industry Standards

Perhaps there are standard rates within your industry that it would be helpful for you to know about. Ask around or do online research, so you don't end up leaving money on the table or scare away potential clients with outrageous pricing. If you can find a set of rates from a guild or trade organization, great. I find it's a lot easier to ask for a specific amount if I can refer to standards from a perceived authority rather than pulling a number out of a hat.

Apart from rates there may be a number of other standards that apply in any given industry. In publishing for example you rarely get asked your rates, they usually present you with a contract that is pretty much take it or leave it. You can negotiate specifics but you rarely get more than fifteen percent royalty as a writer or a fixed rate as an artist.

Client Types

There's a difference between being asked to create a jingle for a friend's YouTube channel and being asked to design a new logo for Amazon. Adjust your rate depending on the client and what value you're adding, not just by how many hours work you put in. Clients are *not* created equal.

Your Own Budget

If you have absolutely no idea what to charge, maybe take a look at how much you need to survive. Look at your budget and how much you'd like to be bringing in every month. Of course you can't expect to persuade clients to pay a premium based on your monthly spending, but it could be helpful for you to know how much you actually need.

You're the Expert

Don't be ashamed of asking for what you're worth, whether you have a degree or not. Remember that the skills you have acquired through years of focused training is not something everyone can do. You are an expert in your field and should be compensated for your efforts.

Preparation, Commute and Equipment

Other than being a skilled professional, maybe you own some high-level gear that normal people don't have access to. You made an investment that needs to be covered over time through what you charge. If you have to spend a lot of time doing research or prep for a particular job, or have to travel hours to and from the gig, remember to take that into account when pricing. The client may offer to compensate you themselves, but if you don't mention that fact when you're negotiating, you'll likely be missing out.

Adjust the Level of Detail

If the client is paying stick figure prices, they can't expect you to deliver a fully-rendered painting. It's perfectly normal to set the level of detail according to the budget. You need to get used to handing in work that feels sub-par to you, if you want to be a creative pro. You need to do the best you can within the given circumstances, which includes the budget.

Scare Away the Clients

An advanced technique if you have too much incoming work (or just want to test your own limits) is jacking up the price. Just think of what the fair price would be and add thirty percent. If this makes the client run away screaming, great! One less item on your plate. If they accept your shameless price, great! More money for you, and more motivation to move things around in your calendar and put in the extra effort.

I usually give the high price first, being willing to go down if I meet resistance. You can steal this tactic:

> *"My going rate for something like this would normally be around (insert high amount)…"*

Take a moment. Sometimes the client will jump in going: "That sounds reasonable." Boom! No need to negotiate further.

If, on the other hand, your hear them fall off the chair on the other end of the line, you can pick up your thought:

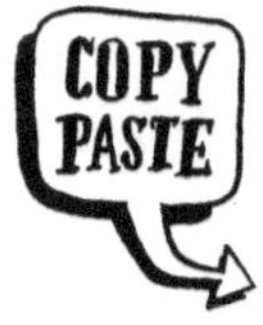

> *"…but since (it's you/it's part of a larger project/it sounds like a relatively simple task), I'm sure we can work out (a discount/ lower rate/some sort of bundle deal). How about (insert lower amount)?"*

Pricing is all about supply and demand. I'm sure you can find plenty of people willing to undercut you. I mean, you can get a freelancer to do almost everything for \$5 on Fiverr.com! You do *not* want to think of that segment as your competition.

If your unique expression is what the client is looking for, price matters a lot less. They're paying for *you*, for your personality and the experience you bring to the table. If a client mentions that they can get the same thing cheaper elsewhere, I'd recommend you simply agree with them and perhaps even direct them to some of your lower paid colleagues.

What you offer as a professional is something other than bargain prices, it's industry experience and a unique skill set. If you speak the same language as the client (culturally as well as professionally), you are great at what you do, flexible and accommodating, understanding of your clients needs—those are reassuring qualities worth paying premium for. Especially if you go the extra mile in terms of showing up in person for a briefing, or get on the phone instead of hiding behind email.

Deliver on your promises every time and the clients will keep coming back, even if some graphic designer in Bangladesh can do the same thing at a tenth of your rate.

Contracts

Depending on what you do and the size of the project, you may want to write up a contract for a specific piece of freelance work. If you're putting half your yearly income on one job or running a risk of losing rights or whatever, a contract might be a good idea. But in my experience contracts tend to complicate things further and bring out conflicts that maybe could have been avoided. Sometimes getting a response in writing just doesn't happen for whatever reason and this can bring the entire project to a halt. I tend to trust professional clients on minor projects and keep the legalities out of it.

If you're wary of a particular client, ask around to see if you can get one of your peers to vouch for them. Or simply use this template when you get off the initial call or back from the briefing:

> *Hey there, nice (chatting/meeting) with you today.*
>
> *I just wanted to make sure I got everything right from the briefing: I will deliver (X number of illustrations/X number of pages/minutes of footage/whatever) by (date) in (format). We agreed on a (total amount/hourly rate) of (X number) for the job, including (X number) of corrections.*
>
> *If there's anything you disagree with or something I misunderstood, please let me know ASAP. If I don't hear back from you, I'll take it as confirmation. Looking forward to get to work on this!*

By *not* asking for confirmation you're letting your busy client off the hook. I can't tell you how many times I've asked a client to confirm getting the files or the scopes of a task and waited days, only to find out they just didn't read my email that thoroughly (if at all). It's stressful and annoying to sit around waiting for a reply. Save everybody the time, and just get to work, leaving it up to the client to object rather than sign a contract or confirm written specs. If disagreements arise at a later time, your email should serve as evidence that you held up your part of the agreement.

Some freelancers have a set of standard operating procedures that they send to the client. But just as you probably don't read the terms and conditions before clicking "accept" on everything, chances are your client won't read yours either. If you do send out a PDF of your terms, at least keep it short, only including the most frequently asked questions and standard rates. Like if you add fifty percent for evenings and weekends, the rights people are acquiring, etc.

On bigger projects, it could very well be a good idea to spend the extra time creating a mutual contract, perhaps including payment in installments, so you can keep yourself fed during the work period. This also helps mitigate the risk of losing months of income if the client goes broke during the project or simply refuses payment after the fact. Most clients are honorable enough but there's no reason for you to act as their bank. Any hint of unprofessionalism or dodgy behavior and you should ask for a portion of the payment up front.

On bigger assignments, chances are the client will be the one presenting you with a contract. The pit falls are different for every industry so you'll have to ask your colleagues what to watch out for and what standards are to be expected. In general, I'd be on the lookout for anything where you sign away rights or IP indefinitely, exclusivity deals preventing you from working for other companies and delayed payments—a classic pit fall in publishing, where some contracts promise royalties only *after* printing costs and other expenses are covered. Since you have no way of checking the clients accounts, these types of deals give the publisher full control of whether you ever get paid or not.

Whatever you're signing, make sure there's a time limit or fixed period after which the rights revert back to you as the creator, or you are able to be free of non-disclosure agreements, exclusivity deals and the like. You don't want to be tied to a bad deal forever and should consult with a lawyer before signing anything that seems the least bit dodgy or unclear.

Bad Clients

"You didn't receive payment? That's weird. Let me talk to our finance department again."

If this sentence seems familiar, welcome to the club.

"Maybe you could come up with a few concepts, and we'll choose the one we like best."

Sure, and pay you for just the one concept. Guess work is extra, my friends. Time is money, for a free-lance artist as well as a consultant or a plumber.

So no, the customer is not always right and you're fully entitled to choose who you want to work with. You're the boss, remember? If you do take on a client, you need to take responsibility for the relationship, not just quietly bitch and moan about all their corrections. Perhaps they don't know any better—educate them! The better matching of expectations you can tackle up front, the smoother the job will go.

Your tolerance for amateurs and grifters may differ from mine. But in the following section are some of the warning signs to be aware of:

Indicator no. 1: Impossible to Get a Hold of

If a client you're working with dodges calls or is unresponsive to email for long periods of time, they're either impossibly busy (which could be a warning sign of bad business culture or imminent burn-out) or are simply evasive. There's a risk they will be just as evasive when the bill is due.

Indicator no. 2: Always in a Rush

I don't mind rush jobs from time to time, especially well-paid ones. But perpetual bad planning and last-minute requests indicates a lack of respect for your work and usually hurt the results. More often than you might think, clients who force you to compromise in order to make a deadline don't even *need* the work at the given time—often times, the files are still not downloaded a week after you handed them in.

Indicator no. 3: Micro-Manages

The client who keeps calling to checkup on you or even insist that you come work at their office lacks a crucial quality: *Trust.* If they don't trust you to do the work you promised, you shouldn't trust them either. Not that they're evil, they could simply be amateurs who aren't used to working with freelancers like you. But if it ends up costing you more time because of constant meetings or corrections, it should cost them extra as well.

Indicator no. 4: Likes to Haggle

Nothing wrong with trying to get a good deal, but for some people, bargain hunting is a game. A game that you won't win. Even if you do give them a discount this time, next time they'll want to haggle you down even further. To paraphrase photographer and influencer Chase Jarvis; it's almost impossible to convert a low-paying client into a high-paying one. Avoid the ones who haggle and consistently try to make you do more for less.

Indicator no. 5: Wants You to Audition

Not every client fishing for freelancers is bad, but be wary. If they need to see a bunch of different people, it's an indicator that they don't really know what they're looking for and that will likely cause trouble down the road even if you get the gig. If they pay you for the time you spend on a presentation or an audition, great. But if you can afford it, consider taking a pass and focusing on your efforts on projects that aren't long shots.

Indicator no. 6: Moves the Goal Post

Constant meetings and internal discussions, a decision to be made higher up in the system, waiting for approval from some unknown entity—these are all common occurrences in the business world. But you don't have to make it part of *your* business, as it has nothing to do with you. If you constantly have to stop and go while they move the goal post and the deadline, consider charging them a stand-by fee or simply let them know that you have to take on other work while they get their shit together. Have them come back to you when they're ready to move forward and reserve the right to blow through the original deadline, since the delay is not your fault.

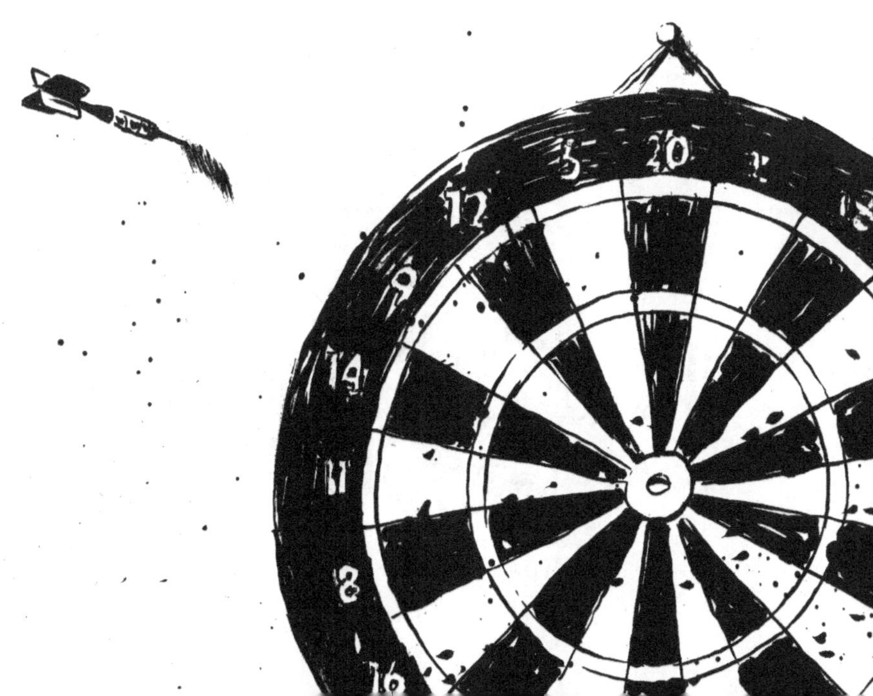

Indicator no. 7: Wants You to Be Someone Else

If a client is dissatisfied with what you hand in and doesn't like the style or the vibe you bring to the project, it's actually not on you—it's on them. They hired *you* for what *you* can do, not for what someone else can do. You should obviously try to accommodate their wishes but you can't buy a horse and complain it's not a canary. If you get the sense the client wants you to change who you are to fit the job, respectfully recommend they find someone else. More about how to say no on page 206.

Indicator no. 8: Won't Foot the Bill

It's a little late to find out about a bad apple after you sent the invoice. Nevertheless, it does happen. Make sure you never work with that client again and consider warning other freelancers of getting in bed with them.

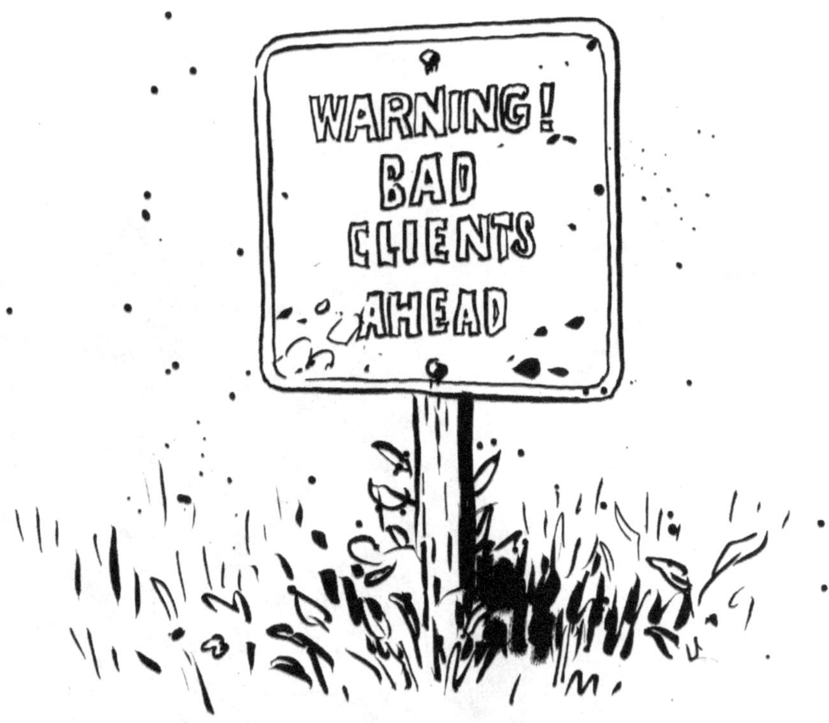

Listen to Your Gut

I know this may come off as new-agey, but I honestly think we pick up more signals than our conscious brain is able to process. You need to trust your intuition, whatever that is. The problem is it can be hard to listen to what your gut is telling you when somebody is waving money in your face. You overlook the warning signs and that little voice in your head telling you that this guy is bad business.

The few times I've been burned by a client who dropped off the face of the Earth or refused to pay, I knew it from the beginning. That is; I kind of knew, but I didn't act on it.

It takes a certain amount of experience to spot where the rocks are underneath the surface. Other than your gut reaction to the job or the person offering it, ask yourself some of these questions:

- Is there a clear scope of this project?
- Is there a clear chain of command or are there many decision-makers?
- Do the people involved understand your craft or working methods?
- Does the client have realistic expectations of what you can do?
- Is the deadline realistic?
- Would I let this guy look after my bag while I went to the bathroom?

With larger projects or people you don't trust a hundred percent, consider asking for part of the payment up front. If they refuse, that's another indicator that you really don't want to be involved with them.

Work Between Work

If you're like most artists I know, you started getting good at your craft because you had a passion for it. A passion that was born out of working by yourself, for yourself. You should work to keep that flame alive, no matter how busy life gets, no matter how much paid work you have coming in. Life as a freelancer is feast or famine, sometimes you got nothing, other times you're having trouble keeping up. That's just how it is. But if you keep working on your own projects on the side, you'll always have something to do. Something you might convert into an asset one day—a book, an album, a series of paintings, whatever. But even if it's just for *you*, it will help you grow as an artist, keep you sharp and help keep the fears at bay.

I've always tried to look at my work as my own projects. Sometimes work-for-hire will come in and interrupt me, but after I finish that, I go back to what I was doing. Flipping my career on its head like that has helped me stay sane over the years, because I don't sit around and worry when no work is coming in. I'm too busy *creating*.

Another way to keep yourself busy and avoid just sitting by the phone or falling down a spiral of worry, is to take care of other stuff that needs doing in your business. Remember, you're the boss, the accountant, the janitor and the PR department—plenty of work to do!

Here are a few suggestions:

Clean Up

When you're knee-deep in work, it's easy to just let things slide around the office. After you hand in a project is a good time to take a day of putting the books back on the shelves, throw out old sketches and notes, and sort out the piles. Having a clean work environment may not be crucial for you in order to be creative, but it might help the cleaning lady (also you, yay!). It's also nice that you can have people in your studio without subjecting them to health hazards.

Filing

No fun, I know, but sooner or later you need to get the receipts, invoices and other paperwork in order. Why not now instead of just before you have to hand it in or while you're in the middle of a deadline?

Learn Something New

Whether you take an online course or read a book that is related to your business or take up Spanish or a baking class, it's bound to help you creatively. The more different kinds of input you have, the more unexpected connections your brain is able to make. And those connections are gold for us creative types.

Grab a Coffee

One of the best ways to learn is through a personal connection to another human being, by asking questions in real time. It could also be an old friend or colleague, you never know what will come of it. I had coffee with a friend recently and mentioned in passing that I didn't really have any incoming work. While we were chatting, his phone buzzed with an email about a job that was too big for him to handle. It wasn't a business meeting but that coffee ended up bringing in half a month's rent for me.

Reach out to New People

Grabbing a coffee with a new acquaintance could provide you with new insights or make you look at yourself and your progress from another angle. During dry spells is a good time to look for new land, new opportunities. Ask someone for a quick coffee, be open and curious to find out how you could help each other out. And pick up the tab. Unless there's an obvious opening to pitch yourself or a project, just take the opportunity to ask a lot of good questions. You'll be wiser for it, and they will like you more for showing interest in them. Win/win.

Update Your Web Page

This is one of those tasks that tend to fall to the bottom of the to-do list when you're busy (unless you use it as procrastination. Not the worst form, I guess). You can update your about page to add the latest projects, update your portfolio, blog or maybe even look at the statistics to see if there's a way to make it more searchable or whatever.

Stock up on Materials

I'm sure you have a lot of tools or supplies you use in your daily work, such as paper, paint, printer cartridges, pencils, coffee, whatever. Maybe use the downtime to stock up so you don't have to run to the store in the middle of a deadline.

SOLO Forever!

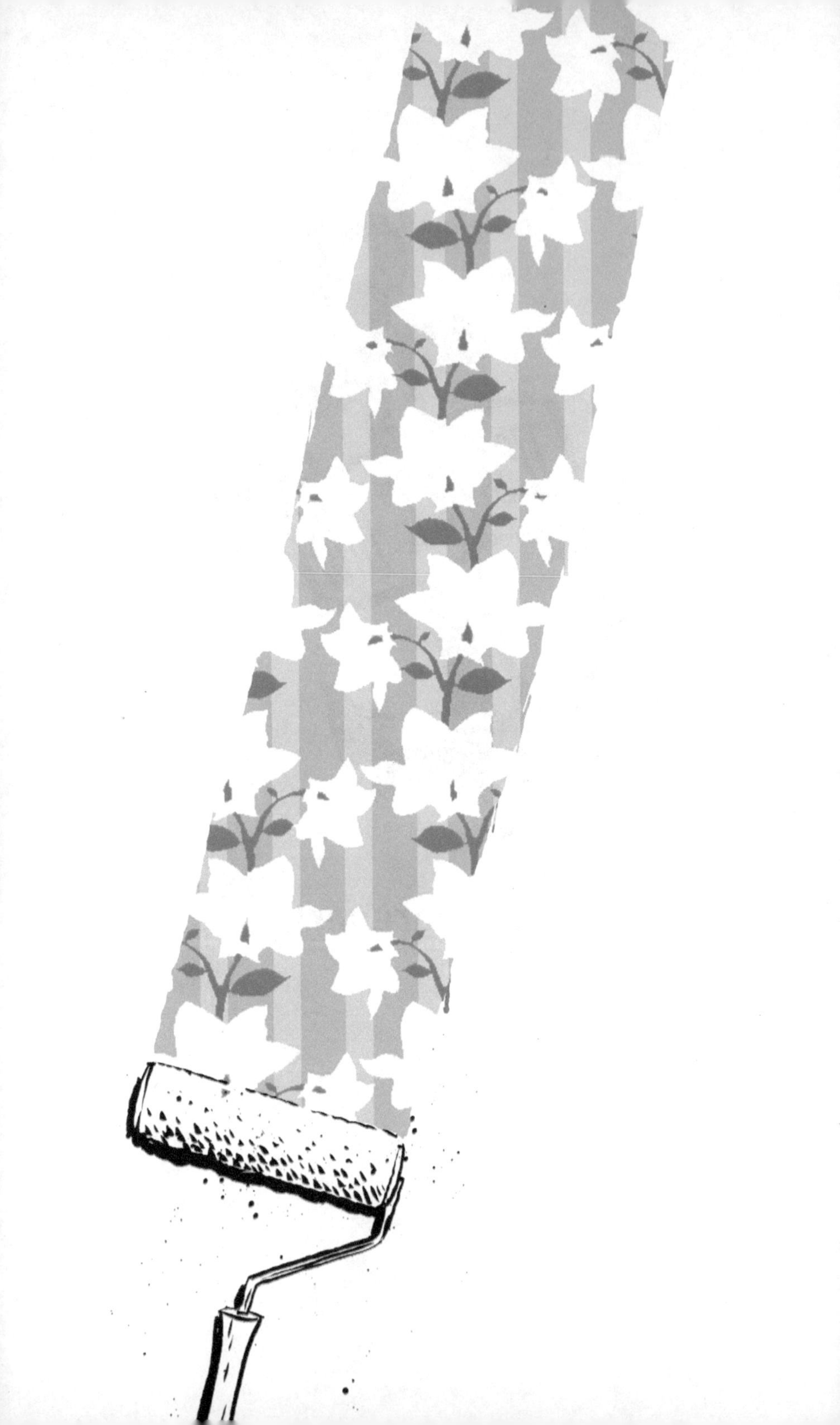

CHAPTER 9

The Art of Being an Artist

During your first year or two as a creative freelancer, the focus should be to build your boat and get in the water. When you're afloat and not taking in water, you can start to think about your destination. Where would you like to go?

In this chapter I get a little more philosophical about this whole creativity business, taking your career, your mindset and your skills to a new level. I'll mostly be talking from my own background as a writer and artist but I'm sure the principles apply to most creative careers.

To many people, art is a hobby. But it's when you really start to take it seriously and treat it as your job that you really pivot. William Faulkner is quoted of saying: "I only write when inspiration strikes. Fortunately it strikes at nine every morning."

Showing up at your desk is when things start to happen. The more you show up, the more likely it is that you'll create something of value. You have to put in the hours, consistently. Painting a couple of times a month won't make you a great painter. You have to build momentum and consistency and daily routines are key.

You can have only somewhat mediocre talent and still have a great artistic career. Just as you can be insanely talented and still struggle making it work. It's not about talent as much as it is about courage, persistence and resilience.

Keeping your ego in check is another important aspect. You need *some* ego to find the belief the song you wrote is so great that everybody needs to hear it. But that ego can just as easily trip you up, if you start to think people don't appreciate your genius enough. Or you strive for perfection in your work, feeling like it's never as good on the paper as it was in your head (hint: It isn't. This feeling never goes away, believe me!).

As an artist, you expose yourself a lot and have to be willing to take criticism. You have to push yourself, and not hold back out of fear of what people might say. You have to be okay with shipping something you're not a hundred percent satisfied with. Chances are you never will be.

In 2011 I sat for a few weeks at Dean Haspiel's Hang Dai Studios in Brooklyn. One of the guys at the studio asked for Dean's advice on whether to take on a particular storyboarding job. He was worried he would fall short and botch the job somehow. Dean replied: "You need the money? Then you take the job. And you fail. HARD. And you learn from that". That attitude was truly inspiring; expecting to fail and being okay with it. I certainly learned a lot from my brief spell at Hang Dai but also from taking on tasks I wasn't entirely ready for.

One of the things I hear tossed around a lot is the idea that you're only as good as your last work. I disagree. You are the sum of all your creative outputs, good or bad. And you're not always the best judge of quality—in fact, you're likely the worst. You just have to do the best you can at that moment and get it out there. You don't end up back at square one because some project didn't turn out the way you wanted it. In fact you learn more from a project like that than you do from a smooth success.

When the process is grueling, frustrating and hard, it's likely because you're evolving and growing as an artist. When you reach that plateau and it feels like you're never going to get better, when you feel like quitting that's exactly when you need to push through.

If you want to learn to swim, you have to go into the deep end of the pool.

The Art of Stealing

I have a friend who has the habit of taking things apart to see how they work. Anything from a radio to a vending machine. To me this is the ultimate approach to art. Find something that works—a film, a novel, a painting—analyze it, break it down, take it apart and figure out why. This is how Raymond Chandler started writing short pulp fiction stories. He took a story from Black Mask, dissected it and identified the various elements and then created a new story by replacing each piece with his own.

You can become a great artist by copying and recreating what you love about another artist. This will teach you a lot. Then after a while, you can bring in other influences and start adding your own voice, thereby creating something new. If you look at my early drawings, you'll definitely see a Mike Mignola phase, a Frank Miller phase and a Sean Phillips phase (which some could argue is not over yet).

My first 48-page comic that was published in Denmark in 1999, was the result of sitting next to Peter Snejbjerg. Peter was a master of the quill (the kind of metal-tipped pen you dip in ink) and all the "real" comics artists out there used it. So of course this young whipper-snapper had to try and copy the technique, with pretty disastrous results. I learned a lot of lessons by sticking it through for 48 pages—the most important being I shouldn't be using a quill. I learned later, that I could use a soft-tipped marker to almost the same effect and that my hand liked working with that way better. Nowadays I listen more to my hand than I listen to my brain.

As an artist it's important to stretch your muscles, draw the things you have a hard time drawing rather than sticking to the things you nail every time. Again, it's a great strategy to just copy. Drawing from life or recreating works from other artists is a crucial way to get better at the craft.

Your Unique Voice

Even though you can learn a great deal by copying others, deep inside of you is a unique artistic vision that you need to cultivate. Let me give you an example from my life, the most valuable lesson I learned at the School of Architecture:

The department was set up like an open office studio in these wonderful old army barracks. My drawing table was across from a guy named Claus. He was hunched over working on the house assignment we'd all been given when the professor, let's call him Mister S., strolled by.

"Ah, drawing a triangle, I see," Mister S. said, commenting on Claus' floor plan. Claus started to explain his thoughts behind the idea, something about lines in the landscape, symbolism and the like.

Mister S. listened and nodded his head before finally saying: "But it could also be round. Right?" Then he turned and left, leaving Claus pondering his triangle.

The week after I was lucky enough to be at my desk when Mister S. stuck his head around again. He looked over Claus' shoulder, smiled diabolically and said: "Oh, what happened to the triangle?"

Claus looked up from his floor plan (you guessed it; the house was now round) and stuttered: "But… You said…?"

"Yes, but who cares what I think," Mister S. said sheepishly. "You need to find out what *you* think!"

That lesson cost poor Claus a week's work. I got it for free and I'll never forget it. In love and art, never listen to what others think. Everybody has an opinion. Yours is the one that matters.

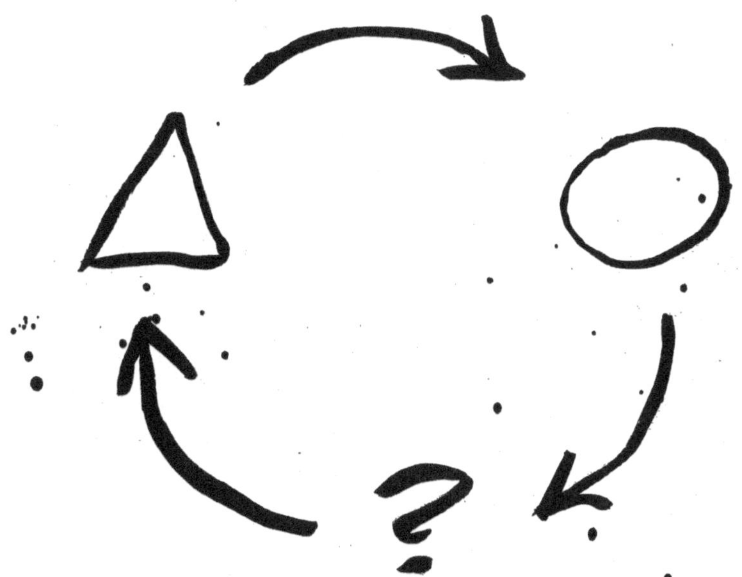

Whatever Works

In art, two plus two doesn't always equal four. Using the same method or the same pen as Stephen King will not make you Stephen King. You need to find out what works for you, by trying out a bunch of different methods.

Some people work within very strict boundaries, setting a timer or planning out everything in detail ahead of time. Others work more intuitively, making it up as they go along. As long as you get a result—and a result that you can be satisfied with—it matters less how you got there. But to make a living as a creative, you need to be able to repeat the process, so it might be a good idea to take a few mental notes along the way. Be conscious of what it is you do and how you spend your time, so you can make the most of it.

It frustrates me to no end seeing other artist just killing it, when their working methods are obviously flawed. I have to remind myself that we're not all wired the same way and what works for me doesn't necessarily work for them and vice versa.

I interviewed a friend of mine who's a very successful writer, after he got a three-year grant from the Danish Arts Council. I was cripplingly envious (can you imagine that? THREE YEARS of rent covered!) and decided I needed to figure out how he got to that place. During the podcast interview it came to light that my friend was envious of the colleagues who could sit down and write for more than four hours. I can personally write for ten hours straight, if the family will leave me alone. So as it turns out, we all have our own struggles and comparing makes little to no sense.

If you want to derail yourself by looking at people better than you and being envious of their success, go right ahead. There's a free resource called Instagram that's perfect for that activity.

It took me many years to accept my own method in writing. Everyone I talked to seemed to write chronologically, apparently that's what you're supposed to do. But when I tried this method I would always get stuck somewhere in chapter five or whenever I hit a point in the story I wasn't able to figure out at that given moment. I completely gave up and walked away from a few books that way.

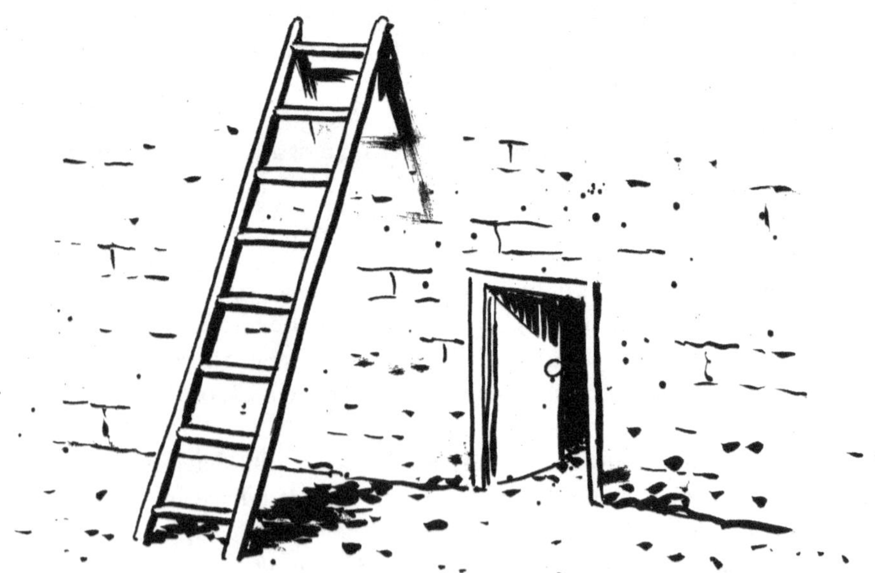

I later figured out that by skipping ahead and writing something I *can* figure out, I'll keep my momentum and avoid getting stuck. I'll get an idea for a piece of dialogue while I'm trying to write a synopsis or get an idea for the end while I'm writing the beginning. Apparently I'm just too much of a scatterbrain to work from A to B to C—and that's OK! As long as I get to the end. Today I'll allow myself to jump around, thereby short-circuiting whatever is blocking my way. I don't care if this is the right method or not, I've become very good at ignoring what other people think.

You have to try stuff and fail a lot before you find what works for you. Maybe you're a night owl and that's when you seem to create your best work. A musician I know consistently sleeps late, while his wife drops their son off at school. He hangs with the family all day and goes to the studio after he put his son to bed at night, working until the sun comes up. Others insist that the morning hours are the most productive.

Perhaps you like working with crayons while your colleagues use markers or watercolor. See if there's anything in their tools or working methods you can learn from, then go do your own thing.

Finish What You Start

I firmly believe in finishing projects, for several reasons. First off, I don't think you can be objective about your work while you're in the middle of it. That novel you feel like abandoning midway could be one of the best you've ever written. You won't learn anything from quitting and you can't sell it either. You need to put a bow on it and get some distance before you can reap the benefits.

I often feel like ditching a project when I'm in the thick of it. I want to go back and redraw pages or change the coloring style. This is just a part of the process.

You grow older and wiser every day, even while you're working, so it's perfectly natural that you would want to do things differently today than three weeks ago. I usually manage to resist the temptation, due to a valuable lesson my friend Sarah taught me twenty years ago.

I was almost finished with my first comic and told Sarah I had plans to redraw the first few pages. Sarah looked at me and said: "If you go back and redraw the pages you're dissatisfied with, you could end up drawing the same ten pages over and over. How about just getting the book done and bring whatever lessons you learn with you to your next project?"

She was bang on. And luckily I was able to take her advice to heart instead of brushing it off. Sometimes I do listen.

The second and perhaps most important reason I harp on about finishing is my theory that it builds confidence. Confidence is crucial for a creative person, it's perhaps our most valuable resource. If you abandon a project out of fear or because you get stuck, you run the risk of damaging your self-confidence in the long run. It can take a while to regroup and trust in your own abilities after you jump ship.

Let's say you set out to create a 120-page graphic novel and you get thirty pages in, before you decide to bail on your idea. I can guarantee you'll at least subconsciously feel like a giant failure. We are our own worst enemy that way, always looking for stuff to beat ourselves up with. Always looking for proof that we're actually useless at our art.

In a second scenario, you set out to create a ten-page comic and actually finish it. You'll feel like a success! You get a little more resistant towards those voices in your head that tell you that you suck. In the first scenario, you drew three times as many pages but gained none of the benefits. Preserve your confidence, guard your core. Always.

My final argument for finishing stuff is *time*. Time is a finite resource. If you're young and free perhaps you can afford to jam for months or even years with no clear goal in mind. If that's the case, I'm slightly envious. I don't have dozens of hours to throw at random projects that don't amount to anything, I have too many things I want to see finished.

Forgive me if I sometimes sound like some productivity robot, but nothing makes me sadder than the sight of someone wasting their talent.

The Phases of Creativity

Decades ago I had the great privilege of working with Lars von Trier (yes, *that* Lars von Trier). While it wasn't exactly pleasant, it was a great learning experience. The initial meetings were frustrating, because it felt like we had to restart every time. I was part of a small team of writers hired to do a pretty simple task (at least that's what I thought—I was young and stupid). We already felt we'd pretty much nailed it before ever meeting with Trier. But he kept unraveling the thing, sending us back with questions and tasks that seemed innate and unnecessary.

I arrogantly thought the man had no idea were the project was heading. It was like he sent us into orbit with lofty, existential considerations that had no place in the real world. But every meeting we were pulled gently back towards Earth where Trier was standing, waving, right in the middle of the spot we were always supposed to land in. He not only had an idea from the beginning, he was smart enough to let us explore concepts on our own before jumping to conclusions.

Most of us can't compare to a creative genius like Lars von Trier, a man of extraordinary intuition and artistic merit. No matter if you like his movies or not, you can't argue that they're always novel and interesting in some way. What the anecdote hopefully illustrates, are the different phases of the creative process. You can't just jump the gun and get a great result. Just as you won't make it past the explorative phase without a clear destination in mind.

I'm sure you know the concept of a brainstorm where anything goes and no ideas are too bad to be considered. Nevertheless, a lot of artists sabotage this phase by sitting with their arms crossed, rejecting ideas because it can't be done or it's been done before.

In the final stages of a project, new ideas can really throw a wrench in the machine. The time to change the movie's location or introduce a novel concept is *not* right before a deadline. I know the voice in your head will try to trick you into accepting that this particular idea is much better and you need to start over. It is lying, trying to trip you up right before the finish line.

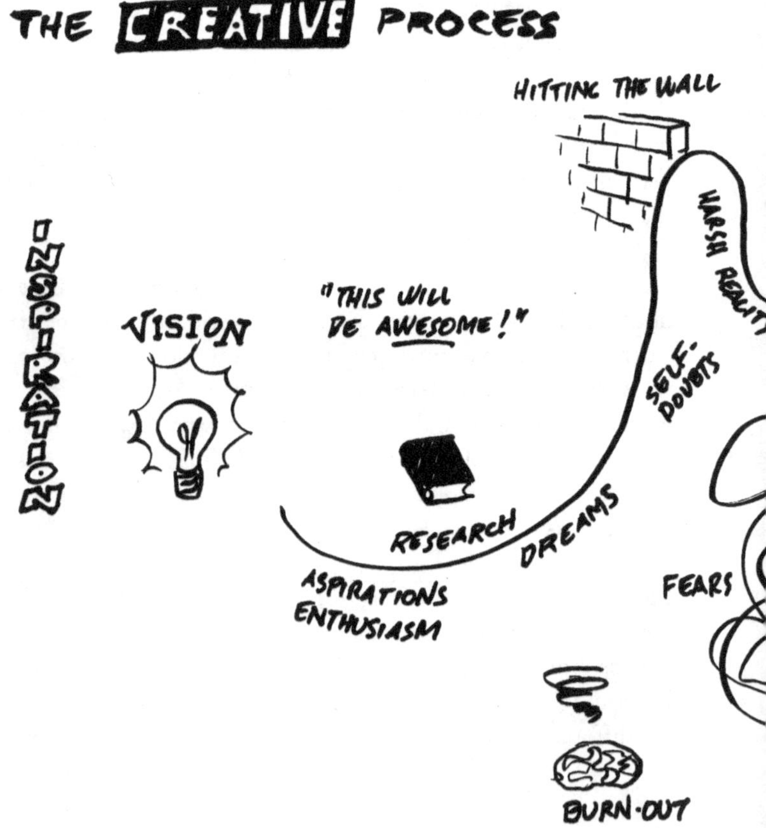

According to Steven Pressfield, that voice inside your head (in his book *The War of Art,* he calls it "The Resistance") is not just trying to prevent you from doing your work, it's trying to *protect* you. A book that is never finished won't get bad reviews, right? Your subconscious self-sabotage could very well be the fear of *finishing.*

I heard a rumor (I tried verifying it online but haven't found a reliable source, sorry) that at Walt Disney studios they have different colored rooms for each part of the creative process. In the blue room you're not allowed to say no or kill any ideas. The green room things get a little more realistic and in the red room they really buckle down and make final decisions.

True or not, this sounds like a great way to avoid confusion and unnecessary arguing. Being mindful of where you are in the creative process is crucial, even when working solo. More on how to deal with your inner critic on page 143.

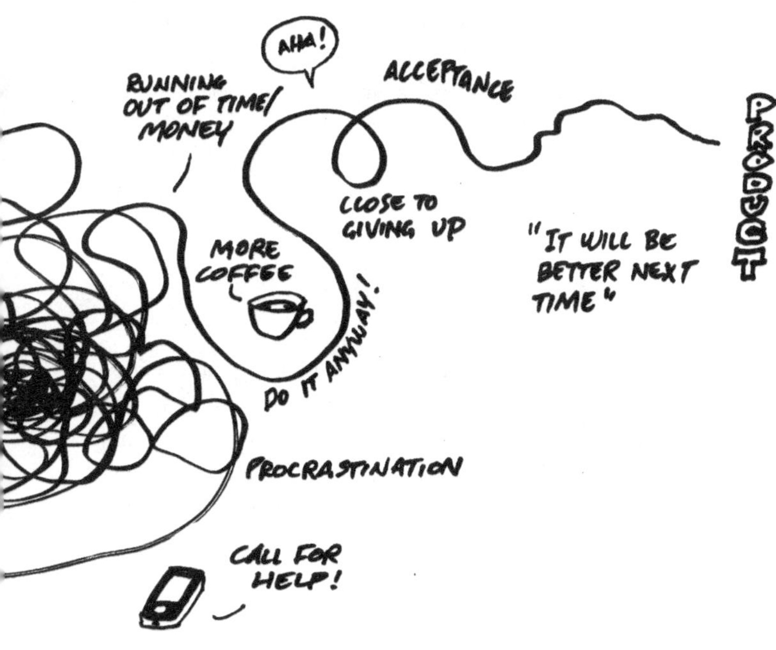

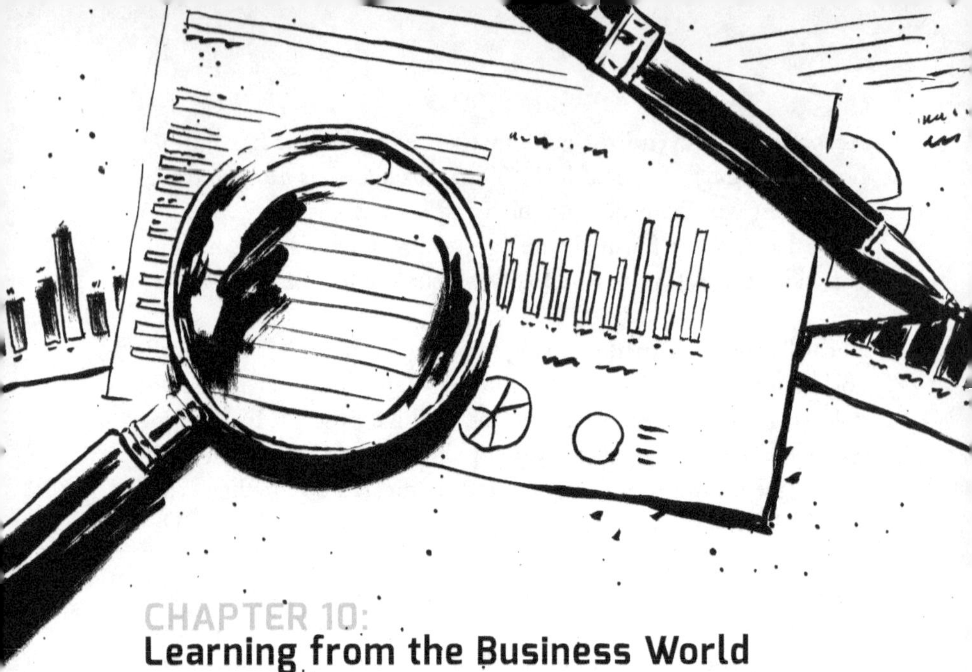

CHAPTER 10

Learning from the Business World

For the past fifteen years or so, I've been frequently hired to do graphic recording or visualization at various live events in both the public and private sector. I've been a fly on the wall at corporate workshops, strategy meetings and research and development brainstorms; learning the jargon of new biz, core values and key performance indicators. I've heard keynotes from consultants, motivational speakers, experts and high-level executives. I've often felt misplaced (not to mention bored out of my skull) at these events, surrounded by people with degrees, neckties and a common language I could hardly keep up with. I've also often felt like it was all talk and no action, hard to find any concrete plans of action in the lingo of benchmarking and scalability.

My daily life is far removed from executive meetings and excel-sheets. There's no clear business strategy, just a lot of fumbling around in the dark, pulling levers and pushing buttons to see what works. There's no formula for art, you can't put art into an excel-sheet. And the whole market analysis and core value system is not something many of us have given much thought to.

Over the years, I've come to think that as alienating and jargon-filled as the corporate world may seem, there's a lot to be learned from it. Even a dumb cartoonist like me is a sort of entrepreneur and maybe a set of goals and a plan to get there isn't such a bad idea.

Where I see a disparity between business and arts is the whole analysis of the customer's needs. When you're selling a product—insurance, shoes, a piece of software—it is crucial to be able to understand the needs of your customer. In arts, it seems to me that the more you think of the end-user and their wants and needs, the less interesting, vibrant and prolific the work will be.

As Andy Warhol put it:

"Don't think about making art, just get it done. Let everyone else decide if it's good or bad, whether they love it or hate it. While they are deciding, make even more art."

Follow the Money

While I don't think you should strive to create according to what the market wants, there's no reason to be downright stupid. Not having any customers means not having any money and no money means you have to get a real job, thereby hurting your chances of creating your own art.

There's a consultancy firm here in Denmark called Workz and the founder and CEO, Ask Agger (not a typo, that's his actual name), is an old friend of mine. On the train ride back from a corporate workshop I had the chance to pick his brain about what creative freelancers can learn from "real" entrepreneurs like him. His main point was: you need to go where the money is.

Ask came up through the same role-playing community I grew from. In this field, we both spent hundreds if not thousands of hours telling stories for a marginal audience. He was one of the creators behind a live scenario that took place over a full weekend, set in an old submarine that was docked in Copenhagen harbor. You could only enjoy the experience if you were one of the fifty or so participants. I myself wrote a scenario for a convention, where I had t-shirts made for every game master, had posters and booklets printed up. I'm sure it was a great delight to the twenty-five people who took part.

The corporate world has a lot of jargon about scalability. I'm sure Ask and I never heard of this back in the early nineties when both of us were spending vast amounts of time and energy pleasing the smallest viable audience, limiting the results from the very start by the choice of medium, not to mention geography. Denmark is not a very big country and you would find it hard to find a smaller niche than role-playing games, even in the nineties.

Ask later took his flair for live action role-playing to the corporate world, basically turning it into teambuilding events. He also used his experience with interactive storytelling and game design to create problem-solving exercises, some in the form of board games. While there may have been few people willing to pay for a role-playing experience, there are huge opportunities within companies looking for ways to get their employees engaged in a new strategy or need outside consultancy in order to think outside the box.

Whatever your artistic endeavors and whatever medium, there's a chance you could squeeze more out of it. Performance theatre for a small, select audience may seem difficult to scale, but you could take the show on the road and sell it again in another city or another venue. You could also film the whole thing and put the show on one of the many video-on-demand (VOD) platforms available today. Or just put it on YouTube to promote the troupe and sell the show to other venues.

Repurposing content is one way of scaling your art. I've written several novels where the basis of the plot came from a role-playing scenario. A few of the chapters in this book are converted blog posts. A comic could appear in an anthology or be divvied up into segments and published as a weekly web comic. Repackaging something you already created rather than create something new can be to your advantage.

You could also give some thought as to how you could expand your audience and meet their needs without necessarily compromising your artistic integrity. At my studio, a couple of illustrators/designers have partnered up and created a new business model. In the weeks before Christmas, a lot of people in the corporate world are struggling to find unique and interesting presents and people in regular jobs are often pressed for time to go shopping. My colleagues have come up with the great idea to set up shop in the lobby or cafeteria at large office buildings (after getting permission from the firm, of course), giving the employees a chance to shop for prints, postcards, original artwork and the like during their lunch break. The products are pretty much the same as what the three artists sell in their respective web shops but the convenience is a service to the customer, aside from the chance for the artists to reach a new audience. Pretty clever.

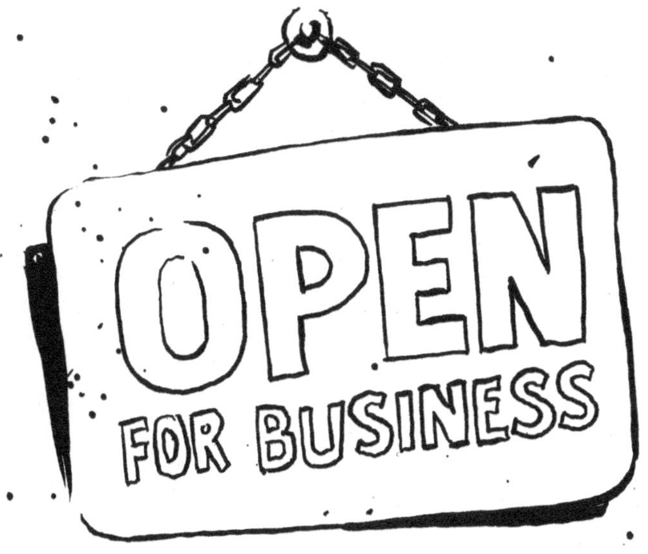

The Sales Funnel

I'd never heard of this concept until a few years ago. You can Google examples that may or may not inspire you, but let me give you the basic rundown.

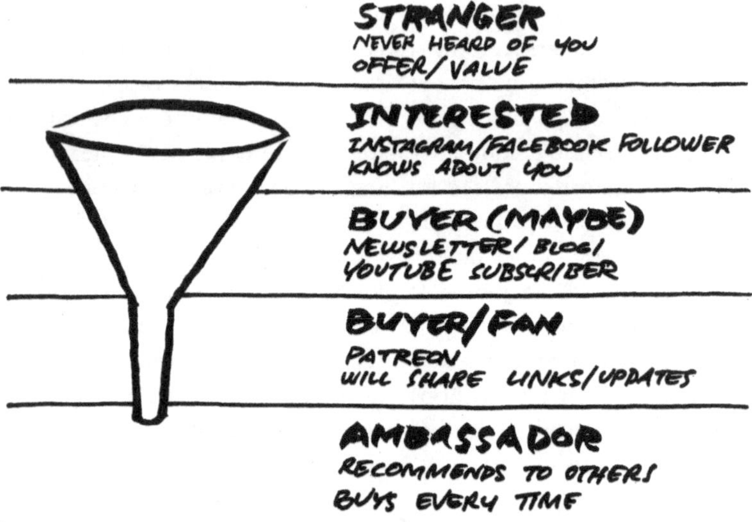

If you have an upturned triangle, the wide part above represents people who have a vague knowledge of you (or your product, if you're in that realm). If you get people in the top of the funnel (likely through social media or other forms of PR) you can start to move them down the funnel (through delivering great content and building trust) until eventually you can make a sale. The very bottom of the funnel represents people who are so committed that they will become ambassadors, recommending other people to check out your stuff, thereby leading new people to the funnel.

Notice how the funnel gets narrower as not everyone will ever buy anything from you, much like not everyone who pass a store will go in and throw their money on the counter. But the wider the funnel, the bigger the chance of somebody checking out the store window, maybe considering a buy sometime.

The challenge is to get people interested enough that they stick around, i.e., by clicking "follow" or subscribing to your newsletter. But all your efforts will be kind of wasted if there's no buy-button in the end.

A few years ago, I was all fired up about getting traffic for my blog. I'd like to get those hours spent looking at stats back, please. In hindsight, I was stroking my own ego and spending time trying to drive people to my site for no good reason. I had no call-to-action on my web page, no buy-button, not even a sign-up box. Sure there's the off chance that someone who followed me for a while online will trip over one of my books one day and might remember my name. Maybe they'll even pick up the book and leaf through it. But it's not really something I can control or even measure in any meaningful way.

If all this talk of markets and strategies is bumming you out, I totally get it. I know it sounds salesy and cynical but you need to eat. Ignoring the sales aspect will leave you starving on a diet consisting of likes.

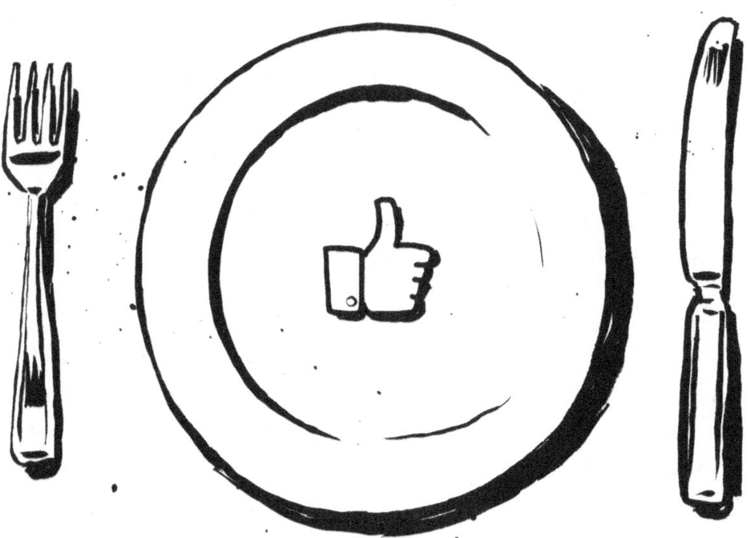

Strategies and Focus

Ask the experts and they will tell you to first plan and then execute. But you could easily wind up spending all the time in the planning phase, on pure guesswork. Your time as a creative is much better spent making stuff and getting better at your craft rather than filling out business plans and doing market analysis. There's a reason the term *analysis paralysis* is thrown around. You have to get the ball rolling, adjust course along the way. Like I heard on some internet business podcast: "Ready, shoot, aim!"

Another thing I learned from the biz world is the idea of an overall goal that you can hold your everyday decisions up against. For a freelancer, every day presents us with a smorgasbord of different options, a to-do list a mile long. In the corporate world they're always measuring progress and performances. While this could be a way of just micro-managing the employees, it can also be helpful for the team to know if they're on the right track. I often dream of having a boss or some branch manager who could coolly evaluate what I'm doing and tell me if I need to be doing things differently or work on a different project. I guess I'll just add one more job description for myself.

Goals, strategies and tactics are not the same thing. You may set your goal only once every decade, whereas your strategy—how you are going to head towards your goal—might change almost on a weekly basis, depending on what seems to be working. Tactics are like the tools and most of what this book is full of. Hope you find some you can steal for your toolbox!

To figure out a strategy, maybe take some time in the beginning of a workweek and think of three simple actions that might take you closer to your goal. Think of who you know or can reach out to who could be able to help, or what you can do *right now* without asking anyone's permission. When evaluating previous tactics, don't beat yourself up if it didn't lead to the desired outcome. Simply register what works and what doesn't. Try to be your own boss, objectively looking at what the employee is doing and see if you can course correct going forward.

A large corporation has the advantage that they can throw time and resources at a problem, have an entire department work full-time on a new initiative for months without creating any income for the company. You try and do that as a solopreneur and you're dead in the water.

What you *can* do, is make decisions. You don't have to get approval higher up in the system, go through a board of directors or get the entire team on board before implementing a new strategy. You can literally start tomorrow. Your resources may be sparse but you're way more mobile than a big corporate entity.

Sometimes you need to climb the mast to see where the ship is heading. In a real business, that is the role of the CEO, to oversee the entire business and have the employees carry out the tasks. As a solopreneur, you are both the CEO and the employee, wearing a hundred different hats depending on what needs to be done.

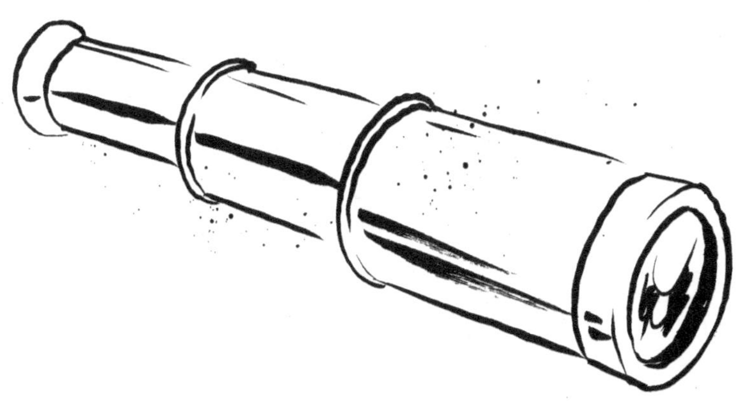

Instead of juggling hats like a crazy person, try to put on the captain's hat once a week and set the course. Write the list of tasks to be done, make the hard decisions. Once your captain's duty is done, hand the list off to the employee (you just changed roles, remember?) and let them get to work. When you're in work mode, don't start worrying about whether the things on the to-do list are the *right* things, just focus on checking the boxes, performing every task to the best of your abilities.

I stole this tactic from the business podcast *The Fizzle Show*, that introduced it as "CEO Mode vs. Worker Bee Mode" and it's really helped me in my daily work, being mindful what role I was in and when I started to drift.

Business Plans

As mentioned earlier I never really had a business plan. If you're a tech start-up or some other business that wants to bring in investors, you absolutely need it. A cartoonist, not so much. Where I'm at now, twenty years in my creative career, having some sort of goal and a strategy for getting there seems like a really good idea. I probably should have done it sooner.

I created this sort of quick-and-dirty business plan that you might find helpful. It won't help you get investors or venture capital but it might help you get a clearer understanding of what next steps you can take and what steps *not* to take.

The following is a list of somewhat existential questions you can ask yourself. Skip the parts that don't make sense for you right now. You can always come back to it later.

- What is your biggest asset as a creative freelancer?
- What is the unique skill or perspective you bring to the table?
- Who are your top three role models?
- What is it those three do that you could successfully imitate?
- What is it they possess that you're envious of?
- Where else could you look for role models?
- Who in your network do you think could help you reach your goal?
- What three clients would you most want to work with?
- What other three clients could you probably land if you gave it a try?
- Where can you find an extra three hours a week?
- What three things could you do tomorrow that would move the needle on your business?
- Which one of those three things will you commit to doing?
- What are three things you should stop doing?
- Who are the five people whose opinion and support you rely on the most?
- Whose condemnation and criticism do you fear the most?
- Is that person on the list of the five you value the most?
- If not, would you please stop paying attention to what they think?

OK, the last few clever questions there I based off this quote from Brené Brown:

"I carry a small sheet of paper in my wallet that has written on it the names of people whose opinions of me matter. To be on that list, you have to love me for my strengths and struggles."

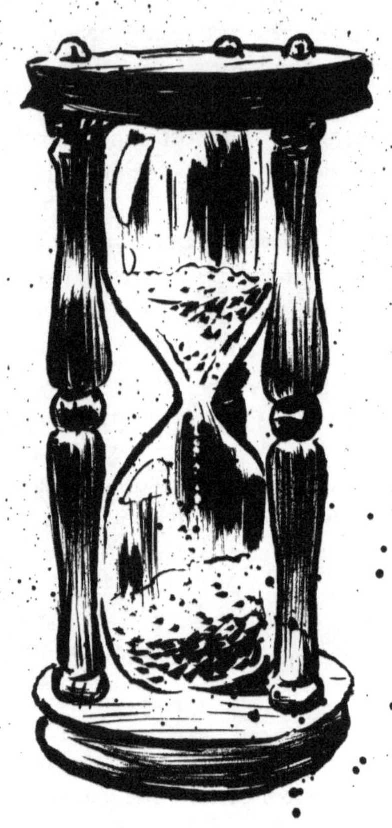

CHAPTER 11

Managing your Time and Focus

The most valuable resource for most of us, is our time. I'm guessing you find it lacking. But it's actually the one currency where all of us are created equally. We all have 24 hours in our days. The trick is finding out how to spend them.

I know you're thinking: "Easy for you to say, I have kids/a stressful job/my sick mom/some other reason why I have less time than you do." But you have to own the fact that how you spend your days is a *choice*. Either a choice *you* made or a choice someone made for you.

I'm not here to judge how you live. Some things are somewhat set in stone, I get it. But if you "have to" work 80 hours a week as a consultant to pay the mortgage, perhaps you're living in the wrong house. No one is forcing you to live in that house. If you "have to" drive the kids to school, to soccer practice or swimming lessons that's also a choice. You chose your kid goes to soccer, you chose where she goes and that taking the bus or car-pooling is not an option, okay, fine with me. So *own* that decision and stop saying you don't have time. You have time with your kid in the car. That's great.

So many people make up excuses for themselves and blame their circumstances for their lack of time. If they timed how many hours a week they spend on Facebook, computer games or watching Netflix, they would realize there's some leeway to be gained here.

We all have dead space during our days; when we're commuting or waiting for a meeting, lunch break at our desk, or just too damn tired to really do anything productive. I'd recommend you keep a pool of low-concentration tasks reserved for these times—reading that article, doing thumbnail sketches, doing light research or simply thinking of the story you want to write. It beats scrolling mindlessly through your Instagram feed.

I usually keep a sketchbook in my bag, sometimes actual pages that I can pull out and do some light work on anywhere. My wife and I spent two months in Paris when our first daughter was three years old. I rough sketched most of my graphic novel *STILETTO* while she was asleep in the stroller. We'd be out walking and the minute her eyes closed, I'd beeline for the nearest café and pull out my script and sketchbook.

Years later back in Copenhagen, I worked on sketches of *Thomas Alsop*, in the café at the *Danish Architecture Centre* while my daughter (same one, around nine at that time) took a course. Portions of this book are written on an iPhone in a darkened bedroom while I was waiting for my youngest daughter to fall asleep. For the longest time she couldn't get to sleep unless me or my wife sat holding her hand. Keeping my phone in the other hand and doing something produc-tive was my way of staying sane. A lot of work communication via texts between my partner Chris and I were handled in those hours between eight and nine pm, when it was still early in New York.

Chris also has an insane work ethic and productivity worth taking some inspiration from. He works in TV and film, where there is a lot of waiting around on set. Where others shoot the breeze, play games on their phone or whatever, Chris finds a quiet corner, opens up his iPad and get's some scriptwriting done. He has consistently generated more scripts per year than almost anyone else I know in the industry and it's this kind of dedication to his craft that has honed him into one of the best writers out there.

I was at Comic Con in San Diego once when an editor looked at me sympathetically when he heard I had fourteen-hour flight home. I laughed and said: "Hey, I have small kids at home. Fourteen hours on an airplane is heaven for me!"

Apart from the discomfort and the excruciating security checks, I *relish* travel time, whether it be by airplane or train. I set no expecta-tions on myself and since no one can get a hold of me, often find myself in a creative flow, scribbling in my notebook like a madman. Or just catching an in-flight movie, I'm not trying to make myself better than I am. I do usually download a few podcasts and always bring a book, so even standing in line at the airport can feel somewhat productive. As long as I move with the cue, I'm able to catch up on a lot of reading this way. (Bonus tip: If you finish a book on the way, you can gift it to someone. Make someone happy and make some room in your bag. Double win!)

My productivity secret? I prioritize the things I want to do and say no to a bunch of other stuff. I say no to a lot of incoming work, for example. How can I afford to do that? I live in a small apartment and keep my expenses low. It's not rocket science, people.

Eating a Whale

When you set out to write a novel, record an album or draw a graphic novel, it can feel like having to eat a whale. You don't know where to start, you don't see how it can ever be done, you wonder why you ever said yes.

I felt this every time I started on a longer comic. I felt like it would be impossible, I felt like I didn't know how. So I had to look at my bookshelf and the pages pinned to my wall to remind myself that I did it before. I sat down with a cup of coffee, calmed myself down and opened up my calendar. I looked at the deadline and the number of pages I had to do, then divided that number by the number of weeks available to work on it. It's stupendously simple when you think about it.

Large projects can be harrowing to tackle, even the ones you yourself set in motion, even the ones that don't have a clear deadline (especially those!). You need to break it down into manageable chunks. Make a plan but be open for the deviations that will undoubtedly arise. Start with the end goal in mind and work backwards. Plant some goal posts along the way, cross every little task off on a list if that makes sense to you, and time yourself if you can.

For my graphic novel *STILETTO*, I decided the book would be 120 pages long. So I created a large sketchbook with 120 blank pages in it and started rough sketching. I had a script, mind you, and I had already broken it down into pages so I sort of knew what I was doing. Still having that sketchbook made it painfully concrete, very easy to oversee the entire book and see how far I was.

As I'm translating this book (which was originally published in Danish in 2017) I just started somewhere one fine morning, and then looked at the word count at the end of the workday. I'd managed to bang out roughly 3,000 words so that became my standard. As long as I keep at it, and manage to swat away the swarming thoughts of inadequacy, I'm able to hit that word count almost every day.

I find that when I'm writing a book, it helps me to set the goal of creating a shitty first draft. It can always be edited later. If I set out to write a great book, I'll never finish anything. In the words of Elizabeth Gilbert:

"A good enough novel violently written now is better than a perfect novel meticulously written never."

For your own projects it's equally important to set goals and deadlines or you'll see it constantly get moved back when other, seemingly more important things come up. If you have all the time in the world, that's exactly how long it will take. You need to make a decision. Saying to yourself: "I'll do it when I get the time," is basically the same as saying you'll never do it.

Time is not something you get. It is something you take.

Focus and Flow

Sometimes you have to completely shut out the world in order to crack a major problem or meet a deadline. We all have different things that work for us, different workflows and ways to trick our brain into focusing. A lot of writers go on a refuge or just a few days away at a hotel. The change of scenery and ability to focus completely on a manuscript can be extremely valuable. You don't have to have access to a romantic cabin in the mountains to be more focused. You could set up office at the local library or a café and not answer any calls for the day.

As I was writing this, an email popped up with a notification for a fundraiser on Facebook. I curiously followed the link, tried to donate by linking up my PayPal, which didn't work. So I ended up watching a couple of short movie clips instead. Suddenly it's fifteen minutes later and I forgot what I was doing. True story. And the story of most of us, most of the time.

Shut that shit off, seriously.

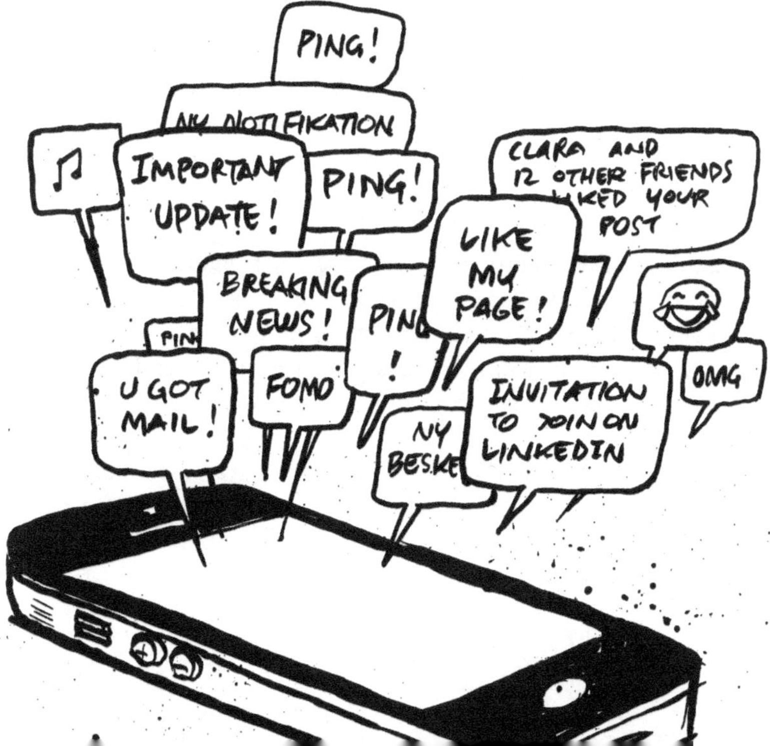

The Power of Habit

Making things a habit is a great way to get things done. Because a habit means it's something you do without thinking about it. The more you rely on inspiration for your creativity, the less likely you are to be creative.

Being more creative is no different than trying to eat healthier or get fit. You need to make it super easy for yourself. Set the bar for success really low. Like "sit down at my desk and look at my comic every day for ten minutes." You can do that, right? You don't even have to work on it, just sit there. But I'll bet you can't help doodling a little once you plant yourself in front of it. Maybe those ten minutes will turn into a good productive hour. Maybe not. The point is to set yourself up for success by lowering your expectations.

You also need to make it hard to fall into whatever traps you tend to fall into. I had a TV addiction once. I had this tiny little TV that fit inside my cupboard, so I coiled the antenna cable around it and put it in there. Every time I wanted to watch TV I had to pull it out from the cupboard, unwrap the cable and plug it in. Bit of a hassle but totally doable. Here's the thing; just making it a little harder to watch TV and putting the damn thing out of sight made me forget I had the option.

The same goes for Facebook. I deleted the app from my phone so now I have to open the browser to check my feed. Again, totally doable. But you bet I go on Facebook a lot less since the app is no longer *right there* every time I look at my phone.

There are several apps for monitoring smartphone usage. I never tried any of them, all my notifications are off anyway and it's always on silent. But we all check our phones more than we need to and it's stealing precious time from us. Time we could spend flexing our creative muscles, even if just for a few minutes.

The most productive habit I have is getting to the studio every day. I walk my youngest to school, hop on my bike and I just *go*. I don't debate myself whether I really need to go in today. Maybe it's raining, maybe I could work from home, maybe I have a bad hair day. Doesn't matter. Just getting to the studio prompts me do some work, no matter if I feel like or not, whether I'm on a deadline or just fiddling with my own projects.

Make it super easy to get to work and super hard not to. Make it a habit.

Put it on the Calendar

If you want to create your own art project that nobody is really waiting for, you need to make it a priority. By putting it in your calendar you're preparing your subconscious mind for the work ahead. If you have something scheduled it's easier to say no to other obligations. You have to stay true to the commitments you make—even the ones you make with yourself.

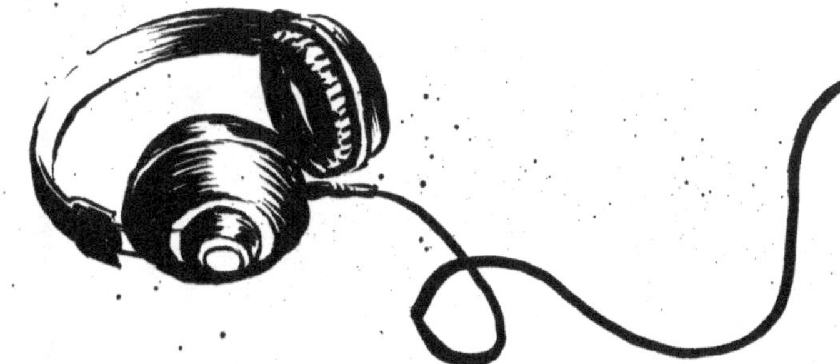

Headphones

In an open office environment or working from a coffee shop, putting on a pair of headphones (even with no sound in them) can help you create the necessary personal space. You can drown out the noise around you and people tend to not talk to someone wearing a big-ass pair of Sennheisers and a concentrated frown.

I have several motion picture soundtracks that I only listen to when I'm writing. By putting the same music on, I'm letting my brain know what we're doing. Recently I found a bunch of drone and synthwave music on YouTube that really helps put me in the zone, but you might have different tastes. I would recommend some kind of ambient sounds or music where there aren't any lyrics, since it's very hard to keep two tracks of words in your head at the same time.

Change of Scenery

Moving yourself to another physical location to do a specific piece of work can really do wonders for your workflow, at least that's what I've found. Especially if you train the primitive part of your mind to link a specific place with a specific kind of work. If you get stuck in whatever you're doing, moving yourself from the office to the kitchen or going for a walk (bring a notepad, you're gonna need it!) will likely shake you out of whatever creative funk you're in.

Triage

So much to do, so little time! So how do you know where to put your focus on any given day?

Just like you and me, army medics have limited resources. During the Napoleonic wars some smart doctor figured out a method to decide which patients should get the attention first. The patients were divided into three categories:

1: The ones likely to live, whether they were treated or not
2: Those likely to die, whether they were treated or not
3: Those likely to live if they got immediate treatment

Category number three was obviously the patient they would try to save.

While trying to save someone's life while bombs are dropping around you is a somewhat more stressful and high stakes work environment than staring at a blank canvas wondering if you should be updating your website instead, you can find inspiration in the triage method. Diagnose your list of daily tasks and inbound communication. You don't *have* to do throw yourself into every online debate or try to solve every problem presented to you. Some (if not most) problems take care of themselves if you leave them alone. Put your energy and focus where you can make an impact.

Shut Off the Interruptions

I already talked at length about turning off email notifications, Facebook pop-ups and text message sounds. Have you turned off yours yet? No? That's what I thought. So let me get back on my soapbox for another sermon.

Research shows that it takes your mind fifteen seconds at minimum to get back on track after an interruption, and some research suggests it can take as long as 23 minutes to refocus in our modern day society where social media and distractions are ever present. Whether it's a friendly colleague asking if she can bring you a coffee from the machine or an email you quickly scan for importance and then delete. Fifteen seconds might not sound like a lot, but think of how many times a day you check your phone or your email and you'll quickly realize it adds up. Many lost hours in a week.

If you need a break from whatever you're doing, having a list of low-energy tasks might be helpful as a remedy for procrastination. If you're like me you are perfectly able to make your own distractions in the form of new ideas for stuff to do. I try to park ideas that come up during my work by jotting them down on a piece of paper or a notebook. Nine times out of ten those ideas or to-do's will never get done, because I sobered up and realized I didn't need to do that particular thing after all. I've also experimented with putting all those little ideas in a pile and pushing it all to Friday, but I must admit I hardly ever looked at the pile again. Perhaps you'll come up with a better method.

Preparations

The days where I lose the battle with Facebook or other procrastination tools are always the ones where I don't have a plan. If I decide the night before what two to three tasks that need to get done the next day, it's a lot easier to just sit down and get to work the following morning.

Productivity experts say checking your email in the morning is the worst thing you can do, since it will likely derail your plans for the day, putting you in reactionary mode rather than action mode. It's true that opening up that email is opening an unknown number of problems (other people's problems), demands and decisions to be made. But no one is likely to die because you wait until ten to open your inbox. By committing the first hour of your workday to the most important task, you might actually start the day ahead rather than being side winded by other people's priorities.

I do check email in the morning, first thing. I find the fear and/ or curiosity of what's in my inbox is just as distracting as taking a quick look. I usually open it up on my phone while the coffee is brewing and it helps wake me up. I'm able to quickly see what needs attending to later, I mark those emails as unread and delete the rest. I love swiping left on my phone and watching notifications, spam and newsletters disappear. And then I can calmly go about my day knowing what I need to deal with *after* I attend to my own agenda.

Figure out what works for you, but be intentional about how you spend your days. Letting other people's agenda fill your calendar is the lazy choice.

All Hands on Deck

When you've been at it for a few years, you've likely created a certain income that allows you to get help for things that aren't your core competences (argh, I caught the biz lingo bug!). Maybe you hate doing accounts, social media or cleaning the studio. No reason to do everything by yourself if you can afford to outsource it.

You can get an intern or a virtual assistant (VA) to perform online tasks. Services like elance.com and virtulstafffinder.com can help with recruiting. You can also hire another freelancer, virtual or otherwise, to help with certain parts of your job. At my old studio I often helped out with coloring or sketching for an hourly rate, when a colleague was falling behind on a deadline or just had too much on their plate. And I've brought on people like that myself from time to time. Better to get help than blow a deadline.

If you use assistants on a regular basis, you might want to mention it to the client. If they hired you specifically because of your skills, maybe they won't like that you outsource parts of it. They likely won't care, as long as the work you deliver is on time and you can vouch for the quality.

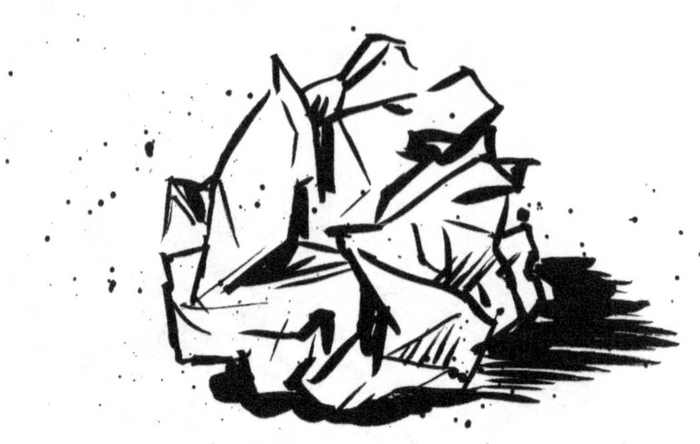

CHAPTER 12:
Cooperation, Critique and Network

Surrounding yourself with peers who are smarter and more prolific than you can be a determining factor in your own prowess. Maybe you can't find any one particular role model in your field, then you just have to go outside and learn from other types of businesses. I didn't learn the techniques and tactics of this book only by talking to other cartoonists, but by listening to podcasts on entrepreneurship, reading books about creativity and talking to writers, screenwriters and business consultants.

Just beware that consuming knowledge can become a form of procrastination and peer support can become a crutch. I used to ask my old studio mates for advice every day, showing them every damn thing I did hoping for their praise and approval. At some point I realized that, despite their best efforts to feign interest, they didn't really care. The person who *did* care was me, and that was the person I really needed to work hard to please.

At some point you have to lose the training wheels and trust in your own judgment.

The Good Critic

We all need feedback to grow, but it can be really hard to take it in. Asking for people's opinion carries a potential risk: They will give it to you! So if what you're really asking for is praise, negative feedback or well-meaning advice can feel like a slap to the face of our precious little ego.

I asked a friend of mine to read the first few chapters of my novel once, asked him what he thought. I wasn't prepared for his opinions and although his criticism was minor stuff, it derailed my writing process enough that the book lay dormant for almost a year after that. I've since learned not to show work-in-progress to people, unless I'm absolute sure they will cheer me on.

It can take years to cultivate a group of reliable readers, whose opinions and expertise you trust. Giving feedback is a learned skill too. And it's helpful if you know what kind of feedback people are looking for when you give it.

You can profitably divvy up the critique in three columns: The Creator, The Product and The Critic.

The Creator:
- Is the maker of The Product and has asked for critique
- Must realize that asking for critique means getting it
- Must listen and be open for suggestions
- Must not take the critique personally
- Must keep quiet and resist the temptation to explain or defend The Product
- Must take notes and sleep on the suggestions given
- Must decide (after having slept on it) what feedback to take in and what to ignore
- Must get used to the discomfort of criticism

The Product:
- The Product is the song, the painting, text or whatever that is being discussed
- The Product is *not* The Creator!
- The purpose of the critique should be to make The Product better, not to kill it or change it into something it doesn't want to be

The Critic:
- Must strive to be constructive
- Must have a basic understanding of what The Product is or is trying to be
- Must have a basic understanding of the medium and genre of The Product
- Must be someone who The Creator respects
- Must not be married to or otherwise emotionally entangled with The Creator

That last point may be stretching it. But in my experience, too close a personal relationship between The Creator and The Critic makes it harder to keep the columns apart. While some are able to distinct between an opinion on the work and the person who created it, I'd recommend going a little outside your close relatives and best friends to find your ideal critic. Do you really trust your mom to be completely objective and give her honest opinion?

A perfect example from my own life: I met the prolific cover artist Dave Johnson (of *100 Bullets* fame) at New York Comic Con in 2011. I showed him some pages from my upcoming graphic novel *STILETTO* and in less than thirty seconds he'd spotted a general flaw in my artwork that I hadn't ever noticed. When drawing a character straight on, I tend to skew the face so the left eye is higher than the right.

Since I hadn't ever met Dave before, I could hardly take his criticism personally. And since I'm in awe of his skill level (let's be honest, I'm a total fanboy) I could hardly dismiss his feedback like he didn't know what he was talking about. He clearly did. I appreciated his honesty and have tried to course correct ever since.

You can possibly dig up an example of a close friend who's both brilliant and sharp in their critique. If you find one of those, hang on for dear life. But if their feedback starts getting in the way of your friendship, see if you can find someone out in the farther regions of your network. The good critic is out there.

Your Inner Critic

I'm sure you know the feeling of looking at your own work and not being able to tell if it's good or not. One day you'll feel like a genius, next day you feel like a complete fraud. The pendulum swings back and forth and staying on the path can be a challenge. You have to be self-critical in order to improve. But if you're *too* self-critical you'll likely dissuade yourself from going on. It's a delicate balance.

One of the biggest lessons I carry with me from the Danish Film School was shutting up my inner critic. The fact that I was even accepted to this master class program, helped convince myself that I had a certain amount of talent. I also quickly figured out that everyone in the class struggled with self-doubts to varying degrees, no matter how long they'd considered themselves writers. In other words, those doubts will likely stay with you, no matter how hard you work. Perhaps they help you stay sharp. But when it's *not* helping, let it sit in the corner with its mouth shut so you can get some work done.

Not all of us find it helpful to have a referee following us around waiting to blow his whistle and shame us for dropping the ball. It has its place in certain phases but here are a few where I think you should do your best to ignore the inner critic:

The brainstorming phase

In the early stages of idea development, you shouldn't judge yourself too harshly. There are no bad ideas in a brainstorm, as even laughably bad ideas could be the springboard for good ones. Just fire away and send the critics out of the room… even your inner critic.

During the first draft

I don't remember when I first understood the concept of a sketch. As a kid I drew with my markers, expecting to either nail it or not. It seemed out of my control. I had the same idiotic approach to writing. One of the biggest revelations for me has been the concept of the first draft, which really has only one purpose: To exist. You can't edit something that's not there.

You can dream all you want, relish in the imagination of this perfect manuscript and the bestselling novel you want to write. But it's when you sit down to actually write the bloody thing that the rubber really meets the road.

I've heard people lovingly refer to the first draft as "the vomit draft," where you just basically get whatever it is out of you and onto the page. I really recommend you try thinking of it that way. Write as fast as you can, no judgment, no shame, no focus on grammar. "Write hot, edit cold" is another expression. Go through the first draft in fiery enthusiasm and once you have something to look at, go through it with your icy gaze and a red correction pen.

Knowing what you're going to write is obviously a huge help. In the movie business they rather rigidly go through phases like pitch, synopsis, treatment and step-outline and you're not supposed to write the script until every beat is worked out. My process is not as structured as that, not by a long shot. I often start with pieces of dialogue or a certain scene (all of which will likely be rewritten). But I tend to think chapters through before I sit down to write them. I don't necessarily put it in writing; I just go over it in my head, usually when I'm doing something else like looking out the window.

This chapter focuses a lot on writing but I'm sure you can apply it to other art forms as well. When I'm doing intro speaks for my podcast, I'll tell myself the first recording is just a warm-up exercise. Usually I'll end up using that first take but I find that it looses me up to know I don't have to knock it out of the park in the first try. I also started "inking" comics in pencil, because I find it loosens me up to know I can just erase any mistakes. I rarely use the eraser but the process is a lot less anxiety-filled than it used to be, taking a quill to a pristine piece of expensive drawing board.

Let the Critic Back in

Here are a few phases where you might benefit from being a little more self-critical:

Early exploration phase

While it's great to play around and try out different styles and expressions in the very beginning, you might want to let the inner critic chime in before you get too far down the wrong path. Asking the annoying questions like: Is this the look you are going for? Are there sources of inspiration you can seek out to raise the bar on yourself? Exploring is great, but it helps to know what you're looking for. The inner critic knows.

Synopsis and treatment

If you are one of those people who likes to thoroughly prepare before you jump in, you need to switch on the analytical part of your brain. Weaving an intricate plot, creating an interesting ensemble cast or planning out your work process; you need the inner critic to shoot down all the crazy ideas and side stories that don't fit in.

Second draft

Sometimes you need a little bit of distance before you can objectively judge the work you did. If I can, I'll put my first draft in a drawer for at least a month before looking at it again with critical eyes. If I can have other people read through it while I'm doing other things, great. Then I can take their opinions into consideration as well, before I start the second draft. Taking a cool, hard look at my manuscript again, I'm sure there are things that need to go or need fixing. My inner critic can help tell me what's good and what's not, and help me decide what feedback to take in and what to ignore.

Last round

When you are putting the finishing touches on a piece of work, you need the inner critic to make sure you cross all the t's and dot all the i's. He's not here to unravel the whole thing and tell you it sucks, we passed that point a long time ago! But you need his scrutiny to weed out the mistakes and make sure the work is as good as can be before shipping.

I'm sure a lot of artists (if not most) have their inner critic present every step up the way. It never really helped me any, I don't need to be more self-critical than I already am, thank you very much. And since I often jump around the various phases I can be deep in some emotional scene one moment and thinking about the marketing aspect in the next. I'm not saying you should copy me—please don't—just be intentional about when you let your inner critic trip you up. He *will* do it if you let him.

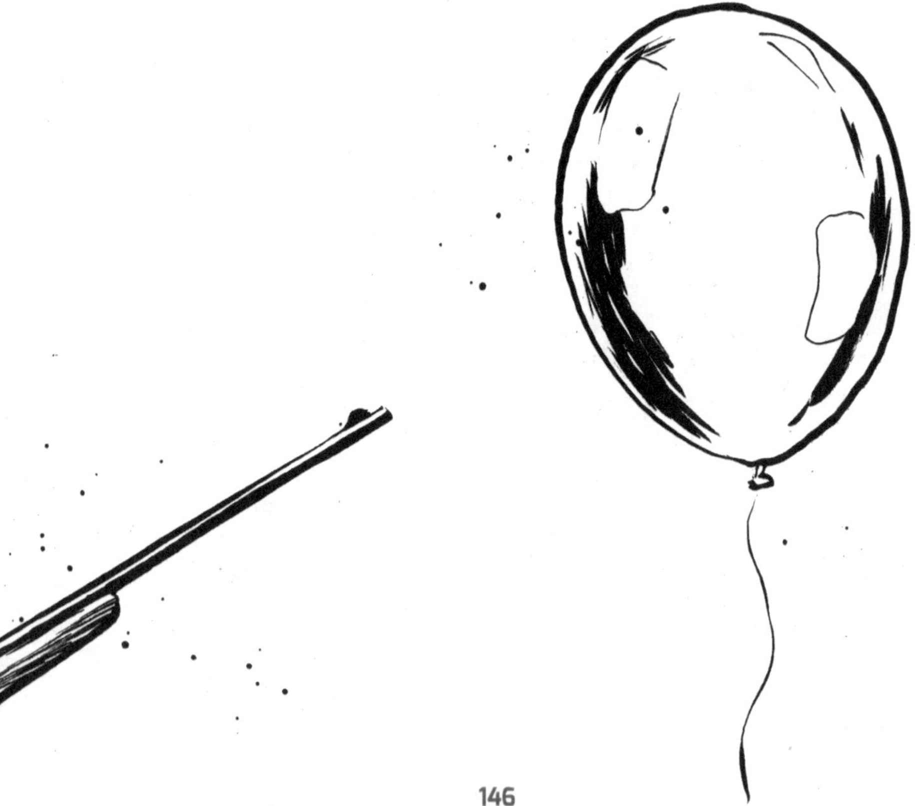

Master Minds

When you've been at it for a few years and want to shake things up a bit, maybe you need to expand your network and bring your career to the next level. A master mind group might be a way to do it.

I first heard of master minds in some entrepreneur podcast, can't remember which. *The Fizzle Show, Smart Passive Income* and Chris Ducker have had whole episodes about it. The idea is to form a small crew of likeminded people to bounce ideas off of and help keep each other accountable. Some meet in person, others do it over Skype or Google Hangouts.

For a little over a year now I've met once every month with four to five other creative freelancers. We see it as a support group, a way of keeping each other in check and helping each other get as far as we can, whatever our individual ambitions are.

Here are some of the elements for a good master mind group:

4-8 members

Too many people in the group makes it hard for everyone to get a chance to speak. Try to find people with similar challenges and/or skill level. You don't have to all be writers or artists or potters or whatever, you can benefit a lot from the perspective of other fields. But if one is a consummate professional while everyone else is just starting out, it could skew the balance.

2-3 hour meetings

Longer than that and member attention starts to drift and energy goes low. Having a set time limit helps with planning and makes it easier to commit to. In my master mind group, we meet the first Monday of every month from 3 pm to 6 pm. Having a fixed day helps planning ahead since we're all busy people.

Moderator

One member is responsible to make sure everyone gets to speak and keeps track of time. I tend to take the lead role in our master mind but I'm thinking of letting it go on rotation.

A Fixed Agenda

It's easier to get people on board if they know what they're signing up for. A fixed structure for each meeting is a good thing to have up front. It could consist of a fifteen-minute round where every member mentions a small victory in their life that occurred recently (we do that every time, to get started on a positive note). Then you could have a round of challenges, group feedback on those challenges and lastly a round of commitments for the next meeting.

Hot seat

If you sometimes need a little more time to really dig in to one member's challenges, you could take turns on who's in the hot seat. Tell the group in advance who will be the focus of the next meeting and give them a chance to prepare. It could be doing research on a topic, feedback on a something sent ahead of time or the like. With 45 minutes in the hot seat, you should have time to dig a little deeper and give/get some valuable guidance.

Show-and-Tell

Instead of the hot seat, a member could prepare a presentation on a specific topic (fundraising, bookkeeping, a certain artistic technique or a piece of software) and let everyone in the group benefit from the expertise of one.

Focus on Problem-Solving

The moderator should strive to keep everyone focused on constructive criticism and practical solutions rather than problems. Give an artist the chance to complain and they will. For hours and hours, unless you stop them!

Guest Speaker

You could have an outside expert come in for a show-and-tell and let everyone in the group benefit from their knowledge.

Commitments

When setting commitments for the next master mind, make sure that it's actually achievable. A commitment like "find a publisher for my book" is not really within the control of the individual member. "Send a proposal to three publishers" is much more doable and concrete. Follow up on last session's commitments at the beginning of every meeting.

Overbook the Meetings

In my experience, it's almost impossible to get everyone to show up every time. So we got an extra man on board to make up for cancellations. As long as four people show up, we go through with the meeting.

You don't necessarily have to start your own master mind, maybe you can find one online or in your local arts community. There are probably also networking events that you could go to (see creative-mornings.com for example) and find a peer group. Or reach out on social media! It's easier now than ever to find your kind of people.

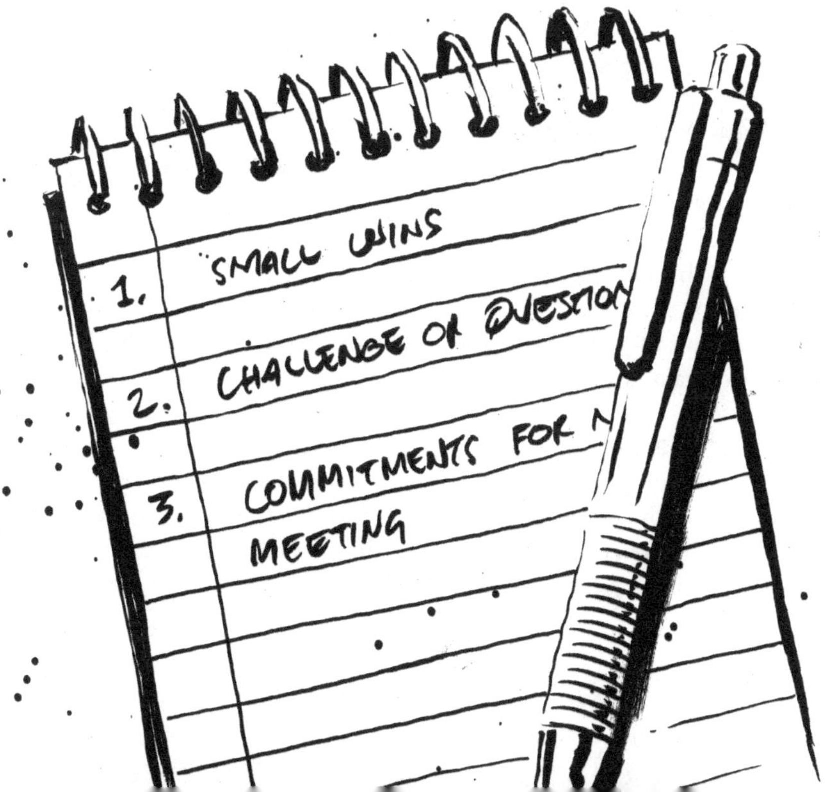

CHAPTER 13

Pitch Your Project

Even a solo artist sometimes needs to get other people on board, especially if the project costs money. Obviously there's a difference between pitching a movie, a book or an eclectic jazz festival, but there are some common denominators:

Keep it Simple

If you can't explain what your project essentially is in one to three sentences, gatekeepers will worry that an audience won't understand it either. So keep all the neat little details in your back pocket and lead with the basic premise.

Unique and Familiar at the Same Time

It sounds impossible, but you need a certain unique quality to sell your idea. It needs to awaken their curiosity; it needs to sound like something new. But it needs to also sound like a tried and tested concept, something they can believe there's an audience for.

Know Your Audience

Knowing the demographic of the end user will really help get an investor or partner to take on your project. Whatever it is needs to eventually find an audience and knowing who they are, where to find them and what they would be willing to pay for is crucial. This goes for who you're pitching to as well; you need to know their tastes and what they've invested in before, so you don't pitch a kids book to a non-fiction publisher.

Bring the Goods

Anyone can get an idea for a book. It's sitting down and writing the damn thing that's hard. You have to do some work up front, both to help persuade a stakeholder that you mean business and to have something that you can protect. Pitching only an idea requires a great deal of trust since ideas can't be copyrighted. You need a written pitch, samples, a keynote presentation, something concrete.

Present the Full Picture but be Open for Suggestions

You have to sell the idea that you are able to pull this thing off, that you've thought it through to the end. You may not have finished the project but you have a plan, an outline, maybe a detailed budget. Simultaneously you need to be open for any changes and ideas that the stakeholder may have. Having some influence will help them feel ownership and get them more engaged in the project.

Pretend to Listen

If a stakeholder starts pitching their own ideas, it's usually a good sign. It means the idea excites them somehow. Perhaps their vision doesn't match yours but if you get too defensive in the beginning, you could lose their engagement altogether. So rather than saying no, listen and take their ideas seriously, enthusiastically taking notes. You might dismiss it later, but at least *pretend* to value their input if you want them to throw money at you.

Explain Your Decisions

When you have an artistic vision all worked out in your head, it can be hard to take in other people's opinions. After all they've only just now heard of the project while you've been living it for weeks, months, maybe years. But hey, they might have a point. Sometimes an objective stakeholder can point out inherent flaws or opportunities that you completely missed. So take notes and think long and hard about the input you get and, if you find it doesn't align with your intentions, have a convincing argument ready.

You are Also Selling Yourself

Other than looking at the qualities of a given project, I'm willing to put my money down that stakeholders are just as focused on who is pitching. They want to know you can actually deliver the goods. So mind how you carry yourself, with confidence but without arrogance. Don't be afraid to mention that award you won last year, the school you went to or the size of your YouTube following—whatever external factor that might help persuade them that you know what you're doing.

Get an Introduction

If you can get someone the stakeholder already knows and trusts to vouch for you, great! It can really help put their minds at ease if you at least have a common friend or someone they can ask about your merits. Just be sure to clear it with that person before you namedrop them in an email.

While pitching in person is likely the most effective way, most people like to be able to look at something in writing. And you need to have a written pitch and/or art samples eventually anyway, if a stakeholder is to take you seriously.

When you approach a potential stakeholder, you can use the following template as a guide:

Hi (name),

I got your email from (trusted mutual friend/respected person in your field) who mentioned the following (book proposal/idea for a comic/exhibition/whatever) might be up your alley.

I'm (ultra-short bio/pitch), I recently (published something exciting/ won an award/finished a prestigious school or class) and right now I'm working on (ultra-short pitch of the project/maybe a link or two).

The target audience is (short description).

I'd love to send you (a detailed synopsis/a demo/a full script/samples of my work) if you're interested. I know you're really busy and don't want to burden you with the details if the project is not a good match. I'd also be happy to (take a call/grab a quick coffee/meet at your offices), whatever is more convenient to you.

Best,
(Your name)

Like the other templates in this book, you should obviously edit and adjust to fit your personal style and needs. But please note that I've kept it short and, like most other templates, I have weeded out the question marks. It allows the stakeholder the option to ignore your email and it allows you to live with not getting a reply. Which is more than likely to happen, by the way.

When/if you don't hear back in a week or two, feel free to send a follow-up email:

> *Hi (name),*
>
> *I don't know if my last email got (lost/ eaten by your spam filter/ buried in your undoubtedly strained inbox), so I just wanted to make sure... I'm enclosing the original email for your convenience. Hope to hear back from you.*
>
> *Best,*
> *(Your name)*

If the second (and maybe third, if you're pushy) email goes unanswered, I'd say cut your losses and move on. Accept the fact that the desired stakeholder is either not interested or just too busy to reply. They likely get ten times the email you do and while you could argue that ignoring emails is not cool (and I would agree), for some people it's simply a survival strategy. It's not personal, you have no idea who or what you're competing against. Don't lose sleep over it. Send the same email again to some other stakeholder or try to pin them down at a trade show or whatever.

If you keep sending the same pitch to people and not getting a reply, it could be that the idea is not really that great, that it's not commercially viable, or that you need a bigger platform. Maybe you could bring in a partner with a better chance of getting attention. Or maybe you should forego the idea of going through the gatekeepers and just make the thing yourself, perhaps after scaling the project down to size according to your budget.

Finding the right stakeholder to pitch to is a whole other can of worms that depends very much on the type of project you have. When I'm looking for a publisher for a book, I will often go to the library or a bookstore and do some research to see who's putting out that kind of thing already. But most of the time I ask my network for recommendations and/or introductions—another reason it's hugely important to nurture a wide network of people in your industry.

If you for some reason or other can't find a home for your project, put it aside for a period, and remember that new opportunities may come up or the market may shift to your advantage. You might meet some new person down the road who could help. You might win the lottery. Don't sit around waiting for it. Come up with a new project and maybe when you're slightly more famous, that first project could resurface, who knows. Keep working, keep churning out quality stuff and eventually something will break through.

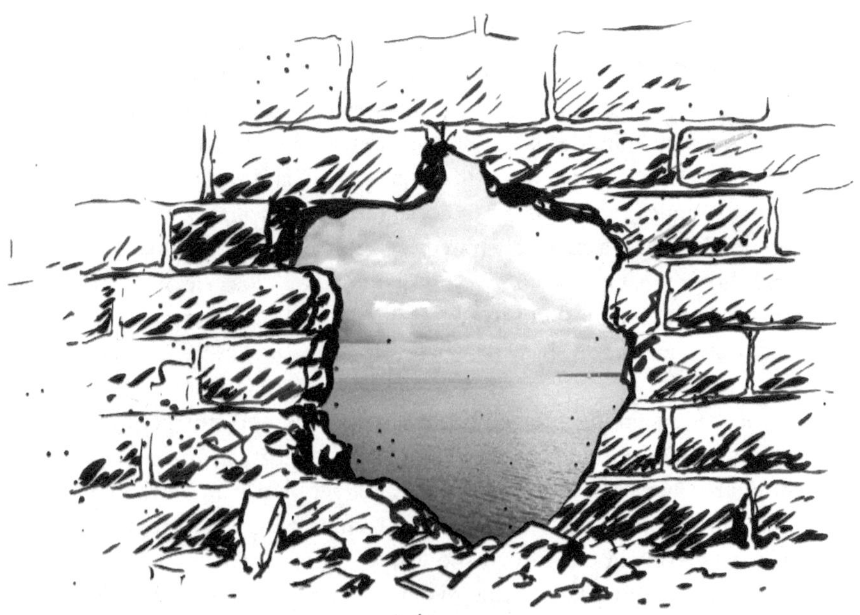

Do it Yourself

Just a few years ago, artists were more or less at the mercy of the gatekeepers—publishers, record labels, production companies, gallery owners, etc. And while we may not have the resources of a big publishing house, nowadays we do have access to the distribution channels.

Musicians figured it out first. Previously you could only get someone to hear your music if you could get a record label to take you on, a club to put you on their stage or a radio station to play your song. Now anyone can put anything on Spotify and build an audience that way. The monetization model has been flipped on its head and now nobody pays for the music. But once they're a fan of the music, they'll pay for the concert and/or t-shirts and other merchandise that the band itself can take care of.

Writer Kevin Kelly has a post on "1,000 true fans" (Google it, you'll thank me), this idea that you basically only need a thousand people—raving fans of your art, who will buy whatever you put out—to make a living. While it may sound like a lot of people (especially for a small country like Denmark!), if you can adjust whatever you make to an international market through the wonders of the internet, the idea of a thousand dedicated people as your fan base isn't so unattainable.

Give it Away

People are used to getting content online for free these days and you could easily argue that the free content model just attracts a lot of freeloaders. Some of those freeloaders might eventually turn into paying customers or raving fans even. Like we talked about in the chapter on the sales funnel (page 122) you need to build trust and a personal connection. It takes a long time to build a following, online or off. And one of the tried and tested strategies is to deliver great content without charging for it. Trying to monetize on day one could seriously hurt your chances of building that following, but once you have a certain number of people who are excited about what you put out, give them the opportunity to give back. Ask them nicely and some of them will be happy to pay you. The end users are the patrons of our time!

I have examples of Danish cartoonists who, after blogging daily for years, release a collection of strips and sell out within days. Even though all the strips had previously been published online for free. Or a comedian I know who does weekly shows on Facebook and then introduced a Patreon-like model, allowing fans like me to finally show our support with a monthly donation. Or another pair of Danish comedians who did stupid skits on YouTube and built a following, eventually enabling them to host sold out events in one of the bigger concert venues in Copenhagen.

I'm sure you can find examples in your area and niche, and obviously just as many who *didn't* make it big. This is not a get-rich-quick game but consistently putting out quality work and bringing it to people for free is certainly not going to hurt your chances of a breakthrough. It's easier to ask for money or make a sale when you already have a following, when you've already proven to people you can deliver the goods.

Do it Yourself – With Others

Not everyone feels comfortable doing everything themselves. Most creatives will likely benefit from having a second pair of eyes on their work and their process. Some need an editor or a producer to help make their work better; others might feel they need the validation of having their work published by a known entity.

I've previously done my books through publishers, both because of the editorial help but also because distribution, marketing and printing seems like an insurmountable task, not to mention costly. But if I'm completely honest with myself, I probably know how to do 95 percent of what the publisher does at this point. And the only thing keeping me from learning that last 5 percent is laziness and fear.

No matter if you choose to go through a gatekeeper or not, you'll need to build your platform. Just a few years ago, if you went to a publisher with a web comic, they wouldn't touch it. Today, a successful web comic is proof of concept. If you have a YouTube following, you have a much better chance of getting a TV show. If you have a successful self-published book, it will likely increase your chances of getting on a big publisher's radar.

An example: I met a Danish soldier who had written a book about his experiences in Iraq and Afghanistan. He had pitched the book to a major publishing house but they seemed pretty unimpressed if not downright arrogant, until they realized he had more likes on his Facebook page than the publishing house had! They quickly changed tactics and put a contract on the table.

Don't Wait

It has never been easier to get your art out to people. Whether you'll become a rock star or not is not the point. The point is you get to play your music and get it in front of an audience. You don't need permission. You don't need to be discovered. The time for finding an audience is not after you write your novel or have enough paintings for an exhibit. The time is now. The sooner you start building your platform the better.

CASE STUDY: STILETTO

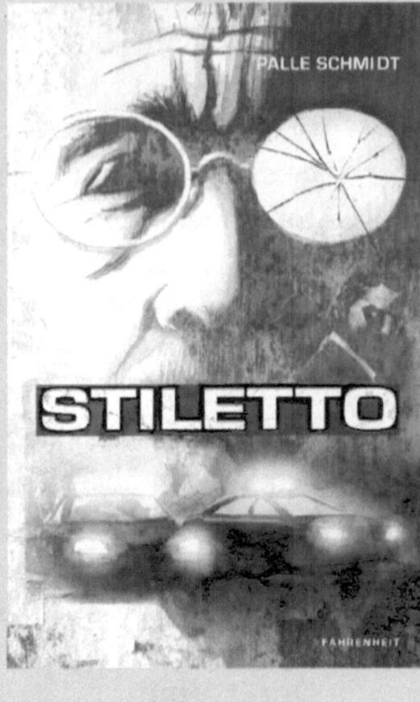

While I was working on *The Devil's Concubine*, I had the idea for sort of a sequel, involving the two cops, Maynard and Alphonse. The story is heavily influenced by 70's cop movies like *Serpico* and *The French Connection* (the sequel being my favorite) and the inciting incident is more or less lifted from *Bullitt*. Where *The Devil's Concubine* was an attempt to make a slick action movie in comic book form, I wanted *STILETTO* to have a more gritty and realistic feel to it.

The style is a great departure from earlier, more inspired from my own sketchbook than anything else. Trying to draw in the very slick style of artists like Eduardo Rizzo or my own mentor Peter Snejbjerg never came naturally to me and the process frustrated me to no end. I decided to try "inking" in pencil and painting the whole thing in watercolor—something I was used to doing in my illustration work.

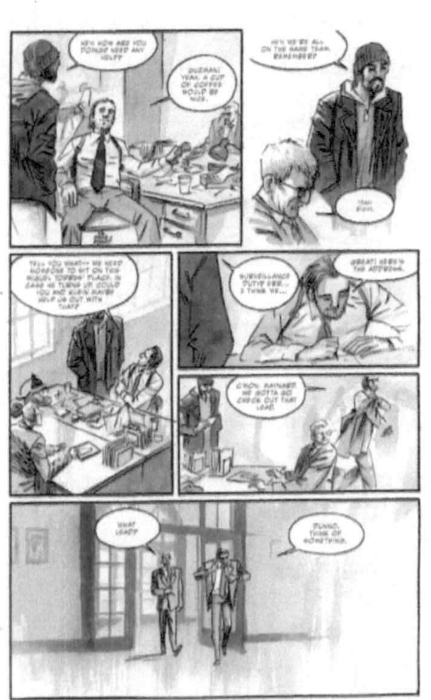

I did a few tests and quickly realized that not only was this drawing process much more fun for me but I could also work way faster. Since making comics takes sooo long, any way to reduce the amount of hours spent on a page is more than welcome.

For the coloring I went for an expressionist approach rather than realism. Since it's a cop story, the use of the color blue would be obvious. So I decided NOT to use the color blue at all! I only use blue for flashbacks and dream sequences. Keeping the whole book in dirty yellowish clay tones creates a much more startling effect when the characters enter a bar where everything is red or there is a flashback or cut-away panel in blue.

By this point I had stopped comparing myself to Danish peers pretty much altogether and focused on the US market. I felt I had an intriguing premise, a solid script and a style that immediately got people's attention when I showed the book to people at cons. So I was surprised when IDW didn't pick up the book. I thought I was in and then it turned out to be a revolving door!

Although *STILETTO* was released in Denmark to rave reviews and an award nomination, it took a few years before the book made it to the US market. It only happened because of Greg Tumbarello, this guy Chris knew who we kept bumping into at cons. Greg was an editor who co-founded Legendary Entertainment's comic book division and I pitched *STILETTO* to him. While Greg really liked it, the company ultimately passed for whatever reason. Eventually, Greg left for a senior editorial position at another company. If I remember correctly, I shot him a note on Facebook saying congrats on the new job and we got to chatting. He asked about *STILETTO*, if anyone had picked it up and I was like, "Er, no. You want it?" To which he said, "Absolutely!"

Working with Greg on *STILETTO* (and this book, btw!) has been an absolute treat and a truly humbling experience. Greg has turned out to be not only a fun guy to hang out with but also a smart and well-articulated editor with a quality lacking in a lot of people working in publishing; he replies to email.

Lessons Learned:
Breaking in is a never-ending process and the quality of the work seems not to matter as much as luck or timing. Sometimes a project that seems like a slam-dunk will have to take the long road before finding a home. Be patient and persistent. You never know where the next opportunity, ally or friendship will turn up. And even if someone passes on it, that doesn't mean they won't remember it and want to help you get it made elsewhere.

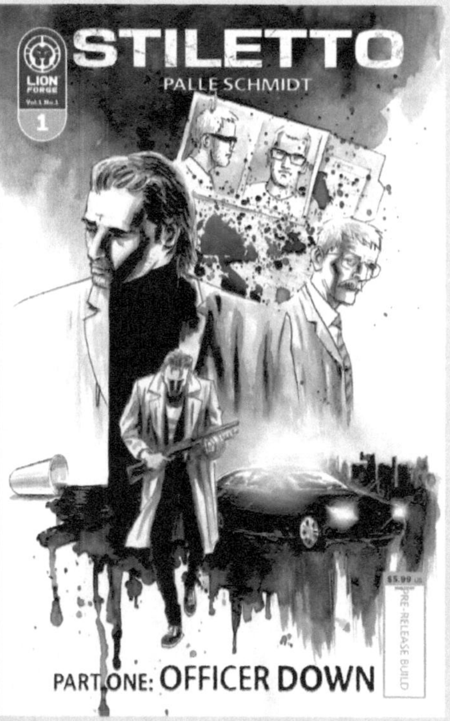

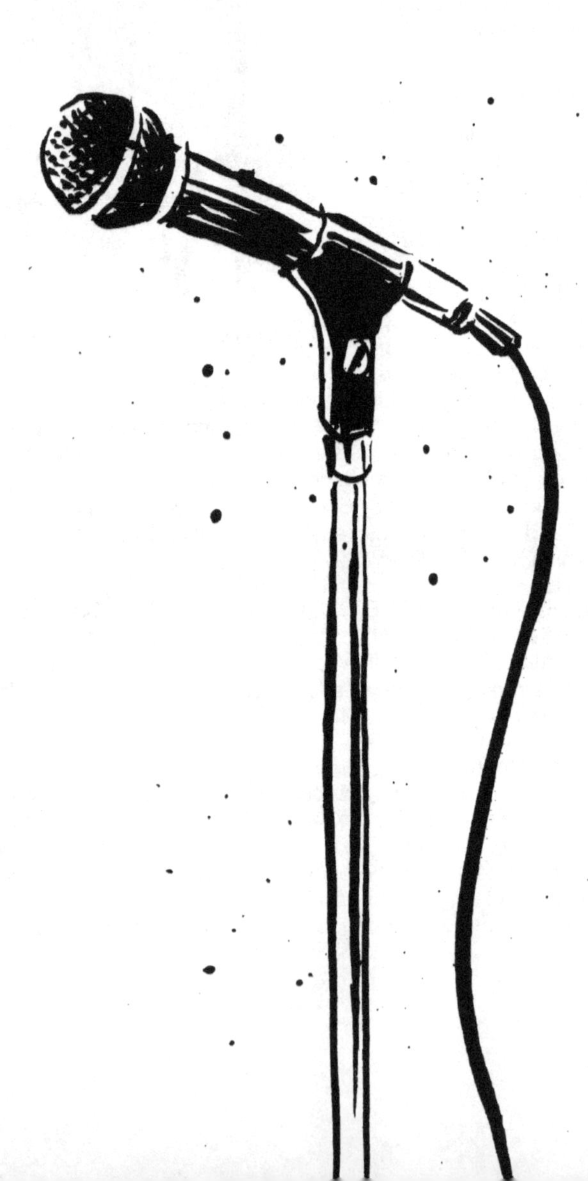

CHAPTER 14

Build Your Platform

Whether you are earning your living from your creative skills or have a day job, you can still build your platform. You can document your progress through Instagram or YouTube. You can sell your stuff through online platforms such as Amazon, Etsy, SoundCloud, iTunes, Gumroad, RedBubble and probably hundreds of other platforms by the time you read this. In this chapter, I'll try to cover some of the ways you can build your own platform both online and in the real world.

Please note, that these are ideas, not fixed truths. I'm no social media guru and things move very quickly these days. As a creative freelancer, you get to choose your own adventure, you don't have to follow some company policy. If you find that using Snapchat or having a Facebook page makes sense for you, go nuts. Just remember to create something you can sell also. It doesn't matter how many people you can bring to the store, if all the shelves are empty.

When it comes to building an online presence and a following of fans, it seems that consistency and clear messaging is key. I'm a bad example because I've got too many things going on, jumping back and forth between posting about a crime novel or a kid's book in Danish and a graphic novel in English. I'm also wildly inconsistent in terms of scheduling, often going weeks between posting anything.

The success stories I see in terms of building an audience are the artists who stick to one topic and post every day or set weekdays. The best advice I can give is find someone in your niche who has a substantial following and try to figure out what they do and emulate their content strategy. Creating (free) content for the web on a schedule can quickly start to feel like a regular job though and you might want to have some way of keeping track of your following independent of any specific social media platform. Which brings me to my next point...

Newsletters

Landing directly in someone's inbox still seems like the safest bet if you want them to actually see your message. Sure, you can reach people through Twitter and Facebook, but you don't own the platform or the connection. An algorithm change could leave you with no means of reaching all the people you've carefully gathered. Or the platform could start charging you to get your posts seen (I'm looking at you, Facebook) or simply go under (remember MySpace?).

Chances of us actually opening an email from a trusted source is way higher than the chance of us seeing a random post on any social media platform. And you likely have access to stats that can tell you if people opened your email or not, how many clicked the link, etc.

This is especially important if you decide to go the crowdfunding route with your projects. Statistics say that only about 3% of your audience engaged through social media will click on your link and donate to your campaign, while engaging via email will give you several times the amount of contributors to your campaign, give several times the amount. It's easy to ignore something while scrolling through your feed, but not as easy to ignore something sitting in your inbox because you have to physically tap to open it or swipe to delete it.

Make it valuable

People rarely sign up to a newsletter simply to "keep in touch." If we're to give up our email, we expect something in return. It could be a promise of valuable content, weekly recommendations or insights, whatever your audience will find interesting. There are examples of sign-up offers and giveaways below.

Make it relevant

Whatever you offer, it should correlate to what it is that you do. If you're a musician, you could offer three free songs upon sign-up.

If you're a chef, offer your ten best recipes. If you're a writer, give away the first chapters of your book or a collection of short stories. If you have a webshop, you could offer a discount code upon sign-up.

Make it easy

The less info you need from people, the easier it is to get them to sign-up. The less hassle it is to log in or provide payment information, the easier it is to get someone to buy from your web shop. There's a reason why iTunes and Amazon are a huge success: the easy access.

How to Create a Newsletter

There are obviously lots of alternatives out there but I have experience with MailChimp, so that's what I'm going to use as an example (I am not affiliated with them in any way). Their service is free for the first 2,000 subscribers (at the time of writing this) which allows you to get your feet wet and try it out, before you commit to a monthly expense. Their interface is also super-simple and easy to figure out. But let me give you a few pointers to get started:

Sign-up Form

It should be self-evident but you need a box on your web page where people can sign up. Once you've created a sign-up form on MailChimp you can embed the form on your site, by copy/pasting an html code into a sidebar or wherever you think it might be best. If you have someone else helping you with web design, just send them the html. It's pretty simple.

If you want to drive people towards your email list from social media, MailChimp also provides you with a direct link to the sign-up form. Please note, that it is illegal to put people on a newsletter without their consent, so you need to direct people to that sign-up form.

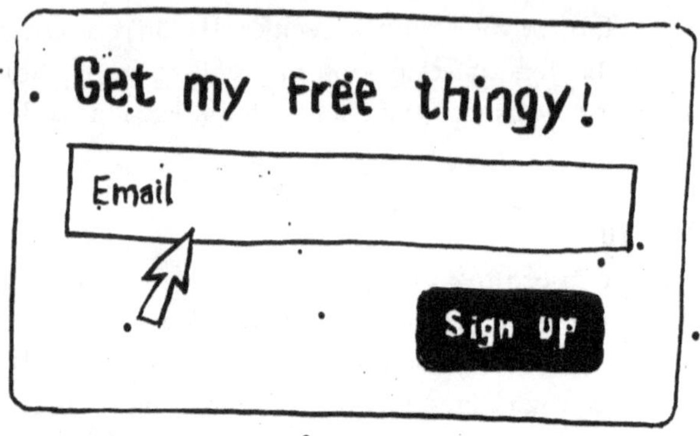

Giveaways

As mentioned above, offering some kind of value or freebie is a good way to get people to give you their email. I've used a free e-book (just a PDF) and a 7-day comics crash course to get people on my Comics for Beginners newsletter. In practice, all I did was put the PDF in a Dropbox folder, right click the file and chose "Copy Dropbox link" and then paste the link into the first email people get upon sign-up. And it could really be a link to anything—a sound file, an unlisted video on YouTube or a sub-page of your website. It doesn't have to be complicated.

After you set up the first email people receive upon sign-up, it will run automatically. You do not need to sit and send every email manually. In fact, for a lot of your email content, you can set it and forget it.

Autoresponders

For a lot of creatives, the task of sending out newsletters on a regular basis seems like a daunting task. I'd recommend you only send out newsletters when you actually have some news to share, rather than think you have to keep posting stuff like you do on Facebook. But if you want to engage with people who just signed up, you might consider setting up an autoresponder series.

In MailChimp, this is currently called "automation" and it allows you to set up a series of emails that people will receive after signing up. You decide when it goes out and how it's sequenced.

The first email could be just a welcome, where you thank people for signing up. You could link to the free giveaway (whatever that is), give a short introduction of yourself or link to your about page, maybe hint to what other content you'll be sending out.

As I mentioned, I offered a free 7-day course upon signing up to my Comics for Beginners newsletter. I basically set up seven pages on the website, each with a video with a task for the day, some work sheets and other helpful tools. Then I set up an autoresponder series, where the link to each page was sent out a day apart for the first week after sign-up (I since changed that approach, since it seemed to overwhelm people more than necessary to get a new email every day. Live and learn, right?). The most time-consuming aspect was creating the videos and the course itself. The autoresponder part requires some concentration but not a lot of skill, honestly.

If I had to set up a newsletter today, I'd sit down and brainstorm what "evergreen content" I could send as autoresponders. Maybe there's a blog post or another piece of content that I'd want every new subscriber to see, some way I'd want to introduce them to what I do. Then I'd write up those emails, including relevant links and feed them into MailChimp and decide when they'd go out. Maybe a few emails the first week, then one every two to three weeks or whatever.

When people sign up for the Comics for Beginners Newsletter, they get emails over several weeks and months. Knowing that new subscribers get dozens of emails of good content that I created years ago helps me feel less obliged to come up with stuff to put in my newsletter—I only send out when there is need.

For our monthly podcast (in Danish, found at PlotCast.dk) we don't offer any freebie upon sign-up, we simply use the list to inform our subscribers when a new episode goes live (the first of every month). I typically create that email the week before and schedule it to send on the morning of the release. I like scheduling stuff like that when I have the time and energy rather than the day of.

CASE STUDY: PLOTCAST

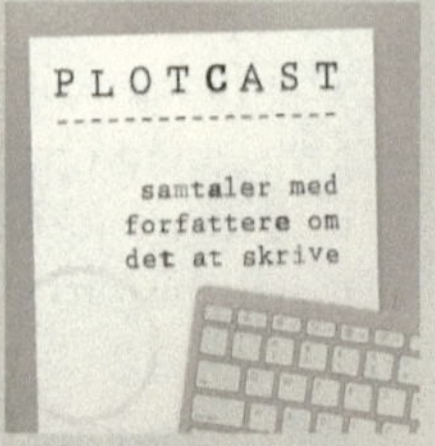

One of my favorite topics is storytelling. While attending Film School in 2012, I thoroughly enjoyed talking to other students and teachers about the intricacies of plot, character and writing methods. When the course came to an end, I wanted to continue that conversation and toyed with the idea of a podcast. I'd been listening to *Scriptnotes* (a weekly podcast with screenwriters John August and Craig Mazin) and dabbled a bit with podcasting for *ComicsForBeginners* but I still felt I was no authority on the matter. Danish writer and plot coach Malene Kirkegaard was very active on social media at that time. She kept popping up in my social feed with excellent writer quotes and good advice for aspiring artists. So although I'd never met her, I reached out to her and suggested we do a podcast together. What I didn't know at the time was she has a background in radio, so beyond her smarts and substantial writer network she was able to edit the episodes.

Malene and I hit it off and started talking about how the interviews should be conducted and decided on some basic rules of engagement, like the length of the episodes and some standard questions. My wife came up with the name *PlotCast* (she's good at pointing out the obvious things I often miss in my attempts at genius). I had a Zoom recorder I bought for *ComicsForBeginners* and recorded one or two interviews, starting with people I already knew. For the first year or so, we only posted an episode every couple of months and didn't do much in terms of promotion. We created a newsletter from day one, I think. The Facebook page came much later, when we already had a bunch of interviews in the bag.

We now publish a new hour-long conversation every month and I've done most of the interviews. At the time of writing this, *PlotCast* has over 50 episodes online. We like to mix things up and talk to both big names, which is good way to draw in new listeners, and people no one has heard of, to let listeners connect to someone closer to their level and to help new writers get some attention.

Lessons Learned:
Having an excuse to reach out to people I admire is a great way of networking. I almost never get a "no" when asking for an interview. I gained a lot of confidence as a speaker and interviewer. Having a bunch of questions printed out beforehand is a great way to put the guest at ease; they can see I come prepared. It also helps knowing who the target audience is (people who are writers or aspiring writers) so we can go off on a tangent and always know to bring it back to the subject. And I don't worry about pressure, allowing myself to be stupid and ask the stupid questions on behalf of the listeners. Bonus Tip—Put your phone in flight mode before you hit record. And consider bringing two recorders, just in case one dies on you. I usually record on my phone and on an iPad, just for safety.

Other Platforms

While email is still the most effective way to communicate directly with your audience, you can obviously build a following on an almost endless number of other platforms. Social media might be where people discover you and then hopefully you can move them over to becoming email subscribers after a while. I'm sure I get a few subscribers for Comics for Beginners through Facebook or Twitter, both of which I rarely touch, but most stumble upon my YouTube videos or some of the podcasts I created. Remember that both You-Tube and iTunes are search engines, where people go and look for content on a specific topic. Every week I get a few new subscribers and every month a couple of people sign up for the premium part of the site, buying access with PayPal. I guess this is what they call "passive income" but as you can probably tell, a lot of work went into creating the site and all the content around it. It's really not that different than having a book available on Amazon that you wrote a long time ago and people still buy from time to time.

Again, I'm no guru or expert. I know there are plenty of things I could do to drive even more traffic and make more sales, but that would mean less time for my other projects, including this book. That's one of the reasons I *didn't* create a classic membership site with monthly payments—I don't want to commit to updating on a regular basis and I myself wouldn't want to sign up for a monthly subscription. I also have a 30-day money back guarantee so if people don't feel the VIP area is worth their dollars, they can get a full refund. So far only one person has taken advantage of the offer.

Podcasts, YouTube and Other Platforms

Today we all basically have a production company in our pocket and everyone can get their own radio or TV-show. You still have to create the actual content but the means of production and distribution channels are almost free. There are a number of platforms to put audio and video content on but the two biggest are obviously iTunes and YouTube.

Earlier in this book I harped on the value of giving stuff away for free, which is the basic model for audio and video online. Maybe you can make a buck doing it (ads or sponsorships come to mind) but most people seem to use it just as a way of getting in front of an audience.

I have a friend who owns a bicycle shop. I couldn't help but come up with ideas on how he could use YouTube to drive people to his store, by offering expert advice. In Denmark almost everyone (at least in Copenhagen) rides a bike, but not everyone is a bicycle mechanic. If my friend was to put out short videos on bike maintenance, choosing the right bike, how to fix a flat tire or whatever, I'm sure it would get a lot of views. And even though people might watch a tutorial in the vain hope of fixing their own bike, they'd most likely realize it's a bit of a hassle and wonder, "Maybe I could just get these guys to do it, they seem to know what they're doing." I still think it would be a great idea for building and expanding their brand. If you know a bicycle mechanic (or a used car salesman, or a book store, a sushi restaurant or whatever, feel free to pass along the idea).

Let me say this though: Your first videos will probably suck. But the sooner you get those first five to ten really bad videos done, the sooner you can start to improve. You could commit to creating thirty videos before you are allowed to delete the first five (bad) videos. Maybe that will help your motivation.

Uploading a video to YouTube shouldn't be too hard and there are a lot of tutorials on editing, lighting and whatever you need, available for free on, well, YouTube. There are a series of video guides from Wistia that you might also find helpful and you can likely find others in your niche that can inspire you in terms of content and style. I would advise against spending too many days researching though, as it will likely kill your enthusiasm seeing that everything you could ever think of doing has already been done. But it hasn't been done by *you*. So dare to suck.

For the premium content (a ten part tutorial series on how to create comics, from idea to finished page) on ComicsForBeginners.com, I got a director friend of mine (Sohail A. Hassan of pure-fictionfilm. com) to help with filming and editing. It was a way to get over my own inhibitions, having someone there to direct me, and I frankly couldn't have made such a high-quality tutorial series without his talent and expertise. We put the first three videos up on YouTube and the first one has 255,352 views at the time of writing this. No, it's not exactly *Gangnam Style* numbers but still pretty good for a complete amateur YouTuber. And I'm sure it helps drive traffic to the site.

Podcasts are easier to do, because you don't have to stare at a camera and remember your lines. You don't even have to put on pants! I've done solo episodes where I basically read from my notes, reportage style shows and interviews both in person and over Skype (using Ecamm Call Recorder). I use a decent condenser microphone (my favorite one is from Apogee) that plugs directly into my iPhone and I've edited entire shows with intro music and everything on the same phone, using the app BossJock Studio. Again, not bad for an amateur, right?

Getting your podcast on iTunes is slightly more complicated than uploading a video to YouTube. You have to have hosting for your episodes (I use Libsyn, but there are plenty of other options) and you need to get approved by iTunes. And there's something about a feed that I never really understood. Yet both the Comics for Beginners podcast I did all by myself and the (over fifty) PlotCast episodes I did with fellow writer Malene Kirkegaard are available everywhere, pictures, show notes and everything.

I'm honestly not a very tech-savvy guy. If I can figure out this stuff, so can you.

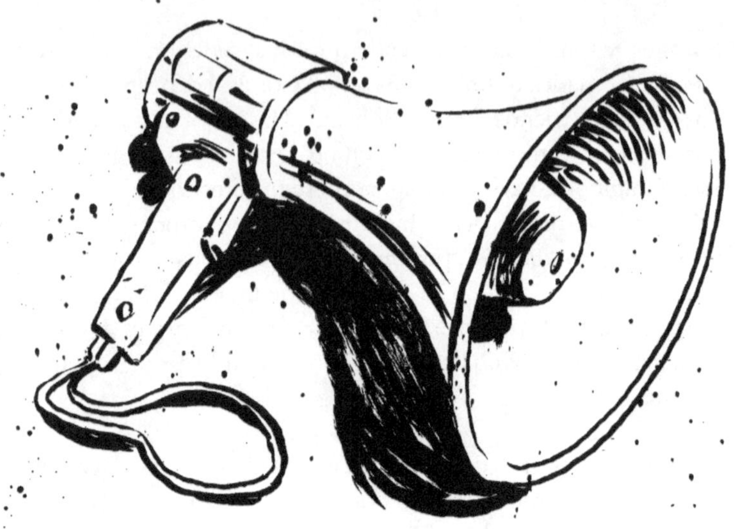

Launching

OK, so you have something coming out and you want to reach an audience. Great! But how do you do that as a one-man army with limited time and resources? You want to avoid burning out and you want to avoid burning bridges—both with your audience, colleagues and other influencers.

We already talked about building an audience and a platform, which is something that can be leveraged when you have a new book, record, exhibition or whatever coming out. Remember that creating a thing and selling a thing is not the same, so if you can bring other people on board to help, do it!

I'm not a marketing guru or a success story to follow but I have read a ton of stuff on launches and done a few of my own (and made a ton of mistakes along the way). Here's some of what I've learned from my latest release:

Plan Ahead

Once your book (or record or whatever) is out, it's really too late to do any kind of outreach. You want to start at least a few months before if you want to get podcast interviews, reviews or help from influencers. I'd like a chance to read a book if the author expects me to help hype it, so I sent my book to a few people two months before it came out. These weren't famous people or anything, just a few trusted fans I wanted to give a first look, but they've all been really supportive and shared content on Facebook, etc. because they already had a relationship with the book.

Reaching Out to Reviewers and Influencers

It goes without saying, that reviews are a good thing. It's also painfully obvious that great reviews are more about validation and ego than producing actual sales.

Be aware that reviewers are extremely busy people and may need weeks or even months to get to your book. Which is why you should send it out waaay ahead of time. For my latest release, I sent emails with a short pitch to book bloggers, enclosing a press release (see below) and a reading sample, asking them if they would want to review the book. (Only after getting a yes did I send them the book, giving them the choice of either E-pub format or physical.) Almost everyone I reached out to in these spheres of influence said yes and have posted reviews—of which I've followed up with a thank you email, further building a rapport with these people. In contrast, none of the media outlets such as newspapers, TV and radio have reviewed the book or even gotten back to me saying they received it. So my take-away is: reach out, ask before sending, build a personal relationship. Sending review copies to the media without a clear recipient and/or a confirmation that they will review it is money out the window. At the very least, you should have an "ATT:" on the envelope.

So how do you find the people to send your book to? Again, do your research. I went to the websites of a handful of successful writers in the same genre and looked at the reviews they had posted. Most writers like to brag about how many stars a book got but oftentimes they will also link to the review itself or mention the reviewer by name.

Press Release

Now that you've done your research, you're ready to send out a press release. It should state clearly what the thing is, who it's for and where people can find out more. A short pitch, price, release date, a pic of the cover, maybe a quote from the creator (you) or some media angle.

Here's the thing about the media: They like to have the story served on a platter. What makes a good media story is a whole topic in itself but let's just say it needs to be interesting to both the media outlet and their readers. "New book out" is probably not that interesting. "New book out about X" is a little closer, but if you can somehow tap into something in the zeitgeist, great. If you've done your planning right, you could schedule the release to coincide with some event like an anniversary or a national holiday. What better time to release a tribute to Picasso than on his birthday or 25 year anniversary after his death, right? (And no, I haven't even bothered to Google when that is, I'm just using it as an example!)

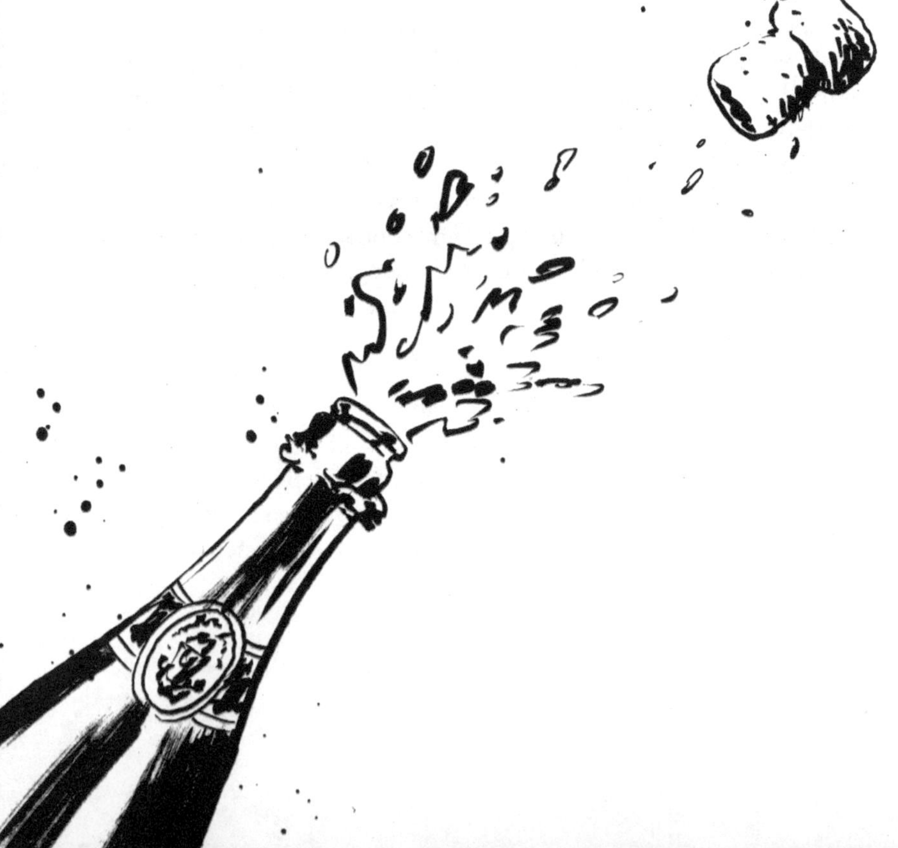

I will say this about press releases: Don't get your hopes up. Spend some time on it, sure, but think of it as an info sheet, a service to whoever might want to write about it. They will most likely ignore it, like 90% of what lands in their inbox. I've heard some people get good result from actually calling up a reporter a few days after to ask if they received the press release and have any questions. I myself would find that a bit obnoxious (or maybe I'm just scared of doing it). But I have on at least one occasion been mentioned in a big Danish paper from sending out a press release and they pretty much copied the text from it. It's something you should do, just expect crickets and be happy if anything ever comes from it.

Launch Mode is Not Working Mode

If I expect to get any kind of work done in the week a new book comes out, I'm in for a lot of frustrating days at the office. I find it helps to psyche myself and set the bar really low. If I'm in launch mode it means I'll be on social media a lot, sending emails, packing books, following up and basically doing a lot of things that feel like procrastination. It's not! While it may not produce sales, it's just a part of the process that I need to make peace with, instead of kicking myself.

Launch Week

I found that focusing most of my efforts on one week is a good way to make sure I don't spend months just fiddling around with social media and extracurricular activities. It also helps people notice. This may come as a surprise to you, but not everyone is on Instagram every day! You can't post one or two things and expect people to see it, you need to put out a lot more hype and self-promotion than you probably feel comfortable with. If you're like me, you will strain to come up with ideas for posts and feel like a massive douche. That's another reason to keep it to about a week. I think your Facebook friends will forgive you for hyping a book the week it comes out but you don't want people to unfollow you because you're that guy who just won't shut up about his Kickstarter.

I've found a service called Grum.co that allows you to plan Instagram posts beforehand, so a few weeks before the launch I uploaded a few pics for each day of the launch week, planned to go up 4-6 hours apart. That way I could focus on other things in the week itself, knowing that at the very least, my Instagram was active even if I got sidewinded. If you have a Facebook page you can plan posts and there are similar services for Twitter. If you're really into social media and have the cash to burn you can get the HootSuite app and take care of all your platforms through that. I've used it and it's a great service, just a massive time suck.

Availability

Why market anything if the product is not on the shelves? One of the first things to focus on is to make sure your thing is available for download, in stores or open for business. Once the orders start coming in, you want to be able to deliver the goods.

Niche Market or Purple Cow?

The term *Purple Cow* is from Seth Godin's book of the same name. He basically says you need to stand out to be noticed. No reason to make yet another run of the mill product, unless you're competing on price in the race-to-the-bottom industry.

While that may be good advice in general, I feel like sometimes it's good to be similar to the competition. At least the potential audience knows what you are! By trying to be unique you may alienate people before they even look at it. Not to mention how grueling it could be in the creation process knowing that you have to come up with something no one has ever seen the likes of before. No pressure, right?

Some friends of mine had a table at New York Comic Con selling their various books. A guy stopped and they gave him the elevator pitch on some of the books. He pointed at one of the covers and asked, "What's this one about?" "Cannibalism," my friend replied and the customer pulled out his wallet immediately. He didn't even bother to open the book, he just put the money down. Why? I guess he liked books about cannibalism. That's an example of a niche rather than a Purple Cow. The problem with a country like Denmark is that it's too small for niche markets. You may find your crowd but there's not enough of them for you to sustain a career.

With niche markets, I think the main goal shouldn't be to stand out but to plainly state what it is. You can have a unique spin on the teen vampire romance novel, sure, but the cover should probably look pretty much like the rest of the books in that genre. Once you're Stephen King, you can afford to have a unique cover but the rest of us probably need to cater to the audience, let them know what genre it is from first glance.

Make it Easy

For my latest book, I dedicated a page on my website to info, pics, bio, trailer, a reading sample, quotes—basically anything you might need for an article, review or whatever. In the press release, I made sure to include a link to that page, so anyone interested could go there and grab a high-resolution jpeg of the cover and copy/paste from the pitch and my bio.

The same goes if you want people to share the content, link to the book on Amazon or whatever. Creating a Tweetable link or at least making your Facebook posts public should be a no-brainer. You'd be surprised how many people talk about their work and set the privacy setting so it can't be shared. Wtf? No reason to create a bunch of hoops people have to jump through to help promote your stuff! Make it super easy.

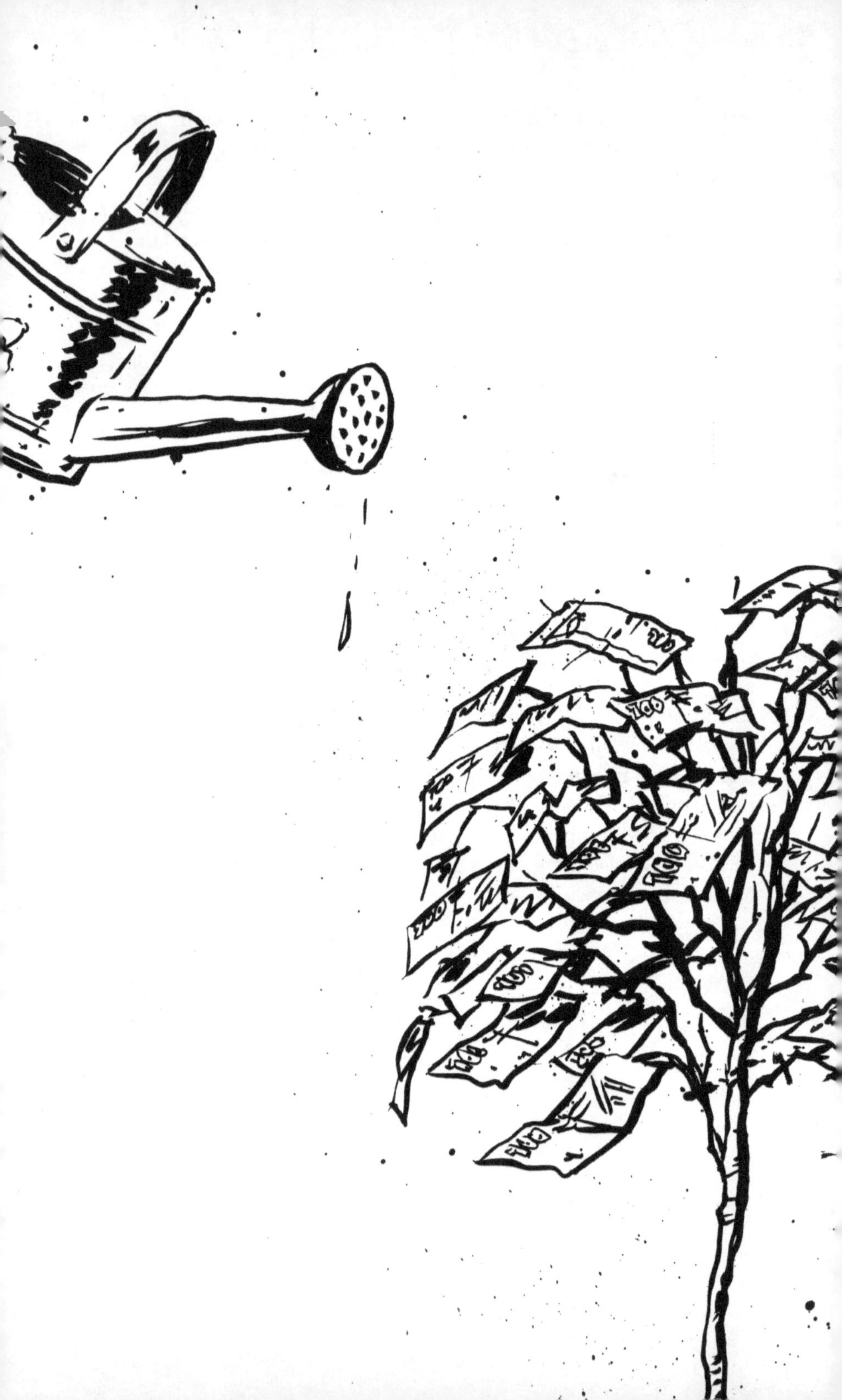

CHAPTER 15

Create Your Own Income

If you walk into a bank and tell them you would like to invest, the staff will likely advise you to diversify. Don't put all your eggs in one basket, right? Oddly enough, when it comes to income, diversification is *not* advised. Better to have one job, relying on the whims of one boss to decide your future. I find this dichotomy very strange indeed.

As I'm writing this in a coffee shop, a couple at the next table are talking loudly. The woman is afraid of getting fired from her job and is now reaching out to friends to figure out what her options are. The man is sympathetic; he has been there before. He mentions a work place where they knew there were going to be cutbacks and everyone had to be at their desk by 9am to receive an email, letting them know if they'd been fired or not. Yikes.

Now the woman is talking about the summer home her family bought last year. Turns out the man is also looking to buy one. These are normal people. I don't get it. How can they have one source of income—an unreliable one at that—and still go get a second mortgage? Why is the bank letting them?

Since I don't know how to be a normal person, I will continue to strike out my own path. Trusting my gut that having several (albeit small) income streams are better than having a boss decide my future. This chapter is intended to give you some ideas on how you can create an income without relying on external factors. Some of it could maybe be scaled up to provide the income of a full-time job but the point is rather to diversify in order to help sustain your career and your lifestyle in the long run.

Pop-up Sales

If you're giving a talk or hosting a workshop, you can bring your books for sale. If you're a musician, sell the CD, t-shirts or other merch. If you're a comics artist, tabling at a con is a way to sell your stuff. Do research within your niche and find out how to set up shop at an already existing event—what are the entrance fees, best practices, tech options. I've seen people use various credit card payment thingies that plug into a phone, so I know there are clever ways to accept payment other than cash. You don't have to be Walmart to be a store, if only for a day or two.

Webshops

Whether you sell physical products (pottery, pillows, clothes) or virtual (movies, music, e-books), having your own webshop could be a good little side hustle. I know a lot of artists who use Etsy or Bigcartel to handle payment, etc. It doesn't have to be a major hassle to set up.

You could also choose a service such as redbubble.com or cafepress.com, where all you have to do is upload your art and they will pretty much take care of the rest. You can use something like lulu.com for print-on-demand books. These types of sites typically take a substantial cut of earnings but better to get 75 percent of something than a hundred percent of nothing, right? On the upside, you don't have to plunk down the major investment of printing a bunch of books, baseball caps, coffee mugs or whatever and risk being left with piles of wares you can't sell. And since they take care of shipping too, you don't have to rush home from a trip when an order comes in to pack merch and stand in line at the post office (if such a place still exists by the time you read this).

If you did invest in creating a batch of products, you could look for a drop-shipping service to handle all orders and shipment. It's probably not worth it if you only have a couple of sales a month, but it's worth looking into.

Grants and Scholarships

In my part of the world, it's essential for the survival of most artists that they have the opportunity to apply for government funding. Because Danish is such a small-language-area (and a pretty wealthy country) the art scene is heavily subsidized. I obviously can't tell you what the situation is in your country, but I'd advise you look into it. I just Googled "art grants for individual artists" and got over 8,000 hits. A lot of private foundations and companies also support the arts. Perhaps your project will fit into their objective, perhaps not. I can tell you for certain that not applying for a grant guarantees you don't get it.

I see grant applications as part of my admin work just like doing my taxes. I just do it. Sometimes years pass where I don't get anything. I keep throwing my hat in the ring whenever they open for applications. I've also found that travel grants and residencies are a way to get funding. Take a look at resartis.org and see if there's anywhere you want to go and qualify for. It's by no means as out of reach as you may think.

If you do find a grant that you want to examine, take a look at who previously received the grant. You could reach out and ask some of them what they did to get the grant, some of them may reply. You can ask your peers what grants they know of and if they got funding in the past, see if you can bribe them into showing you their application. Calling up the foundation and asking how you can be considered for the individual grants could also be a way of doing research. You may not get through to the person in charge, but often the secretaries have valuable insights as to what they look for, maybe even smaller grants with fewer applicants. If you're a member of a guild or trade organization they might be able to help steer you in the right direction. Or you could go to your local library. Librarians are an often-overlooked resource and they're usually extremely friendly and want to help.

Grant applications are like lottery tickets. Don't expect to win and don't spend months fiddling over your application, just ship it. The more applications you fill out, the better chance you have of getting

a grant one day. You'll learn the necessary skills (like taking rejections in stride) and build a pool of material to recycle for further
applications.

Public Speaking, Live Events and Workshops

While giving a keynote presentation might be a different skill set
than you feel you've built, you likely have an expertise and a unique
experience that some people would like to hear about. Artists are a
rare breed, an object of curiosity and envy for a lot of normal folks.
If you put some effort into it, you could probably come up with
a presentation or a workshop where you can teach some of what
you've learned along the way.

The first few times you give a presentation, you could do it in a
small, private forum for free, so you have a chance to try out your
approach and build your confidence. You could also offer your
workshop to the local community center or library, wherever people
go for live events like that. And while you're there, grab one of their
catalogues and see what else is on the schedule—there could be
some inspiration to be found.

To sell yourself as a public speaker, you have to consider the target
audience. Do some research into the demographic so you have
a chance to pitch a talk that scratches a particular itch. Hearing
about the work process and considerations of a local artist might
be interesting enough in and of itself but you need to adjust it to fit
the venue. An audience of pre-teens are different than a bunch of
elderly women at the community center. To find out what unique
story or set of skills you can bring to the table, ask your peers,
a journalist friend or maybe even a business coach. They tend to
know what angles to look for.

Hosting your own live event has also gotten a lot easier with services
like Eventbrite or Ticket Tailor. But you still have to book the venue
and find the audience. I did a small live podcast event a few years ago
and it was a lot harder to fill the seats than I had anticipated. With
so much free content available online, people seem less inclined to
pay money and actually commit to leaving the house at a specific

time and date. If you want to host your own event, I'd recommend having a solid plan and maybe getting some friends to help out. You could also pre-sell the event through Facebook ads or the like and not book a venue before you know if people will show up.

Whether you're hosting or just piggybacking off another platform, remember to bring copies of your book or CD or whatever for sale. Not just for your own sake—sometimes people really want to purchase right away and support the artist that way. It would be a shame to have to direct them to a store rather than sell and sign on the spot. Bonus tip: bring five books rather than fifty. It's way better for your confidence to sell out than having to drag home a box of unsold books.

Crowdfunding

Platforms like Kickstarter and IndieGoGo have greatly advanced in recent years, allowing artists to see their ideas through without having to go through the traditional gatekeepers. Using videos, images and tempting giveaways, you can sell your idea directly to the end user rather than a middle-man. It seems like there is no limit to what can be funded as long as you have a large enough platform or you're willing to put in the legwork of running the campaign.

A successful Kickstarter campaign requires a lot of hard work. You need a clear strategy and you need to put in the hours. If you look at how many projects are listed as "unfunded" on the various platforms, you'll soon realize that it doesn't come easy. Updates, outreach and daily promotions are necessary if you want to reach your goal and you run the risk of burnout while alienating your friends and fan base. Continuous appeals to support your projects will strain your relationships with people who follow you and finding a new audience who are willing to put money down is no cakewalk.

My own experience was a short-lived IndieGoGo campaign to raise funds to finish the artwork for my graphic novel *STILETTO*. I managed to raise $535 via 11 backers out of a $5,000 goal. I quickly realized that the results were not worth the effort I would have to put in. I could make my money easier elsewhere and not have to ask my friends for money. It just didn't sit well with me and as a one-man operation, I was not able to put in the work needed. I also had no idea what I was doing so I very quickly ran out of steam.

When setting a monetary goal, don't forget to factor in the costs you will assume responsibility for. That includes your time, any fees associated with that site, production costs to create the physical media you're using to incentivize donors — Not to mention shipping costs, which are constantly rising.

Even if you manage to raise the funds needed, your work is far from over. The thing has to be produced and after that comes fulfillment of the perks or giveaways you promised during the campaign. You need to take all the production, packing and shipping into consideration too. Crowdfunding can be a great way to realize your projects, but while the campaign is running it's pretty much a full-time job. Be mindful of the actual workload and consider bringing in help— before, during and after.

Royalties, Licenses, etc.

A widespread source of passive income, royalties are checks coming in from work you already did. A book on the shelves, a movie in theaters, an album on Spotify. The key word here is ownership. I rarely get royalty statements for illustration work, only for books where I am the author. You need to take a look at the contract, see if you can negotiate a royalty—preferably one that isn't dependent on the net proceeds. How this is all set up is different for every industry, so you need to ask your guild organization what the standards are. But as a rule of thumb, if you provide content that you are the sole owner of, you are more than likely due some kind of percentage of sales or a set (albeit miniscule) amount every time your song is played on the radio or your movie is shown on TV. It might not amount to much, but every little thing you produce is an asset that could provide a tiny income every year.

Equipment or Studio Rental

If you're a photographer, you may own some fancy equipment like cameras, lamps or a studio space you can rent out. Perhaps you can sell your time as an on-site technician as well. If you have a home podcast studio, you could rent it out to an author who wants to record an audiobook. If you have a huge hi-res scanner, perhaps a local cartoonist will pay to use it from time to time. Look around you; see what you have laying around that most people probably don't. It could be a small source of income.

Committee Work

If you're an expert in your field, there may be an opportunity to get paid to be on a city committee or school advisory board. After all, if you have a certain artistic talent, you're likely to recognize it in others and could help decide where local funding should go, which students get accepted to the local arts academy or what kind of community arts projects the city should develop.

Blogging for Money

I know I said earlier that blogging was likely a waste of time. But not if you get paid for it! Sponsorships and affiliate marketing can be very profitable for fashion bloggers, food bloggers and review sites. If you're not dead set against ads, there might also be an opportunity there. Of course you need a certain amount of traffic to make efforts worthwhile. And if driving traffic to your website can actually generate revenue, then getting an SEO expert to help out may not be such a bad investment after all.

Sponsorships

A lot of podcasts make a profit from sponsorships and some film productions cover part of their budget via product placements. Depending on what you do, there may be opportunities to get a sponsor on for mutual benefit. Again you probably need a sizeable audience to persuade a potential sponsor to get on board. You'll likely get rejected a ton if you start reaching out too soon. If you think you can handle that, knock yourself out. You could also use the build-it-and-they-will-come approach and not reach out at all, just focus on growing the platform.

Micro-funding

Another form of sponsorship can come directly from your fan base in the form of monthly donations. Platforms such as Patreon allow pay-what-you-want funding in exchange for tier perks and privileges. As with crowdfunding, you need to think through the obligation to steadily provide extra content before you jump in. Even if you only have three people pitching in every month to be part of your community, they still expect some value for their money. Updating a Patreon page or sending out a special giveaway every month can quickly become a chore. There are people who make a living from their Patreon page but they also spend a great deal of time cultivating and nursing their community.

Mentorship

Helping others reach their full potential is extremely rewarding. It's the main reason I wrote this book! Nothing greater than to see the light bulb go in someone's eyes when they suddenly get an insight that will help them going forward. I created comicforbeginners. com in order to help people get started creating their own stories, to help with some of the hurdles and provide some pointers in incremental steps. I now get emails from people all over the world asking for practical advice or guidance and I happily reply to all of them. It gives me immense joy when someone gets back to me a year later or I see their stuff online and can see they implemented some of my advice. I don't take credit for their artistic merits in any way, but I'd like to think I helped steer them in some small way. And that gives me pride and joy.

Beyond the simple human joy of helping others, providing mentorship can also be a source of income. A friend of mine who is a successful writer has a lot of aspiring writers reach out for advice. Of course he can't read everybody's manuscripts so he charges a fee for editorial feedback. The fee is substantial enough that it weeds out the amateurs who aren't really committed to the craft and, at the same time, my friend gets compensated for his time.

Having expert knowledge and skill is an asset. An asset that people should pay for. If you've been at it for while, you likely already have people reaching out for advice or feedback. Consider having a standard fee or at least a standard reply for what kind of mentorship you take on.

Online courses and other digital resources

I know quite a few artists who have a side business teaching their craft through membership sites, paid tutorials or other types of online teaching and I have some experience in that area myself (ComicsForBeginners.com). While it certainly takes a loooong time to create the content for an online course or webinar, the long-term benefits of having a digital product for, sale can be huge. If creating a full course is not something you feel up for you could consider putting some digital tools you created up for sale. Like Photoshop brushes, filters for After Effects, short guides or checklists that will be helpful to another creative in your field. Gumroad is one venue to sell products like that but there are plenty of options.

CASE STUDY: COMICS FOR BEGINNERS

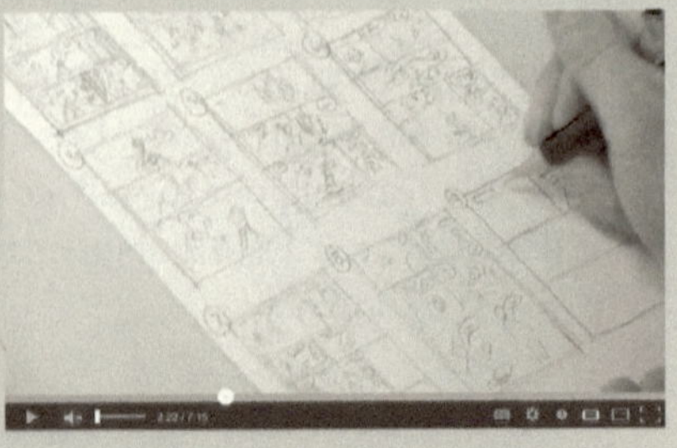

Around 2010 I was feeling kind of stuck in my creative career. I had seen a lot of success as an illustrator—so much in fact that it seemed to fill up my entire work calendar— but I was weirdly unsatisfied and frustrated with the whole thing. By this time I had also become a father for the second time, which was taking its toll as well.

I changed studios in order to give myself a good kick in the pants. Leaving Gimle Studios was one of the hardest things I had ever done. It felt like I was cheating on my wife or something to even consider leaving the place where I had felt so at home for over a decade, leaving the network of people that had helped shape my career. I had learned everything from those people. But I knew it was time to take the training wheels off.

Not long after I joined my new studio Republikken, I had the epiphany to create a video course on how to make comics. I'd read books on writing and books on drawing, never anything that really combined the two. I didn't know anything about e-learning, teaching or making videos, really. I just figured I knew how to tell stories and I knew how to draw. And I wanted to save other aspiring artists from making the same mistakes I did, like starting to draw pages without having written the story yet. Since comics is such a visual medium it made sense to do it in video form. I'd obviously seen a few tutorials on YouTube but I wasn't aware of any real competition in the market.

I did some research and talked to my web designer about the idea and between us we started putting a plan together. I reached out to director Sohail A. Hassan who I knew a little bit and asked if he would be interested in filming and editing. I had no idea what I as getting into, blissfully ignorant of all the work that laid ahead.

I first tried to break down the process by deciding on the lessons to teach. I figured ten lessons was a good round number. I wrote a full script for each episode and with the help of Sohail decided on which parts should be direct to camera and what parts would be better served with animation, screen dumps or still images. At the same time I was trying to get a website and payment method up and running, researching membership sites and online marketing all the while. I found that having a blog on the site was likely the best way to attract traffic and a newsletter was the best way to connect with interested people. Every day I discovered new aspects and the to-do list kept getting longer.

Not long after I'd launched the first video, I saw a post from a big name artist announcing his upcoming drawing master class. My heart sank and I immediately thought: I'm dead. If this guy who is both way more talented and famous than I am has a video course, why would anyone want to watch mine? I clicked the link and watched a few minutes of the tutorial. I didn't understand any of it. I figured if the lessons went over my head and I've been a pro artist for 15 years, no beginner would have a clue either. So I went on my merry way, chugging along.

I decided against the monthly membership model, because I didn't want to feel obliged to update all the time and because I myself wouldn't sign up for a recurring payment (because I know myself well enough that I'd forget I had it and keep paying for it way longer than intended). I also decided not to charge anything for sign-up for the first few months, just to get some people in the door. It ended up staying free for over a year, while we tried to fit in filming and editing the remaining videos. The pay wall went up only after all ten episodes were online and we knew everything worked.

I can't tell you how much work went in to every episode. Being on camera, remembering lines in a foreign language and delivering it in a natural way did not come easy. Neither did the marketing aspect. I certainly doubted myself more than once during the whole thing, but once people started signing up and interacting with the site, I knew I had something valuable. You can find the 10 video tutorials (first 3 are free), the free newsletter, templates and lots of other stuff at comicsforbeginners.com.

Lessons Learned:

Almost all of what's in this book.

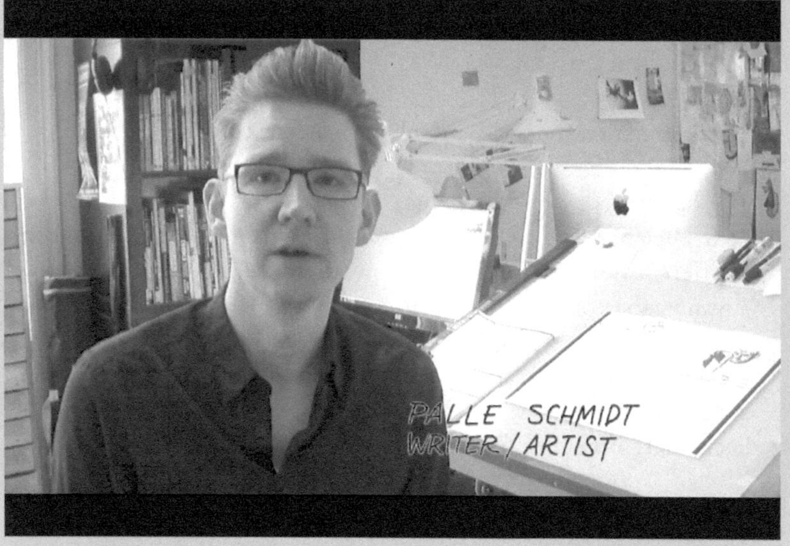

CHAPTER 16

Setbacks and Failures

The old saying "what doesn't kill you, makes you stronger" is not always true. Adversity in and of itself doesn't make you stronger, but overcoming and learning from it definitely does. I firmly believe the deciding factor of a successful freelance career is how you handle rejection, setbacks, writer's block and other types of low points. Some give up when faced with adversity, others get back up and dust themselves off to continue on their path all the wiser from it. Of course you shouldn't mull over it and beat yourself up. In the words of Elizabeth Gilbert: "You don't need to conduct autopsies on your disasters."

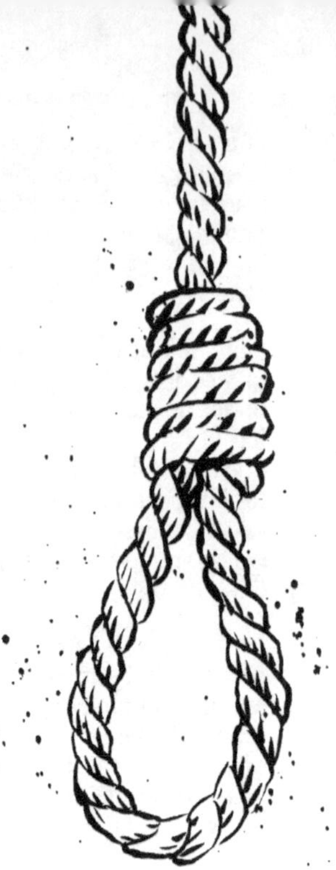

There is no set path to creative success. Whatever that is for you, you need to set your own definition. But when things go great, you don't really learn a lot.

Here are ten reasons why I think you can't learn from success:

1: What works for another artist is not necessarily going to work for you. They have a different background, a different skill set, maybe a different home life or financial situation putting them in a more advantageous position than you.

2: Success is personal. You might perceive another creator as hugely successful while they see their career as less than perfect—most likely that's how they feel!

3: You can't measure success. We as artists have an embedded dissatisfaction with where we are. That's what motivates us to get going! So the feeling of success we might have quickly fades and gives way to new dissatisfaction.

4: No one mulls over success. The more time you spend thinking about something, the bigger the chance of learning from that experience. Who lies awake thinking of their successes? We're much more prone to miring over what went wrong or how we're not good enough. Let's use that in a constructive way and at least learn something from those self-doubts.

5: What worked for you once is not necessarily going to work again! The world is constantly changing and so are you. The circumstances that made a success could have shifted or the artistic side of you refuses to repeat the process.

6: The learning you could subtract from a previous success is usually hidden somewhere in the big picture. What you think made the success and what actually made it happen is probably not the same thing.

7: Success is 80% timing. Okay, I have no scientific evidence for this, but I do believe a lot of what makes a success is out of our control. It's not just meeting the right peers or editors, being up for the task when opportunity arises. Any work of art needs to hit home with an audience and the market is constantly shifting. Serial killers or cute ponies might be in vogue this year, but next year no one cares about the topic.

8: To be really successful in art, you cannot just be replicating what you did last. You need to be constantly pushing yourself.

9: Success is outside of your comfort zone. If you are any good at what you do, you will constantly be introducing new methods, new tools and new influences on your work. See how the list of ingredients is constantly changing? You can't repeat the recipe, it's just impossible.

10: No one succeeds from day one. So if you want to learn from success you have to wait a loooong time. Failure happens all the time, especially in the beginning. Great learning possibilities!

Learning from failure is a much better strategy than trying to copy your own success or the success of others. And luckily, failure is bound to happen on a regular basis.

Here are a number of different types of setbacks and failures you may trip over:

Career Standstill

When you're in the very beginning of learning something new, you'll see a lot of progress over a short period. Once you've reached a certain level you might feel stuck or like you've plateaued. At times, when it feels your art is not going anywhere, it's important to look behind you. Look at where you where a year ago, five years ago. You'll likely realize that you've made a lot of progress even though it feels like a complete standstill. Maybe you need to learn a completely new skill or change directions to get to the next level.

I myself had sort of an existential crisis seven or eight years ago. Maybe it was in part because I was pushing forty, maybe I had simply been sidetracked by my success as an illustrator and lost sight of my own ambitions. I certainly wasn't happy in my work life, I felt stuck and was unable to see a way out of it. My wife (who is also a writer) told me: "If you keep doing the same things, you can't expect a different result." And even though at the time it felt like blatantly obvious advice, it was also painfully true.

I started to force myself in a new direction, asking myself at every opportunity: "Have I done this before?" If the answer was yes, I turned it down. If the answer was no, I jumped in.

I moved to a new studio (a painful decision, as I'd been in the same spot for twelve years and was surrounded by people I loved and admired), starting seeking out new knowledge and a new network of people. I started new types of projects such as Comics for

Beginners and PlotCast, and took a master class in screenwriting at the Danish Film School. In hindsight it was maybe less a change in direction and more of a pivot, but my feeling of stagnation eventually led way to new challenges and experiences.

The biggest breakthrough probably came from the US release of my graphic novel *The Devil's Concubine* by IDW in 2011. The release prompted me to go to comic cons in the US (starting with the MoCCA festival in New York 2011 and later that year San Diego Comic Con and New York Comic Con). For some reason I'd never been able to justify travels like that. It seemed like a long shot, a hassle, both expensive and time-consuming. Not knowing exactly what I was looking for, I managed to find not only myself but new insights, inspiration and collaborators—and a few friends for life.

I know I kind of scoffed at the education system earlier but, that said, I'm a huge believer in self-education. We're blessed to live in an age where all the information known to man is available from the device in your pocket. The trick is to be vigilant about what it is you want and need to learn, rather than give way to distraction. You need to set your own curriculum.

Artistic Impasse

If you struggle to get any creative work done at all, it could mean a number of things. If it feels like the well is dry, maybe you need to fill it up. Seek inspiration in other art forms or simply allow yourself some time off. If you're feeling completely burnt out, it could be a sign of depression, but most likely it stems from some kind of fear. The fear of failure, the fear of finishing. When a work is finished and put out into the world it can feel like a loss of control and setting yourself up for criticism. It can be hard to live up to the expectations of the audience as well as your own.

If you're not able to "dance with that fear," as Seth Godin puts it, you are dead in the water. It could help to trick yourself into thinking of the work as a jam session rather than a large scale concert where nothing must go wrong. We talked about this idea earlier, but the fear of the blank page is real and tangible. You need to splash some paint on that canvas, put yourself in a situation where you don't freeze up. I still have a ton of doubts about whatever I am creating. Experience has taught me to push through those doubts and distract my primal brain in the process just putting on a pair of headphones and doing one task at a time, going for progress not perfection.

When I was working on my graphic novel *STILETTO*, I made a rule for myself; I was not allowed to redraw or make significant corrections until after I had finished all 120 pages of artwork. I made mental notes whenever I was dissatisfied with a panel, promising myself I would fix it later. But guess what? When looking at the book as a whole, redrawing those panels didn't feel so important any more. I ended up redrawing maybe a handful of panels, all because of continuity or for clearer storytelling, not because I didn't like the art. I was able to keep myself from getting derailed by postponing judgment. It also saved me a ton of work.

Attempts to cheat your own brain like that don't always work. If you feel you lack ideas or lack the drive to create, go do something else. I always used to think of my creativity as a bonfire that had to be kept burning. I was afraid the fire would die out if I left it alone for too long. Now I feel like walking away from it for a day, a week or even a month is the *best* way to get a bigger fire burning. Seeing new places, having different experiences and learning something new are almost surefire ways of getting out of a creative funk.

On a day-to-day basis, I also try to use the approach of getting a different perspective. I bring my notebook while I walk along the lakes or stop in a cafe. I flip my drawings over on the light box, look at the mirrored image and immediately spot mistakes I was blind to before. I print out my manuscript and go sit in another chair or in the kitchen rather than stare at the computer screen. Going back and forth between digital and analogue as well as changing scenes can help you get out of whatever rut you're stuck in.

CASE STUDY: HARD EVIDENCE

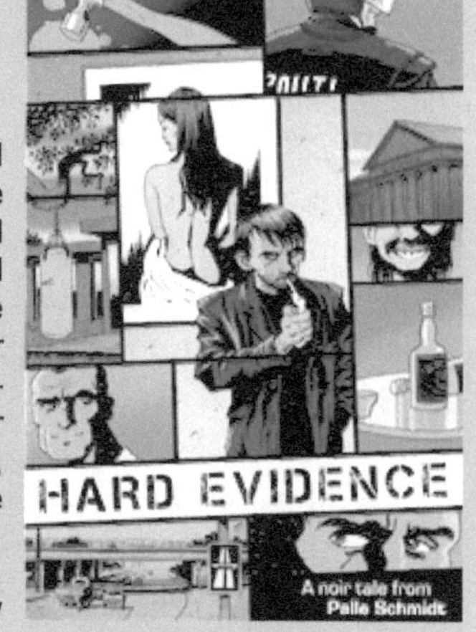

In the year 2000 my friend Malik Hyltoft and I published *FUSION the roleplaying game*. The first two books in the series were produced through a major Danish publisher and a third was self-published. This was not just a niche product, but a niche within a niche. I'm super proud of what we put out there, but I found myself wanting to do something a non-roleplayer could pick up and enjoy. But at the same time, I knew I had something of a fan base in the RPG underground. What to do?

I think it was at some convention a guy showed me a White Wolf comic, based on the *Werewolf* game, and encouraged me to do something similar with *FUSION*. I completely dismissed the idea (because I'm an idiot that way). And then changed my mind less than 24 hours later.

The plot for *Hard Evidence* came from a roleplaying game session. Well, two actually. My friend Thomas Bjerregaard came up with the story of a man who seemingly murdered his wife, and a sinister conspiracy beneath it all. First time around, the setting was America in the 1950's and the investigators were FBI agents. I re-hashed the plot for our *FUSION* campaign, the setting now a near-future Copenhagen and private investigators on the case.

We took turns as game masters in our campaign, like different directors on a TV show. My character, ex-con Hauge, wasn't in the session as it played out, but took the stage for the graphic novel. I enjoyed playing this guy so much, I thought he should have his own show. I toned down his thick-headed personality and made him a bit more articulate for the graphic novel. I wanted the dialogue to be zinging and tough, like Raymond Chandler at his best.

In a way, this project was a stepping-stone for me. It got me back into comics when I thought it too hard. *The Devil's Concubine* was scripted and thumbnailed and just laid there, like a mountain waiting to be climbed. *Hard Evidence* seemed like a less daunting task. Drawing it got me back into shape and rebuilt my confidence. The story originally ran as a weekly web comic on the *FUSION* website, thus forcing me to get the damn pages done in time. I can highly recommend this method. The only downside is that people have read the book before it comes out. I coerced a few of my peers into doing art for a pin-up gallery in the back, so buyers would get something new for their money.

Lessons Learned:
Sometimes it's a good idea to do a smaller project, almost like a throwaway thing rather than trying to tackle the most ambitious thing you can think of.

The Recurring Crisis

After a few years of working as a pro, you might feel a certain pattern start to emerge. An empty feeling of unease after a big project is finished is perfectly normal. The more you pour yourself into a work of art, the more you're likely to experience that feeling of disappointment. What was the point of it all? If your project is a live event or a concert, at least people clap at the end, but you can still get that empty feeling, when the party is over and everyone has gone and you're left sweeping the floor.

The first few times I published a book I felt high for days. But eventually it fades, when there are hardly any reviews, no one is calling to congratulate you, life remains pretty much the same as before. You spent all this time pushing a giant boulder into the well and stand waiting… and waiting… and waiting…for the splash.

The only remedy I know for this recurring post-release funk is to keep myself busy. Once the project is launched, I'm already deep into the next. It's hard to be excited about a new book and simultaneously disappointed over the results of the one you just released. I try to focus on the work; doing the best I can with my limited abilities. The rest—sales numbers, reviews, fame and glory—is beyond my control.

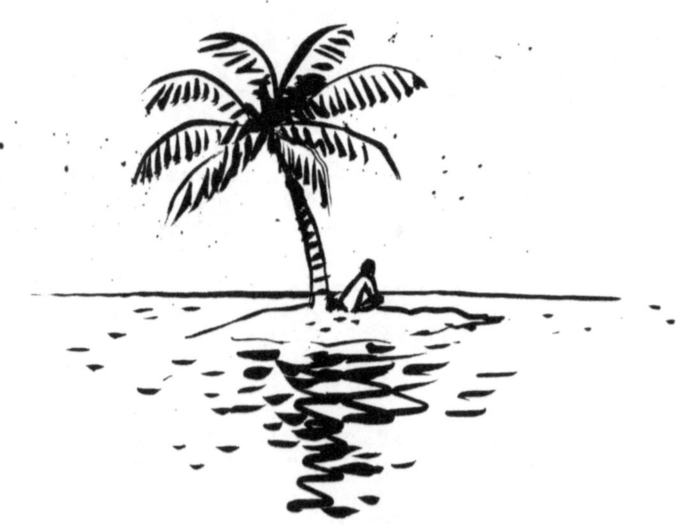

Con Fatigue

Whether you're a writer, an artist, a musician or a filmmaker, there's a good chance you have an introverted personality. I don't think anyone would call me an introvert but I can tell you for a fact that being "on" for days on end really drains me. I need alone time to recharge.

At Angoulême in 2012, I wrote a blog post on the phenomenon I later started calling "con fatigue." It was day 2 or 3 of the comics festival. Sure, I had a hangover. But the hangover was more of a psychological kind as I walked around the exhibition tents that were packed with comics fans in all ages and genders. I should have been thrilled to see all this interest for my field. I should have been enthused at looking at all this great art and inspired by the spirit of the festival. Instead, it all felt overwhelming and my own role in all this seemed completely redundant.

I don't know everything about how the creative brain works but it does seem to reach a point sometimes where it cannot process any more information and just wants to shut down. Where you can't look at any more art or meet any more interesting people. It creates a sinking feeling that I suppose is not unlike depression. I say this here, because we need to know it happens, and that's okay. It's part of the human condition.

So there I was in Angoulême, feeling sorry for myself, just wanting to go home and hug my kids. I felt like no one was even remotely interested in looking at my work and I completely understood why. It's useless! Look at all this other stuff! How can I compete, why even try? In other words, I was being a self-centered little cry-baby.

Frustrated, I went into a crowded lunchtime café and got a soda at the bar, tried to check my email but couldn't log on to their Wi-Fi. Of course.

Then, in the door walks Brian Azzarello.

I've been a fan of Azzarello's since his early work on *Hellblazer*, that was so scorchingly cynical and hardcore I'd never read anything like it. I was working on the layouts for *The Devil's Concubine* when *100 Bullets* started coming out—Azzarello's stark writing and Eduardo Risso's slick line art blew me away. The pages were so perfectly balanced, the blackness bled across panels and the colors were vibrant and bloody awesome. It looked exactly like my book! It was like they had plugged into my brain and pulled out the look and style that I was unable to put down on paper. Looking at *Bullets*, I knew how my book should be done. I tried putting it away and I tried to create my own style, but the damned thing had etched itself in my mind so permanently that *The Devil's Concubine* in certain places looks like—let's be brutally honest here—a rip-off.

Bumping into Azzarello like that, I had to shake his hand and thank him. I was able to fumble a book from my bag and give it to him, along with my sincere apologies. I said it with a smile and I hope he took the fact that I was so inspired by his work as a compliment. We had a nice little chat but I didn't want to outstay my welcome. I just felt honored and privileged to be able to give something back.

As I left the café, I left my inner cry-baby behind.

Later I met writer Joe Keatinge whom I'd recently met in New York, and he was nice enough to introduce me to a couple of French editors he knew. Suddenly my visit at the festival seemed to make sense again. You can't plan things like these. But if you're not there, they certainly don't happen.

Later on in the evening, I ended up at dinner with a bunch of comics guys. We discussed the topic of hitting the wall. Feeling so small and useless in a sea of talent that you just want to pack up and go home. I don't know if we broke a taboo subject but it seemed Danes and Americans alike lit up at the reveal that we all at one point or another had shared the same experience. When you hit that wall, you just have to recognize it for what it is and wait for the sensation to pass through you. And it will.

Economic Crisis

When the coffers are near empty (which they will be, believe me) it's often too late to really do anything about it. You have to plant seeds *way* before you need the fruit from the tree. And some seeds never grow at all.

If you see economic crisis looming, here's a template for an email you can send out to select business partners:

> *Hi (name),*
>
> *It's been a while! I've been super busy with (my own projects/ moving house/parenthood/other work) but I'm now getting back in the game and have some room in the calendar for incoming assignments. Let me know how things are going with you and let's maybe grab a coffee some time in the near future.*
>
> *Best,*
> *(Your name)*

Of course I can't know what relationships you have with your clients, or what the best way to reach out may be. But I hope you recognize the above as a respectful and not too pushy way of asking if they have any work lying around they could throw your way. Letting them know you're available is not desperate or annoying, it's a service you provide. Own it.

By the way, be sure to change the wording a bit if you intend to carpet bomb your contacts. Editors compare notes, you know.

The best way to brace yourself for periods of low to no income, is to have a buffer. Keep an emergency fund for rainy days, have several sources of income and ideas for how to generate new income should the shit hit the fan. Even if it's just a garage sale or sleeping on a friends couch for a week while you rent out your apartment on AirBnB. Don't flush your freelance career down the toilet because you have a few bad months.

I would advise against panicking and getting a steady job—unless you want to! Just as it rains on the day you leave your umbrella at home, freelance gigs tend to come in just when you've given up and plumped yourself down in a cubicle.

Dealing with Rejection

You could mark this down as "recurring" as well, since it's hard to have a creative career without having to deal with rejection on a regular basis. The trick is to not take it personally.

I've certainly had my share of rejections, from grant applications to book proposals. Sometimes I'll get a critique that hits home and I need to rethink and regroup. Mostly it's been a standard email, where it's obvious they didn't read the material I sent. I take that as a sign that I'm not a bankable enough name in their book, or that they don't currently take projects on of that type. Whatever the reason, I'll never know and I don't care.

Here are three good reasons not to think too long and hard over a rejection:

1: You can't expect an honest reason for the rejection. An editor would never admit that their publishing house is struggling financially. Or that they don't have the clout to bring a project to the bosses. Or that they never got around to reading your proposal. Or that they don't like you personally.

2: The reasons don't matter. First off, you can't trust what they tell you (see above). Secondly, even if they do take the time to tell you why your project sucks, it doesn't matter what they think, unless you agree with the criticism. Here's the thing: *They already said no.* Adapting your project to their critique is a complete waste of time. The next gatekeeper might fall in love with the exact parts the first one wanted taken out.

3: Rejections from one or several gatekeepers doesn't necessarily say anything about the quality of the project. Maybe it's the way you pitched it, your brand name, the market or the state of the business, who knows. Remember that William Golding's classic *Lord of the Flies* was rejected by *twenty-one* publishers.

Of course you should listen to constructive criticism and strive to make the best possible product. But ask ten people and you'll likely get ten different opinions. If a publisher is willing to take on a project and have ideas for changes, that's a different situation entirely. I'm more than willing to listen to people who are interested in building something together. But the opinions of people who say no? My life's too short to listen to those.

Here's a real life example: My first novel was rejected by a major Danish publisher, the first one I sent it to. They were very nice about it and gave me a few pointers. They said the plot was so-so but my characters were so interesting that you just had to finish the book to find out what happened to them. Still, no thanks.

The next publisher I sent the manuscript to thought the plot was very original and exciting. But the characters were flat, clichéd and uninteresting. They turned down the book as well. The thing is even though I got the almost completely opposite response, I hadn't changed a comma in the manuscript after the first rejection.

As I mentioned in the chapter on pitching (page 150) you can obviously benefit from listening to expert opinions. And if you get the same type of comments from several people you'd be wise to listen. But even if they put their finger on something that's broken, their ideas on how to fix it are likely off. Unless it's a trusted editor or collaborator giving the critique, *you* need to decide what needs fixing and how.

Let's use the paper boat from the cover of this book as a metaphor. Fold a couple dozens of those boats and put them in water. Most of them will likely sink. Who cares, just fold some more. Unless you're being overtly sloppy, for every boat you make and carefully put in the water, the better your chances of making it. The metaphor should also help underline the fact that if a boat sinks, it's not your fault. And you can't really blame the water either. Don't take it personally, don't carry a grudge. Just fold more boats. Or salvage the sunken ones and put them back in the water. That rejected novel I mentioned earlier eventually found a home at a small publisher and I've just put out another book with that same publisher.

If you keep several boats in the water at the same time, you care less about the ones that sink. And even if they all sink, you'll be better at folding boats. You're learning, building your skill set and becoming more resilient to failure—that's a valuable skill too.

The Comparison Game

Sometimes it feels like everyone else in your business is killing it, leading perfect lives and success just drops in their lap. It's obviously not true, you already know that. Comics writer Jim Zub said it best in a tweet:

"You see everyone else's career like a highlight reel while your own is lived out in slow motion. It's a flawed perception. Purge it."

I've struggled with envy a lot. Like anger, it was this emotion that I felt wasn't helping me at all and I didn't know how to control it. But as my wife taught me, envy could be a *good* thing. It's your subconscious telling you what your ambitions are. It's a way to identify your own goals. If you continuously feel envy looking at someone else's success, maybe you could try to figure out what they did to get there. How you could model what they do to get some of what they have.

Most of the time, comparing yourself to others is obviously a dead end. We don't all have the same amount of talent, opportunities, mindset or even luck. And what works for someone else might not work for you.

I know plenty of artists both more talented and more successful than I'll ever be. Let me tell you; They still struggle, they still strive for recognition, more sales or more TV time. That hunger you feel cannot be satisfied, no matter how much you eat. No matter how many five star reviews, bestselling books or number one albums, you'll always want *more*. It's just human nature, better learn to live with it.

Dealing with Success

While dealing with failure is an important topic, I think there are pitfalls in success as well. When you have a huge hit, you have all the more eyes on you, all the more pressure to perform. Not only that, but now *you're* the one your colleagues are looking at with envy.

You might think the danger lies in becoming complacent and slacking off. That's not my experience. Most of the creatives I know will just plow ahead and find something new to be dissatisfied with. The success is quickly forgotten and the goal post is moved ahead.

I need to constantly remind myself of the things I actually accomplished, to be grateful for where I *am* rather than frustrated with where I'm *not*. Every year around Christmas I send out an email to friends and collaborators with sort of a yearly round-up. Not to brag, but as a reminder to myself. Looking at the things I got done in a year always blows my mind. It's my way of celebrating (without the hangovers).

Ego

As I probably mentioned, you need to think highly of yourself to attempt to be any kind of artist. You have to believe that what you have to offer is valuable and high quality enough for people to want to pay for it. At the same time, you have to be humble and realize you're not the best artist ever and there is always room for improvement.

Here's an embarrassing story about ego: I was on a train, sitting in the silent section and heading across the Danish countryside to do a talk. The Danish version of this book had just come out and I had already gotten a few speaking gigs as an "expert." I had my headphones on, was listening to music and scribbling notes for my talk, when a young man approached me from a few seats ahead. I saw him coming towards me and he whispered, "Excuse me?" I immediately thought he'd recognized me from the book or something and was ready to talk. He pointed at me and continued to whisper: "Would you mind turning your music down a bit?"

I of course obliged, feeling silly for thinking some random stranger on a train would recognize me. I'm not a celebrity in Denmark, not by a long shot, why would I think that?! Because of ego. Because I was preparing my talk and living in that mind set, I guess. But a sobering experience, for sure. I wasn't special. I was just that annoying guy on the train who plays his music too loud.

It can be a challenge to stay grounded and humble if you suddenly strike it big and everybody seems to think you're the second coming. Dave Grohl was asked in an interview, what keeps him grounded. His reply:

"Having kids that don't fucking care that you're a rockstar. My kids don't give a shit if I'm in the Foo Fighters."

On the other end of the spectrum, you have someone like Kanye West. I know, neither of us are likely to become Kanye West (or Dave Grohl for that matter). But still, we might have more success than we're equipped to handle. If you've been struggling and looking for recognition for years, suddenly getting it is likely to make your head spin. You need to redefine your entire sense of self.

Thinking of the long game and not dwelling on the current success is probably the best strategy.

Keep your long-term goal in mind. It will help you navigate the opportunities and offers that might follow. It's easy to get bedazzled if you start getting offers from people you admire and you could get flattered into doing something you don't really want to do. Of course you need to ride the wave and cash in while you can— just don't spend it all at once.

There is no such thing as "making it." You don't just suddenly hit a place where you never have to work for it again. Having a hit, winning an award or getting some form of commercial success is like wind in your sails. You don't know how long it will last and you still need to be at the helm, keeping an eye on the horizon and be ready to adjust the course.

Prepared for it

Life sometimes drops opportunities in your lap. You meet a particular person, get a shot at something big, a door opens. You have to be ready to go through that door when it happens. When it happens for someone else it's easy to perceive it as just dumb luck. But you know what they say—it takes ten years to become an overnight success.

When Chris Miskiewicz and I pitched *Thomas Alsop* at Comic Con in 2013, the circumstances in which we met the right people *were* just dumb luck. But we'd done our homework and knew what we wanted. Both of us had spent twenty years of honing our craft and we had something to show for it. I had drawn the entire first issue of the book and Chris had written scripts for the entire 8-issue volume as well as pitches for the next four books. He'd even shot a live action trailer (viewable at thomasalsop.com) with animations and special effects, selling the idea of a possible movie or TV series based on the property. We had also had extensive talks between us about what parts of the story were essential and what parts could be negotiated.

Preparation, confidence and courage are some of the elements that determine whether you are able to take advantage of the opportunities when they arise. The opportunity in and of itself is *not* enough.

I heard a story recently about a couple of Danish filmmakers (no names, since I don't know them personally) who won an award for a short film and were subsequently invited to London to meet an acclaimed director. They happily flew to London but hadn't realized that it wasn't just a social call. Several producers and decision makers where seated in the conference room when the filmmakers arrived, eager to hear what the Danes had planned for their next movie. The problem was, they didn't have anything. No pitch, no ideas, nothing. An awkward meeting, indeed. While meeting the famous British director might make for a good bar story, the missed opportunity is painful to even hear about.

The Follow-Up

I know several people who have struggled with the second novel or the follow up to a success. Some of them are *still* struggling. You are suddenly up against a different set of expectations the second time around, fans are eagerly awaiting your next work and you feel the pressure to deliver at an even higher level than the previous.

A trick to avoid this expectation escalation is to create something else entirely. Quentin Tarantino famously wrote *From Dusk till Dawn* as a "no-brainer," a purposefully bad movie to reset the expectations of his audience. David Bowie seemed to reinvent himself every couple of years, jumping from art form to art form, which made it impossible to pigeon-hole him or compare to his latest success. How do you compare a panting to a pop album?

When Bob Dylan played the Newport Festival in 1965, he shocked his fans by playing an electric guitar rather than sticking to the script of folk music at that time. Half the people booed and the other half cheered. What seemed to matter to Dylan was not pleasing the crowd but pushing the boundaries of his art, damn the consequences.

This type of shape-shifting or willingness to try new things I think is key to longevity in an artist. Make sure what you're doing always interests *you*, rather than worry what the critics might think. If you want to be a prolific artist, mindlessly trying to repeat past successes is a faulty strategy.

CHAPTER 17

The Art of Saying No

There is such a thing as too much success. Meaning you go through periods where there is simply too many things on your plate and you have trouble keeping up. You have to take care of yourself and avoid burnout. Your energy is the most valuable resource of your company. Don't squander it.

If you ever had a goldfish, you'll know you have to take care not to overfeed them. The stupid things will keep eating until it kills them. Freelancers are basically like goldfish. We say yes to way too many incoming jobs because we're afraid of starvation. You never know when you'll be fed again, right?

While the stress it brings to take on more than you can handle probably won't kill you, it *could* seriously damage your health both mentally and physically. If you crash and burn and need months to recover, it will also hurt your business. As a creative, you can't just hire someone to do your job for you. Better to divert some of the incoming work before you're unable to live up to your obligations.

When you say yes to one thing, you're saying no to something else. While it's tempting to take on every client, because we never know when they'll stop calling, it's a short term strategy that isn't sustainable. You know how your computer slows down if you have too many open windows and programs running? Your brain is the same way. You don't want it to crash on you taking you out of rotation for months, unable to work on bringing in any income. Better to say no up front.

Here's a template you can use to get out of work:

Dear (name),

Thanks for reaching out! I'm sorry to say I can't currently take on any more work as it would hurt obligations I already have.

I'd like to refer you to (name of colleague/other freelancer) who is both (reliable/insanely talented/great to work with) and (has a similar style to what you're looking for/not too pricey/smells nice). You can find examples of (his/her) work at (website/Instagram page).

I'm sorry I'm unable to help out this time. Don't hesitate to reach out again if the opportunity to work together should arise sometime in the future.

Best,
(Your name)

Giving a respectful no is a tricky thing. Now I just saved you the trouble of figuring out how. You're welcome. Please note that the above template is also applicable to any type of pro-bono work.

The Great Big No

From the very beginning of my career, my own projects have always been my top priority. Sometimes work comes along and interrupts me, but when that is done I'm back doing my own thing. For quite a few years I had so much work interrupting me that I wasn't able to focus on creating stuff for myself and it made me bitter and resentful. Until I realized who was really to blame for what my calendar looked like: Myself.

So I started saying no, instead of listening to the scarcity-driven little voice inside me that wanted me to think of the money.

We all need money to live, but how much do you *really* need? And is it possible to create your own money? I mean legally. It might take longer to monetize your music or your web comic, but it is ever more satisfying. I don't make any money from my podcast, but knowing I put something of value into the world, something that didn't exist before that I thought of, brings me great joy and pride. Much more so than a well-paid storyboard gig.

These days I'm very picky with what I take on. Saying no to money is still friggin' hard. But if I say yes to every little thing, I won't be able to say yes when something truly interesting comes along, because I'll be too busy.

Too much incoming work may be one of those problems you think of as a luxury, fair enough. And in the beginning of your career you should absolutely say yes to as much as you can, to build your skill set, get your battle scars and create an income. Just beware that the kind of work you do, is the kind of work you'll get offered. So if you realize you really don't like making radio jingles or airbrush posters or whatever, consider passing on those types of gigs or you will further brand yourself as the radio jingle/airbrush guy.

Every incoming gig has the opportunity to take you closer to your goal or further away from it. If you need the money, there's not much of an option. But if you can afford it, try saying yes to things that kind of lead in the direction of what you want to be doing long term. Having some of that in your portfolio will attract the clients you really want.

A way to get better clients is to fire the bad ones. If one client responsible for like five percent of your income is causing you eighty percent of your headaches and anxiety, get rid of them. Right now.

You don't owe a bad client anything. Just because someone wants to hire you, doesn't mean they're entitled. I'm writing this as reminder to myself as well.

Here's what I'll tell bad clients in the future:

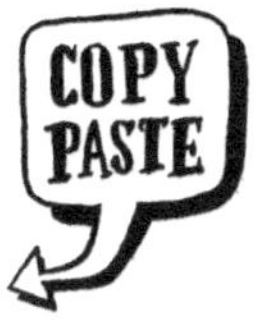

Dear (name of client),

*Thanks for reaching out. I'll have to take a pass on this.
Right now my focus is elsewhere and my interests have changed from
when we started working together.*

Thanks again and best of luck going forward.

Best,
(Your name)

Referring to another freelancer is optional in this case. Depends on
how horrible the client is and how much you like the person you're
referring them to.

The Long Term Goal

When you don't have a boss, no one is patting you on the back and
telling you you're doing good, or just good enough. As mentioned
earlier, us creative types have a tendency to be wildly self-critical
and quickly revert to feeling like a failure.

But to convincingly call yourself a failure, you first have to define
what the opposite would be. What is your criteria for success in
the long run? Is it to make a living doing your own projects? Is it
improving your craft on a daily basis? Is it to make one record or to
head up a big music festival?

An overall goal is nice to have, not just to decide smaller objectives
or benchmarks, but also to prevent you from getting derailed by
other people's agendas, usually in the form of incoming work.

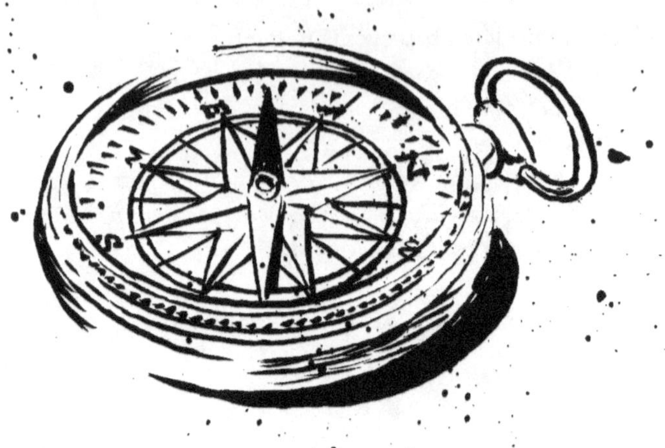

Think of it as a long sea voyage. You need provisions (money) but you are heading in a specific *direction*, not just aimlessly floating around. You have to do little detours to collect provisions but be wary of straying too far off course.

When deciding your ideal destination you need to be ambitious but realistic. And be mindful of what's within your control and what isn't. A goal like "sign a big record deal" could certainly be something to aim for, but it could be even more concrete. Like "sign a record deal with a big company in the next five years." The goal is still not a hundred percent within your control and you might feel like a failure if for some reason it doesn't happen. "Finish the recording of an album" *is* within your control, and you need to do that anyway—so how about making that the goal instead?

Personally, my goal of success is prioritizing my own projects as much as possible. As long as I'm working on something, I'm a success on a daily basis.

The less you're dependent on the grace of others, the better. The sooner you can escape the notion that self-worth can be attained through praise, rave reviews and media attention, the better you can focus on the important stuff: Creating the best possible art with the skills you have, to the enjoyment of your core audience—yourself. If others like what you do too, that's icing on the cake.

The Art of Selling Out

We all have that thought that pops in our heads, when we see some low level celebrity on a daytime reality TV show or doing an ad for laxatives: "There goes his street cred." At the same time we all totally understand the reason behind it. You gotta eat, right?

Just because you need to make a freelance living, doesn't mean you have to bend over and accept every offer you might get. You're the boss of your company and you decide what's ethical and what isn't. I have a short list in my head of people and organizations I would never work for (and a silent hope that one day they might call, so I can let them know in no uncertain terms why I would never touch them with a ten foot pole). But mostly you will need to decide on offers as they come in.

One time a job was referred to me from a friend, almost as a practical joke. It was a storyboard gig for Kinder milk slice and my friend was certain I would be offended and turn them down. Nope, not at all! I gladly accepted and did a good job, if I dare say so myself. Whatever I might feel about the product, I wasn't the one endorsing it on TV and if I didn't do it, someone else would have taken the job and the money, which was obviously what I was in it for.

On the other end of the spectrum, I recently declined the invitation to attend a networking dinner with a major client, because the keynote speaker was a right-wing politician I absolutely loathe. I felt I was standing up for my integrity. My wife thought I was nuts.

The point I'm trying to make is this: You have to be the judge of what "selling out" means to you. Don't worry too much about what others might think. This goes for business as well as life in general.

CHAPTER 18

Sustainably SOLO

SOLO with Kids

I'm insanely privileged to live in a country where school and health care are paid by my taxes, so my situation is probably different from yours. I understand why a lot of creatives see having kids as a hindrance for building a career in the arts. Especially musicians, theatre people and others who work nights or do a lot of travel for work might find it challenging to juggle these things unless they have a very supportive family or can afford a regular babysitter.

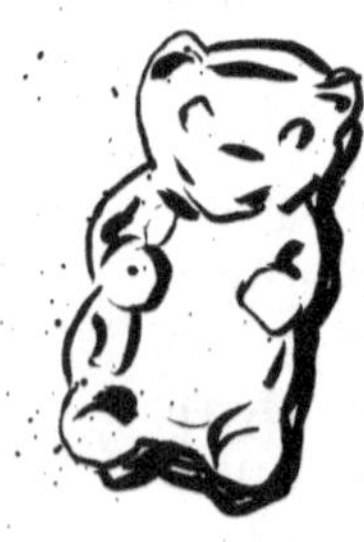

On the other hand, working freelance also means you have the ability to decide when and where you work, allowing you to have time with your kids. Regular working people don't have that option. I can easily take a day off or work (less efficiently, but still) from home if one my kids gets sick. I can bring them to the studio with me whenever I want, something they see as a field trip and an absolute joy. My youngest daughter helped me scan a bunch of comics pages recently, at the rate of a gummy bear a page. She was so proud of helping out, and I was no less proud.

You might fear that your art projects will be derailed by the arrival of kids. That hasn't been the case for me, on the contrary. I've become much more *intentional* about how I spend my time. I want to be the best possible version of myself for my kids, and that dictates having a more joyful work life. I don't want to come home grumpy and depleted because I spent all day doing something I hated only to make a living. And I honestly think that provides my kids with a happier childhood than having more money and the latest iPhone. I've also managed to combine travel to conventions and residency stays with vacation-type activities, which helps make some of the expenses tax deductible. Going on a family trip with some sort of work-related activity baked in, helps me feel better about taking time off—something I'm not naturally prone to do.

Having less time has also made me *way* more efficient. Before we had kids, I would get to the studio at around 11am. After coffee, chatting with studio mates and checking my email, it was basically lunchtime. So in reality I was at my desk at maybe 1pm and used to work till about 8 or 9pm. But because now I have two 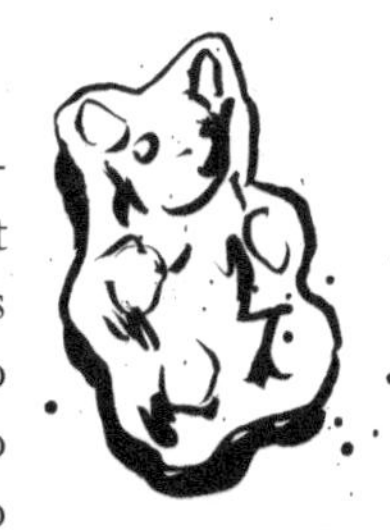 girls who need to be in school by 8am, I'm usually at my desk at 8:30am. If I'm picking my kids up, I have to leave around 4 pm, but precisely because I *know* time is of the essence, I spend less time goofing off during the day. Working nights is no longer really an option (I'm pretty much worthless after 9 pm now) unless I stay at the studio and keep at it.

Obviously your life gets turned upside down when you have kids. You have to be more systematic and you're no longer the center of the universe. I see that as a good thing—creatively as well. Instead of pouring all your energy and focus into your art, you now have to push a stroller around, sit on the floor and play with Legos or help with homework. Your art may be important to you but your toddler does not care. At all. If you can embrace this shift in focus I think it's really healthy— and might feed your creativity in ways you can't predict.

How affected your work life will be from having kids depends on the help you can get from your spouse, family and friends—and what kind of kids you get. I often tell people that parenthood is less about teaching your kids stuff as it is about getting to know *them*. That takes time and effort. You also have to learn how to be a parent and find a new balance in your relationship. Your priorities might change, you might find it harder to live with the insecurity of freelance life. You might feel like a bad parent because you can't offer the economic stability or luxuries that other kids get. Maybe you'll sometimes feel like you're failing as a parent. In fact, I can pretty much *guarantee* you'll feel that way, no matter what you do. Do the best you can and ignore the nagging feeling of inadequacy as a parent just as you ignore the feeling of inadequacy as an artist.

Do the best you can and keep on truckin'.

CASE STUDY: SOLO

For years I searched the shelves of Danish bookstores, online and in libraries for
a book on how to juggle being a creative
and a freelancer. How to squeeze more
creative juice out of myself and have a
more reliable source of income. I never
really found the book I needed. Then one
day it dawned on me, I knew how to write
that book!

I decided to go for a wildly personal style
and tone rather than try to pass myself
off as an expert with the research to back
up my thesis. At the same time, I wasn't

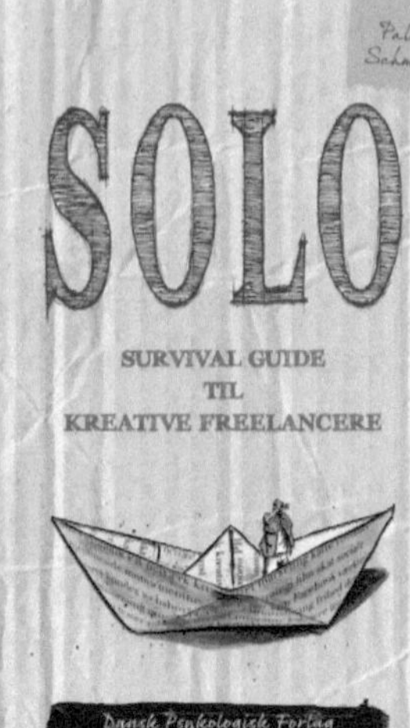

entirely confident that a publisher would take my expertise at face value.
So I reached out to a handful of Danish creative pros I knew—writers,
comedians, musicians, photographers, designers—and asked them to
answer a few standard questions. Not only did their answers confirm my
own ideas (though better formulated) and shone a light on some aspects
that I had missed, having some big names attached to the project might
have helped me sell it.

The first few publishers I approached got an 8-page proposal detailing
the project and the intended audience along with a few test chapters.
It took a few months for the rejections to come in, at which time I had
decided (perhaps wrongly) that the idea for this book was so good that it
would be easy for a publisher to reject it and then go off and hire a ghost
writer or a big name author to do it as an in-house project. So I finished a
first draft, including 10-15 mini-interviews and presented a finished book
to the next publishers rather than a proposal. I wanted to make it harder
for them to turn it down.

I got some interest from a publisher but the editor-in-chief changed jobs
halfway through negotiating and it took almost a year from our first contact until a contract was finally on the way. As it turned out, the publisher
didn't seem to know how to sell the book to the Danish market. The
editor admitted that I probably had a much better understanding of my
audience and I ended up doing most of the PR myself. I'd written about
how to do it all in the book so I felt I had to take my own medicine!

For the English language version I again decided to finish the whole
thing before showing it to anybody. I debated myself for a looong time
whether to translate it myself—or whether to even do it at all. After all,
who was I to tell people in the US or anywhere else outside Denmark
how to conduct themselves? With so many other books on the market

covering this topic, what did I have to add? After wrestling with these questions of self-doubt and imposter syndrome I finally just sat down one day and tried translating a few chapters. As it turned out I was able to bang out a lot of words and I figured any spelling or grammar could be fixed later. It also turned out that I had learned a lot since the Danish book came out so I did quite a lot of editing along the way, throwing out entire sections, adding to others and including whole new chapters—something that wouldn't have been possible had I sent it off to a professional translator.

Rather than try to approach a US publisher directly (which seems like a daunting, if not impossible task unless you first have an agent attached) I sent the first draft to my STILETTO editor Greg Tumbarello, who ended up giving the final thumbs up for the text. I also leveraged my ComicsForBeginners newsletter and solicited feedback from a handful of people across the world—total strangers who were willing to read the manuscript and let me know their thoughts. Quite a few edits came from this process which further shaped the book you now hold in your hands!

Lessons Learned:
In many respects, this book came easy to me. I didn't have to make anything up and it's written very much how I sound when I talk. For the English language version I had to learn to leave self-doubt at the door when I step inside my creative zone. Listen to my gut, just do the damn work, and let others decide the quality after I'm done with it.

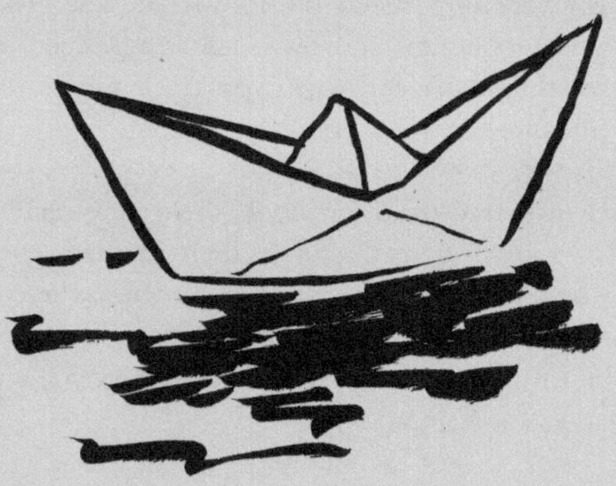

SOLO Forever?

It's hard to predict what the future holds for creative freelancers (or for humanity in general) but I don't see a decline in the need for arts and entertainment, whether it is film, games, music, painting, poetry or pottery. We live in an age of artist empowerment, where the tools of production are pretty much available to everyone. More and more people strike out on their own while others are pushed, as "steady jobs" disappear. And as we've discussed earlier in the book, freedom to create your own work life is just as viable an ambition as making a ton of money. People are starting to catch on to this idea.

In terms of retirement, I'm not really qualified to give advice. I don't have plans to retire and will likely keep doing something creative until the day I die—because that's what I *like* doing. I don't have a retirement fund or stocks or anything. We own an apartment that's pretty much paid out and we have public retirement funds in Denmark, so I'm not too worried. Maybe I'm just super naive but I believe in having many small sources of income from assets that I create, rather than believe the fear-based marketing of banks and insurance companies. Last year I created an e-book publishing house and started doing audiobook versions of older works that I was able to get the rights back for. At the time of writing this, income is a very slow trickle but it's MINE. The great thing about these types of income sources (such as described on page 177-185) is that they don't end when you reach age 65 or whatever the retirement age is where you live.

As you've likely gathered from this book, there is no secret recipe for success. There are many paths, just as there are many goals. You have to define (and redefine) your own goal. In times when the goal posts seem to be moving or it all becomes a bit murky, reach out to your peers. Return to the section on mentors (page 37) and look to other industries for inspiration.

I hope this book has been as illuminating and inspiring for you to read as it has been for me to write it. The key lesson I'm taking away is that my initial goal of making a living from my own projects was flawed. I'll be happy if I can make a living doing things that thrill me, that feel important and challenging, no matter if the project originates with me or someone else.

I'll leave you with one last quote, from boxer Mike Tyson:

"Everybody has a plan until they get punched in the face."

Just as even the best laid plans can't stand up to a well-placed right hook, this book can't prepare you for everything that might come in the way of your freelance career. Hopefully you've learned some strategies that will help you roll with the punches. And hopefully you've gotten some ideas for how you can create a sustainable business, balancing the need to eat with your artistic ambitions. There are many, many opportunities available as the examples of this book should allude to. According to Wikipedia, there are ten million creative freelancers in the US today and tendencies point to a rise in that number. So while you may be going SOLO, you are definitely not alone!

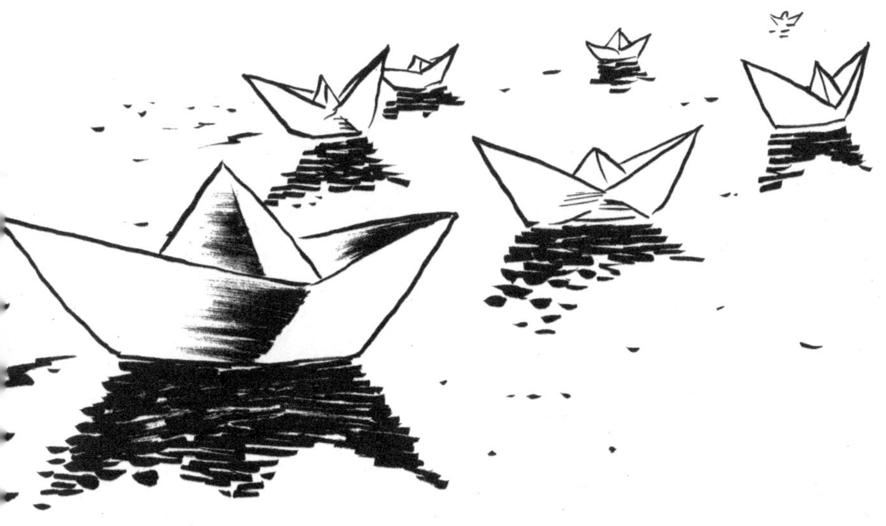

Oh hey, one last thing; If you think this book might be useful for others, pay it forward! Give your copy to another aspiring or struggling freelancer, gift it to someone or let people in your network know about it on social.

You could also use this template for an email:

Hey (name),

I just finished reading this book; SOLO - Survival Guide for Creative Freelancers, have you heard about that? It's full of really (useful/interesting/actionable/controversial) ideas for us creative types. It's a quick read and I think it might be up your alley.

Anyway, check it out at your bookstore or get it here: (link).

Hope things are well (with you/in your business/in the suburbs/whatever).

Take care!

Best,
(Your name)

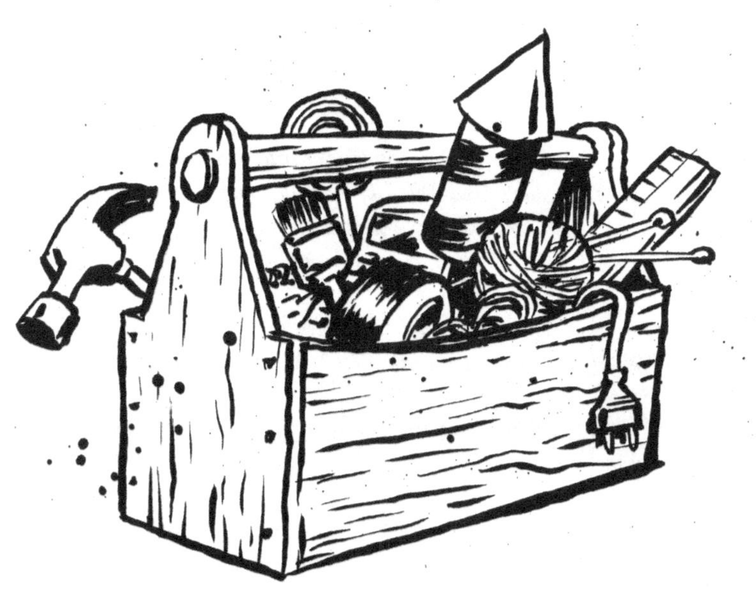

Resource Section

Templates

Email to potential mentor:

Hi (name),

I've been following your career as a (cartoonist/writer/musician/ whatever) for quite some time now and I must say I'm floored by your (results/skills/work ethic/ability to keep upping your game). I'm heading towards becoming a (cartoonist/writer/musician/ whatever) myself and would be eternally grateful if I could (buy you a coffee/buy you lunch/get you on a quick call) some time. I have a handful of short, concrete questions I want to ask you.

Let me know if it's at all possible to (meet up/sit down/hop on Skype) some time in the coming weeks. Whatever is convenient for you!

I know you have a busy schedule but a few pointers from you would mean the world to me.

Best,
(Your name)

Questions for your mentor

- How did you get to the level you're at in your career?
- What do you think would be a logical next step for someone in my situation?
- Where do you see my art needing improvement?
- Is there anything I'm missing in how I perceive this business?
- How can I improve my online presence?
- Any resources or people you can recommend I reach out to?
- What's the one piece of advice you give most to people who want to achieve what you have?

What to say when you approach a publisher/producer/ stakeholder at a show or whatever:

"Hi, I'm (name), I see you've got some (great books/cool products/ interesting stuff going on) very much in line with what I do. Do you mind if I leave (a portfolio/some samples/a card)? Or maybe you can tell me who it would be a good idea to reach out to?"

Follow-up email to potential work relationships:

Hey (name),

Great to meet you at (the book reception/your store/the trade show) the other day! I think I gave you (my card/a sample of my work/a portfolio/my latest demo) but just in case you lost it, here's my info again.

You can find more of my work at (link to homepage/link to You-Tube channel/Facebook page/LinkedIn profile).

Thanks again for (your time/a great chat/an engaging conversation). Hope to see you again some time!

Best,
(Your name)

Open-for-business email to friends and contacts:

Hey (name),

I just wanted to let you know that I've taken a leap of faith and started out as a freelance (designer/artist/musician). Visit my website at (link) to find out more. You can still get in touch with me at (phone number/email).

Hope this finds you well and that you're enjoying (what's left of the summer/your work at whatever/life in general)!

Best,
(Your name)

Interview tactic (advanced solicitation strategy):

> *"I figured out I have some blind spots and would really love to get a deeper understanding of how the business works on your end of things."*

Examples of questions you can ask are:

- - Where do you see the big challenges for your company in the coming years?
- - What tasks consume most of your time on a daily basis?
- - Where do you see your industry heading?
- - What core competences are you looking for in a freelancer?
- - How do you prefer people contact you with business opportunities?
- - What's the worst thing a freelancer could do in terms of retaining a work relation?

Pricing tactic:

> *"My going rate for something like this would normally be around (insert high amount)…"*

Take a moment. Sometimes the client will jump in going: "That sounds reasonable." Boom! No need to negotiate further.

If, on the other hand, your hear them fall off the chair on the other end of the line, you can pick up your thought:

> *"…but since (it's you/it's part of a larger project/it sounds like a relatively simple task) I'm sure we can work out (a discount/ lower rate/some sort of bundle deal). How about (insert lower amount)?"*

Work brief follow-up:

Hey there, nice (chatting/meeting) with you today.

I just wanted to make sure I got everything right from the briefing: I will deliver (X number of illustrations/X number of pages/ minutes of footage/whatever) by (date) in (format). We agreed on a (total amount/hourly rate) of (X number) for the job, including (X number) of corrections.

If there's anything you disagree with or something I misunderstood, please let me know ASAP. If I don't hear back from you, I'll take it as confirmation. Looking forward to get to work on this!

Pitch email:

Hi (name),

I got your email from (trusted mutual friend/respected person in your field) who mentioned the following (book proposal/idea for a comic/exhibition/whatever) might be up your alley.

I'm (ultra-short bio/pitch), I recently (published something exciting/won an award/finished a prestigious school or class) and right now I'm working on (ultra-short pitch of the project/maybe a link or two).

The target audience is (short description).

I'd love to send you (a detailed synopsis/a demo/a full script/samples of my work) if you're interested. I know you're really busy and don't want to burden you with the details if the project is not a good match. I'd also be happy to (take a call/grab a quick coffee/meet at your offices), whatever is more convenient to you.

Best,
(Your name)

Pitch email follow-up:

Hi (name),

I don't know if my last email got (lost/eaten by your spam filter/ buried in your undoubtedly strained inbox), so I just wanted to make sure… I'm enclosing the original email for your convenience. Hope to hear back from you.

Best,
(Your name)

Unsolicited looking-for-work email to contacts:

Hi (name),

It's been a while! I've been super busy with (my own projects/moving house/parenthood/other work) but I'm now getting back in the game and have some room in the calendar for incoming assignments. Let me know how things are going with you and let's maybe grab a coffee some time in the near future.

Best,
(Your name)

Reminder email for unpaid invoice:

Hi (name),

I was just going through my accounts and as far as I could see I haven't received the payment on the attached invoice. Would you check to see if something went wrong on your end?

Thanks!

Best,
(Your name)

Polite way of turning down
incoming work (temporarily):

Dear (name),

Thanks for reaching out! I'm sorry to say I can't currently take on any more work as it would hurt obligations I already have.

I'd like to refer you to (name of colleague/ other freelancer) who is both (reliable/ insanely talented/ great to work with) and (has a similar style to what you're looking for/ not too pricey/ smells nice). You can find examples of (his/ her) work at (website/ Instagram page).

I'm sorry I'm unable to help out this time. Don't hesitate to reach out again if the opportunity to work together should arise sometime in the future.

Best,
(Your name)

Polite way of turning down
incoming work (permanently):

Dear (name of client),

Thanks for reaching out. I'll have to take a pass on this. Right now my focus is elsewhere and my interests have changed from when we started working together.

Thanks again and best of luck going forward.

Best,
(Your name)

Essential business-related questions to ask yourself:

- What is your biggest asset as a creative freelancer?
- What is the unique skill or perspective you bring to the table?
- Who are your top three role models?
- What is it those three do that you could successfully imitate?
- What is it they possess that you're envious of?
- Where else could you look for role models?
- Who in your network do you think could help you reach
your goal?
- What three clients would you most want to work with?
- What other three clients could you probably land if you gave
it a try?
- Where can you find an extra three hours a week?
- What three things could you do tomorrow that would move the
needle on your business?
- Which one of those three things will you commit to doing?
- What are three things you should stop doing?
- Who are the five people whose opinion and support you rely on
the most?
- Whose condemnation and criticism do you fear the most?
- Is that person on the list of the five you value the most?
- If not, would you please stop paying attention to what they
think?

Useful Links:

CROWDFUNDING AND MICRO-FUNDING:

KICKSTARTER.COM
Crowdfunding platform.

INDIEGOGO.COM
Crowdfunding platform.

PATREON.COM
Micro-funding for artists.

WEBSHOPS AND PAYMENT SOLUTIONS:

GUMROAD.COM
Sell your own digital products online. Cheap and easy to use.

CDBABY.COM
Online music sales for indie artists.

ETSY.COM
Sell physical wares at a percentage.

BIGCARTEL.COM
Simple webshop solution.

REDBUBBLE.COM
Webshop solution for selling prints, merchandise and other products. They handle manufacturing and shipping.

PAYPAL.COM
Worldwide payments solution, enabling you to receive money through your site with no credit card payment set-up.

ACCOUNTING:

FRESHBOOKS.COM
Online accounting and invoicing software.

QUICKBOOKS.COM
Online accounting and invoicing software.

VERIFY
App for handling receipts (links up with QuickBooks).

FORRECEIPT.COM
App for handling receipts (links up to Google Drive).

PRINT AND OFFICE SUPPLIES:

MOO.COM
Quality business cards, etc. Print-on-demand.

LULU.COM
Print-on-demand webshop service for books.

KA-BLAM.COM
Print-on-demand webshop service for books.

GREKOPRINTING.COM
Print-on-demand webshop service for books.

FILE-SHARING, ETC.:

WETRANSFER.COM
Free service, allowing you to send up to 2 gigabytes of files free.

DROPBOX.COM
Cloud storage software. First 2 gigabytes free.

PR, PRODUCTIVITY AND OTHER TOOLS:

MAILCHIMP.COM
Newsletter service provider, free for the first couple thousand subscribers. Easy to use.

EVERNOTE.COM
Keep track of notes and to-do lists across devices. Free and premium version.

TALKWALKER.COM/EN/ALERTS
Free service, alerting you when your name (or keyword or phrase) is mentioned online.

SURVEYMONKEY.COM
Easy to set up to set up user surveys. Free and premium version.

DOODLE.COM
Online calendar service for arranging meetings etc. Free and premium version.

TRIPIT.COM
App for collecting travel info in one place. Super convenient. Free and premium version.

SQUARESPACE.COM
Simple website-solution with lots of templates. Monthly prices of $8 and up.

EVENTBRITE.COM
Online ticketing platform.

CANVA.COM
Online design software. Free and premium templates.

INSPIRATION, NETWORK, ETC.

CREATIVEBLOQ.COM
Design focused blog full of inspiration for creatives.

CREATIVEMORNINGS.COM
Blog, podcast, events in your area.

STARTUPNATION.COM
Useful advice for starting a company.

LYNDA.COM
Online course platform.

SMARTPASSIVEINCOME.COM
Blog, videos and podcast focused mainly on online sales.

LIFEHACKER.COM
Productivity tips, creativity and more.

UPWORK.COM
Hire freelancers everywhere.

CREATIVELIVE.COM
Hundreds of video courses for creatives and entrepreneurs. Paid content.

CHASE JARVIS LIVE
Podcast and YouTube channel with entrepreneur interviews.

COMIXLAUNCH.COM
Blog and podcast on crowdfunding, specifically for comics.

RESARTIS.ORG
Find artist residencies everywhere.

NUMBEO.COM
Compare living cost between different countries and cities.

MY WEBSITES:

PALLESCHMIDT.COM
The main hub, blog and portfolio.

COMICSFORBEGINNERS.COM
Video tutorials for aspiring comics creators.

PLOTCAST.DK
Podcast (in Danish) with writer interviews.

THOMASALSOP.COM
The website for the comic I did with writer Chris Miskiewicz.